Derrick & Brenda Holmes
@ James Grieve. 2001

The Dejected Soul's Cure

Tending to Support Poor, Drooping Sinners

with

Rules, Comforts, and Cautions
in Several Cases, in Seventeen Sermons

and

A Treatise of Angels

by

Christopher Love
Minister of St. Lawrence Jewry, London

Edited by Dr. Don Kistler

Soli Deo Gloria Publications
. . . for instruction in righteousness . . .

Soli Deo Gloria Publications
P.O. Box 451, Morgan, PA 15064
(412) 221-1901/FAX 221-1902
www.SDGBooks.com

*

The Dejected Soul's Cure and *A Treatise of Angels* were first published in the 17th century. This Soli Deo Gloria reprint, in which spelling, grammar, and formatting changes have been made,
is © 2001 by Don Kistler and
Soli Deo Gloria. All
rights reserved.

*

ISBN 1-57358-112-7

Contents

The Dejected Soul's Cure

To the Reader	v
Sermon 1 *The Text Opened and the Doctrine Stated*	1
Sermon 2 *When Are God's People Too Cast Down for Sin?*	20
Sermon 3 *Why Are Wicked Men Not Cast Down for Sin?*	32
Sermon 4 *Christians Ought to Check Their Own Hearts*	53
Sermon 5 *Why Are the People of God Cast Down?*	69
Sermon 6 *Why God's People Should Not Be Too Cast Down*	85
Sermon 7 *Scripture Rules to Recover a Sense of God's Love*	100
Sermon 8 *Things That Disquiet the Soul of a Child of God*	113

Sermon 9	129
A Use of Exhortation	
Sermon 10	143
The Calamitous Condition of the Church	
Sermon 11	161
Reproof to Three Sorts of Men	
Sermon 12	174
Uses of Instruction and Trial	
Sermon 13	186
Differences Between a Natural Conscience in a Wicked Man and the Conscience of a Godly Man Who Is Troubled for Sin	
Sermon 14	203
More Differences Between a Natural Conscience in a Wicked Man and the Conscience of a Godly Man Who Is Troubled for Sin	
Sermon 15	216
Why are God's People Too Disquieted for Sin?	
Sermon 16	228
Practical Application	
Sermon 17	241
Further Rules	

A Treatise of Angels — 253

To the Reader

Christian Reader,

You are desired to take notice that the end of this, our epistolary preface, is not to strew the flowers of our praises upon our deceased brother, whose praise is in all the churches of Christ; nay, "his works praise him in the gates." We wish to say no more of him than Christ did of Lazarus in Luke 16:22: "The poor man died, and was carried by angels into Abraham's bosom"; but there is this double end in it:

1. To assure you that these seventeen sermons on Psalm 42 are, though posthumous, yet a legitimate issue, they all having been diligently compared with and revised by Mr. Love's own notes, except the last two on Psalm 42, the notes of which could not be found. Yet the very context of them shows they are a thread of the same spinning. This we thought good to inform you of because forged pieces have, in all ages and in all fields, been obtruded upon the world under the name of persons of any worth or eminence. Nay, Jerome tells us that diverse apocryphal books were vended under the names of the apostles themselves. The same principles of pride and avarice are busy in such impostors at this day. These sermons we publish and justify as being his. They were prepared by him for the pulpit, not for the press; had he lived to publish them, no question but they would have been more polite. But because we would publish nothing but what was purely his, we have

therefore sent them abroad as they were left by him, without the addition of any considerable sentence more than what was in his own notes, that you may conclude that you have him speaking in these treatises and nobody else. Whatever mistakes or literal faults you may find, impute them either to the oversight of the corrector or the printer; and if you have a measure of knowledge to amend them, exercise so much charity as to cover them. We do not care at all to satisfy censorious critics.

2. The next thing we aim at in this epistle is to remind you of that which, if you have any savor of the knowledge of the gospel, you yourself will discern, and that is the spiritualness and seasonableness of this discourse, which is to raise and elevate the spirits of the saints under their faintings and despondencies of spirit; to pluck the sick feathers out of the wings of faith and prayer; to hold out some spiritual pulleys to a weak Christian to raise up himself by; to buoy up those radical graces of faith and hope in the waters of affliction, temptation, and desertions. Our beloved brother had been himself long in the school of temptation and desertions, under the nurture of God's rod. So there is no question in these sermons but that he felt what he spoke, and spoke what he felt, being enabled by God to comfort others with the comforts wherewith he himself was comforted of God. You will find several common, useful, practical cases of conscience distinctly propounded and judiciously resolved, to satisfy the scrupulous, resolve the doubting, and comfort the dejected Christian. In this treatise there are three very considerable things.

(1) You will see a singular dexterity in comfort-

ing troubled, dejected souls, which is certainly one main work of a gospel ministry. God would have His people comforted, and the gospel is a dispensation checkered with God's glory and His people's comfort. The whole chain of salvation is enameled with these two, that our hearts might be ravished with it. God has inseparably linked these together, and so they are to be held out in the dispensation of the gospel, which is called "good tidings of great joy" (Luke 2:10); "the gospel of salvation" (Ephesians 1:13); and "glad tidings of peace, of good things" (Romans 10:15). But who is sufficient for these things? It is a piece of singular skill, not learned in the school of philosophers, no, nor yet at the feet of Gamaliel, but under the pedagogy of the Spirit Himself, who is "the Comforter," to be able to "speak a word in season to him that is weary." Such a one is an interpreter, a messenger one of a thousand. And Isaiah 50:4 speaks of it as a special gift. Though Jerome and other ancient expositors understand these words as referring to Christ—who is indeed commissioned and fitted by God for this work of binding up the broken in heart (Isaiah 61:1), being that true Samaritan who pours His cleansing wine and supplying oil into wounded spirits—yet the words by the Jews, Calvin, and Aquinas are interpreted as referring to the prophet; and no question but that God does, in a more than ordinary manner, furnish some of His ministers with this gift, according as His church has need of them. Though there are many good surgeons in London, yet not all are masters of the hospital; and there are many good physicians in England, yet not all are public professors. So, though God has given to all His ministers a charge to seek that which is lost, and to heal that which is sick, and bind that which is broken, yet every one is not in a like measure able and fit for these works. How much is here spoken to satisfy and settle a doubting Christian, we would rather you should find by your own experience than our report.

(2) You will find here a sweet mixture of law and gospel, bittersweet, at the same time purging out your corruptions and yet deliciously affecting your spiritual taste. If any are offended at this we shall only say look to the end, and that will put a luster upon the means. If the Word wounds, it is to heal; if it casts down, it is to raise up. You may thank your own corruptions that call for corrosives before lenitives can be applied. It is the proper work of a surgeon to heal; that he lances and bleeds and scars is by accident because of the malignant distemper of the patient. It is the proper work of a carpenter to build; that he sometimes pulls down is by accident. So if the ministers of the gospel sometimes wound and trouble you, is the fault theirs or yours?

If a prince sends a messenger to a condemned man with a pardon, provided that he confesses his crime and humbles himself and commits himself to become a new man, and all this while the messenger cannot get him to acknowledge himself as guilty or desire pardon, but he stands out till another warrant is sealed for his execution, who is at fault, the messenger or the condemned man? The parallel lies plain. Oh, how glad would the servants of Christ be if they might be always pouring out the precious ointment of the gospel! Oh, how sweet a theme is the grace of God, the love of Jesus Christ! How sweet and delightful would our ministry be if we might always walk among these sweet perfumes! Do you think ministers are delighted to hear the cries

To the Reader

and groans of souls when they are put to pain by sound and clear convictions? Nay, are they not rather astonished to converse every day with so many carcasses that prick them, cut them, wound them, burn them, threaten, do what you will, and feel just nothing? Verily, were it not out of faithfulness to God and souls, they would not insist so much on such subjects. Certainly, as it is the glory of a surgeon not to make wounds but to heal them, so it is the glory of ministers to heal wounded consciences.

(3) A third thing observable is the sweet directions that here are scattered up and down as to how a Christian should behave himself in the vicissitudes of providence. You are taught here your spiritual postures, how to rise in thankfulness, how to fall in humility, when you must go to your closet, and when to be in the open. Here is a straight rule by which you may measure your excesses and defects when you are too much or when too little cast down; for we are very prone either to overdo or underdo. It is so hard to hit upon the middle. Here you may learn when you are active or when you are passive in your own dejections. You may meet with some particulars twice, but remember, he who shoots the same arrow twice and both times hits the mark has well shot.

Now the other treatise on the ministry of angels was not intended for a philosophical, but for a Christian audience. It is a high subject, and there is room enough for speculation. Too many in these days have been wantonly busy to converse with angels out of pride and curiosity, but the good angels will not be spoken with upon those terms; or, if they do speak, to be sure it will be no comfort to those persons. For the apostle, by laying down a supposition, has given us a certainty that the angels will speak no other doctrine than he did. Therefore such spirits as are intruders into things not seen are vainly puffed up in their fleshly mind (Colossians 2:18), however spiritual they seem to be. As for that opinion that every man has his particular angel, if any think it not sufficiently answered in this treatise, we shall add only this: when the maintainers of it have agreed among themselves as to whether every man has two angels (a good one and a bad one), or if every man has but one (whether that is a good one or a bad one)—if it is a bad one, what comfort is there in that doctrine? If every man has a good one, how can this stand with the text that limits their ministry to the heirs of salvation? When these riddles are unfolded, no question but a further answer will be given. This author practically handles that subject, and with great sobriety.

To draw towards an end: As God has always in His family some sick and weak children, so He provides comforts and attendants for them, for He will not leave them comfortless. And certainly He will not leave them helpless. Be of good comfort then; there are more with us than against us. While we have visible enemies warring against us, we have invisible angels taking our part; and therefore the Psalmist, after he had spoken of the protection of angels in Psalm 34:7, adds in verse 8: "Oh, taste and see how good the Lord is."

Go therefore, and chide yourself for your unbelief, for your despondency of spirit. Say to your heart, as did David, "Why art thou cast down, O my soul?" And as God said to Jonah in another case: "Dost thou well in it?" Is it for kings' sons, for God's children, for those who have angels to guard and serve them, who have hidden manna, to walk so sadly and dejectedly? It is enough for those poor, low spirits who dwell in the lower region of sense and reason to be dejected. If these treatises tend to your comfort, give God the glory. Grace be with all who love the Lord Jesus in sincerity. Amen.

So pray the servants of your soul and your faith, in the work of the gospel:

Edmund Calamy   *Simeon Ashe*
William Taylor   *William Whitaker*
Matthew Poole   *Joseph Church*

Sermon 1

The Text Opened and the Doctrine Stated

"Why art thou cast down, O my soul? and why art thou disquieted within me? Hope thou in God, for I shall yet praise Him, who is the health of my countenance, and my God." Psalm 42:11

Although the book of Psalms is compiled into one volume, and called in Acts 1:20 "the book of Psalms," in the Hebrew there are five books of Psalms; they are divided into five books.

The first book of Psalms, according to the Hebrew, is from the first Psalm to the end of Psalm 41. And it is concluded with "Amen, and Amen."

The Hebrews account the second book of Psalms to begin at Psalm 42 unto Psalm 72. And that you find also to conclude with "Amen, and Amen," and the end of David's prayers.

The third book of Psalms goes from the end of Psalm 72 to Psalm 89, and there you find it concludes with "Amen, and Amen."

The fourth book of Psalms extends from Psalm 89 unto Psalm 106; and there also it is concluded with "Amen," "Hallelujah," or "Praise ye the Lord."

The fifth or last book of Psalms is from Psalm 106 to Psalm 150, the last psalm in the book of Psalms, and this also ends with "Hallelujah."

My text falls under that psalm that begins the second book, and interpreters differ greatly about the occasion on which this psalm was penned. Generally, interpreters agree that it was penned by David either when he was fleeing from Saul (for then David was sorely troubled, and driven from his house and habitation, and was by reason of his enemies driven from the worship of God, from the place of God's public worship) and was forced to hide himself in dens and caves of the earth—in that sad condition that he was then in, it may be supposed that he made this psalm—or else it was written in that time when he was fain to flee for his life before his son Absalom. Most agree that it was composed when David was deprived of the public worship of God.

But I now come to the words themselves: "Why art thou cast down, O my soul?" My text contains in it a pathetic soliloquy that this psalmist used for his own soul, between two friends, as it were, when he reasons and confers with himself; and that is when the more supernatural part of man, the more excellent and more noble part of man, confers and reasons with the more inferior part of man or the outward part of man: "Why art thou cast down and disquieted within me?" As a man who would direct his speech to one whom he desired to reason with, so here David, to commune with his own heart, uses such like reasonings as he would under all his afflictions and all his troubles, asking why he should be troubled, and why his soul should be troubled and cast down and disquieted within him. "Why art thou disquieted?" These words are a soliloquy whereby he labors to cheer himself under all the trouble of soul that he found to be within himself; these are exceedingly useful to your souls. This course you find

The Text Opened and the Doctrine Stated

David took in other places at other times. Psalm 103:1: "Bless the Lord, O my soul, and all that is within me, bless His holy name." See here how the psalmist calls to his soul to bless the name of God. And at another time when he would check his own soul for his negligence and his miscarriage before the Lord, he said, "I was as a beast before him." And the Scripture tells us that the people of God should, and do, check their own hearts before God for any one sin. When they find the least miscarriage in themselves, they then check themselves for it: "Why art thou cast down, O my soul?"

Now in general, I shall lay down these five particulars to be considered about the words.

1. What is the reason why this text is used three times in this psalm and in the next? You do not find two verses of the same length used in all the book of Psalms besides here. In the fifth verse of this 42nd Psalm, and in the eleventh verse, and then in the fifth verse of Psalm 43, there are the same words: "Why art thou cast down, O my soul?" There is no psalm that makes such a repetition of words (but only Psalm 107) besides this in the whole book of Psalms, and there is often repeated: "Oh, that men would praise the Lord."

Now what may this teach us, that David so often makes mention of his own soul, why it should not be cast down and disquieted and troubled? Now surely, the frequent mention of this text and these words argues and points out to us the weightiness of the matter. Things of lesser moment are less spoken of, and are but touched on, but things of greater moment are more thought and spoken of, and are repeated more often, with the greater eagerness and earnestness, as are these words: "Why art thou cast down, O my soul? and why art thou disquieted within me?"

2. When and on what occasion were these words spoken? Was it at that time when David was persecuted by the hands of Saul, when he was banished from his own house, and from the public and set assemblies of the worship of God (verse 2), and for this cause was it that his soul was cast down and disquieted within him, when he had holy breathings after God in his public worship? "O when shall I appear before God? and when I remember those things, my soul is troubled" (verses 2 and 4). This surely was one thing that troubled his soul.

David was in affliction and trouble when affliction came upon the church of God. Some deep and great calamity, one after another, one deep affliction comes after another: "Deep calleth to deep at the noise of the waterspouts" (verse 7)—one after another, trouble after trouble, sorrow after sorrow, affliction after affliction. This was that which troubled his soul. As one wave in the sea follows another, so did one trouble follow another, as in verse 7.

Again, when he wrote this psalm, it was at the time when deep sorrows and troubles of the church lay upon him, and that by reason of great enemies that he met with, as is recorded in verse 9: "Why hast Thou forgotten me? why go I mourning because of the oppression of the enemy?" And yet even then, in this great and sad condition of trouble that was upon him, he breathed out this sweet ejaculation or soliloquy: "Why art thou troubled, O my soul? and why art thou disquieted within me?"

Therefore, observe that the people of God have many times, to their great comfort, cause, in the midst of their greatest troubles and sorrows, to have these di-

The Text Opened and the Doctrine Stated

vine meditations in their minds so that their souls are not cast down too much under trouble. "Why," said David (notwithstanding that he was in great trouble) art thou cast down, O my soul?" So you read that Paul wrote most of his epistles when he was under bonds in prison and in trouble; yet even then was his heart filled with joy to his great comfort. So David's heart was better within him at that time when he was in a cave than at that time when he was in a palace; and though troubles were upon him, yet he could then call to his soul not to be troubled within him.

3. David's trouble was from the devil and from wicked men who oppressed him. Wicked men oppressed him and the devil tempted him, yet David chided his own heart and nothing else. David did not chide Saul, nor did he chide Absalom. But he checked and chided his own heart: "Why art thou cast down, O my soul?" Though the devil and wicked men tempt and oppress as instruments of punishment for sin, yet we, with David, are to chide our own hearts. David had cause to chide Absalom and Saul, yet he did not do so, but instead chiefly checked his own heart: "Why art thou cast down, O my soul?"

4. Consider that though in our translations the words are translated and rendered positively, "Why art thou cast down?" yet in the original they are rendered actively. We read it, "Why art thou cast down?" but in the original it is "Why bowest (or pressest) thou down thyself, my soul? and why tumultest thou against me?" And the words so read intimate that God's own people may be cast down too much for the sense of sin, and they are most active in their own defection. It is neither God nor the devil who casts you down, but "Why dost

thou cast down thyself?"—creating more trouble for yourself than either God inflicts or the devil tempts you to.

In the words themselves there are three particulars to be considered.

First, two levels of distress are here complained of, differing in degree from each other, disquiet being more than to be cast down.

Second, there are two duties to be performed: hope in God and praise of God.

Third, here is a twofold encouragement in these distresses: "He is the health of my countenance, and my God."

"Why art thou cast down, O my soul?" Or, if you read it in the active voice, "Why dost thou cast down thyself, my soul?" Believers are agents in their own sorrow and trouble. Neither God by inflicting nor the devil in tempting so much troubles us as we do ourselves. Proverbs 12:25: "Heaviness in the heart of man maketh it stoop." The sense of sin casts him down in God's presence.

Casting down is sometimes in a good sense, that is, when the soul is duly humbled before God for sin and for judgment. 2 Corinthians 7:6: "God that comforteth those that are cast down," that is, that are cast down in humiliation for sin, under the sense of sin and misery. And in this sense David did never, nor does he here check his heart, for he never held his heart back from the exercise of grace and doing his duty.

It is also sometimes taken in a bad sense, where sorrow for sin is inordinate and more than is required and enjoined. Where this is found it is not to be cherished but checked. And so it was for this that David checked himself, as in the text: "Why art thou cast down, O my soul? and why art thou disquieted within me?"

These words, in explaining and treating them, will be of singular use to the people of God. Therefore, I intend to spend some time upon them. I shall at this time make entrance into the first part of the text: "Why art thou cast down?" or "Why dost thou cast down thyself, my soul?"

DOCTRINE. The children of God, though they cannot be cast off, yet may be cast down. "Why art thou cast down, O my soul?"

There are five particulars in this psalm as to why David's soul was cast down.

First, he mourned because of his enforced absence from God's public worship, that they could not gather together in the place where God was to be worshipped. See the breathing of this good man in Psalm 42:2: "My soul thirsteth for God, for the living God; when shall I come and appear before Him?" So in verse 4: "When I remember these things, I pour out my soul in me. For I had gone with the multitude; I went with them to the house of God, with the voice of joy and praise, with a multitude that kept holiday." David was deprived of the public worship of God, and this made him mourn.

Second, his soul was cast down under the sense of sin that he had committed against God, and the evil effects of sin, to remember what he had done against God. And he felt the sense of the wrath of God in the remembrance of sin.

Third, he lay under the eclipse and sad suspension of divine favor. Verse 9: "I will say unto God, my Rock, why has Thou forgotten me?" The apprehension of the suspensions of God's favor caused David's soul to be cast down within him, because he lay under the loss of God's love and favor, and he lacked the light of God's countenance. This made him mourn.

Fourth, because of the oppression and prevailing of the enemies over the people of God (verse 4).

Fifth, he was grieved more for sin than personal afflictions, because of the reproach, blasphemies and dishonor that were cast upon the name of God by other men. This made him say, as if he were being stabbed or killed, "In my bones, my enemies reproach me, while they say daily to me, 'Where is thy God?' " (verse 10). So likewise in verse 3: "My tears have been my meat day and night, while they continually say unto me, Where is thy God?" All this showed that he was more troubled about spiritual troubles than outward afflictions of the body. Blasphemy against God was as a sword in his bones, while troubles for himself were but as a scratch in the flesh. And this should teach you all that if you are troubled and cast down, be sure that you are, with David, cast down and troubled more for spiritual things than for outward personal sufferings. The dishonor that was done to the name of God was as a sword in David's bones.

In the handling of this doctrine I shall show you why it is that the souls of the children of God that are not cast off may be cast down. And that I shall lay down more generally, and it shall be as the foundation of the following discourse, in these four particulars:

First, though they may not be cast off, yet they may be cast down for the greatness and grievousness of sin. That is the great cause why the souls of the people of God are cast down.

Second, they may be cast down because of the want

of the love of God and the assurance of pardoning grace.

Third, they may be cast down because of the afflictions and calamitous condition of the church and people of God.

Fourth, they may be cast down because of those outward and personal afflictions of the body. These I shall only name because they are as the foundation of the following discourse.

First, the souls of the children of God may be cast down, though they cannot be cast off, under the sight and sense of sin. The great reason why I treat this subject is that it may be as an appendix to that subject concerning the pardon of sin.

In handling this doctrine concerning the casting down of the soul for the sight and sense of the greatness and grievousness of his sin, there are six particulars to be considered.

I shall show you what this casting down for sin is.

I shall show you what sort of men God casts down and humbles in the sight and sense of sin.

I shall show you when God's people may be said to be too cast down in the sight and sense of sin.

I shall show how may we distinguish between the casting down for sin of the godly and the casting down for sin of wicked and reprobate men, seeing that God's people are cast down for sin and wicked men are not cast down for sin at all.

I shall show what reasons may be given why the souls of God's people shall not be cast off, yet may be cast down under the sight and sense of sin.

I shall show what rules may be laid down unto the people of God that they may not be cast down too much under the burden and sight and sense of sin, and so run into dejection of mind by reason of sin.

I will now begin to address these questions:

1. What is casting down for sin? I told you in the beginning that there is a casting down for sin, first, when God casts down the soul by way of humiliation for sin. And this I told you is a casting down for sin in a good sense, where sorrow for sin is mixed with faith.

Then, second, there is a casting down for sin in a bad sense. And that is when the soul is so cast down for sin that it cannot at that time look towards Jesus Christ with an eye of faith for pardon of sin and be fully persuaded of taking the forgiveness of sin by Jesus Christ. And this sort of humiliation is that for which you are to check your hearts.

2. What sort of men are they whom God most casts down for sin? This I shall lay down by nine particulars. There are nine sorts of men whom God most humbles and casts down for sin.

(1) Those who have been most notorious and most infamous for sin, who have been most scandalous in their lives before conversion. God usually brings them home with tempestuous alarms in their consciences. Manasseh was high in sin and great in iniquity and abomination, but he was low in the sight of his own sin. And God uses more harsh and rough means to bring in gross and notoriously ill livers, those who set their faces against heaven, enraged persecutors, and defamers of God and His truth, who go on resolutely and stubbornly and forwardly in the ways of sin. When God calls such home He lays them low, and humbles them deeply under the sight and sense of past provocations.

The Text Opened and the Doctrine Stated

Paul was a high, great, and notorious sinner before his conversion. He was a great persecutor of the church and people of God. He was an injurious person and a blasphemer. He did not care what wrong and what havoc he made of the church of God. He persecuted God's people from one city to another, cast them into prison, and labored to put both Christians and religion out of remembrance.

Now when Paul—being such a notorious sinner and so abounding in sin—was brought home by conversion, God had to deal with him more severely and more sharply, and humble him greatly and lay him low in the sight and sense of his own vileness, and under the greatness of his own sinfulness. God had to unhorse Paul in meeting him in the way. He was riding to accomplish his evil designs, and he was going to vex the people of God. I say, God cast him down to the ground and laid him upon his face, and made him cry, "Lord, what wilt Thou have me to do?" You may read the history in Acts 9. And the great reason is that, as his cruelty was manifest, so God would make his repentance and humiliation as manifest as his sin was. Not only as his sin was against a great God, so his humiliation and repentance should be manifested to be great, but also as his sins were so great an offense to men who feared God, so his humiliation and repentance should be great and manifested before them who were so offended at his course. This humiliation and horror are his spiritual penance to the world and make repentance more visible.

And if I now speak to any of you here who have been or still are notorious in sin and wickedness, who have sinned greatly, if ever God brings you home by effectual calling and conversion, He will lay you low by humiliation and cast you down greatly under the sight, sense, and sorrow for sin. As your sins have been great, so your sorrow shall be great.

That instance spoken concerning Lydia is worthy of observation in Acts 16:14–15. There you read of two persons who were converted, yet in a different way one from the other. You read of Lydia in the fourteenth verse: "A certain woman named Lydia, a seller of purple, of the city of Thyatira, which worshipped God, heard us, whose heart the Lord opened, that she attended to the things that were spoken of Paul." This woman was converted in a very easy way and manner in coming to hear Paul preach; and at this time the Lord opened her heart. Here was conversion without any mention made of terror and trouble of conscience, of casting down for sin or deep humiliation under the sense and sight of sin. No mention is made of casting down in the sense and apprehension of her former life, but she was brought home to God in a very mild and gentle way.

But in the same chapter (16:27–30) you read the story of the jailer, how he called for a light and sprang in, and "came trembling to Paul, and fell down before Paul and Silas, and said unto them, 'Sirs, what must I do to be saved?'" This was one who a little before dealt cruelly with Paul and Silas, put them in the inner prison, fastened their feet in the stocks, and was a man of a wicked, rugged temper against the people of God, as you may read in verse 24.

Therefore, when God would bring him home by conversion, He made him fear and quake. He made his conscience tremble and his heart ache. He made him spring in, fall down on his face, and make a great inquiry what he must do to be saved—and all of this because of the wickedness of his doings. This is the way God takes to bring in stubborn and stout sinners unto Himself.

I may allude to what Solomon said in Ecclesiastes 10:8: "He that diggeth a pit shall fall therein, and whoso breaketh a hedge, a serpent shall bite him." I know that this passage means chiefly that those who tread down and break the hedge of government, kingdoms, or the church shall be broken down themselves sooner or later. But I may allude to this verse here. Therefore, O man, who has broken down the hedge of God's commands, even broken every command of God by your sinful life, be sure that a serpent shall bite you. You shall be laid low in the sense and sight of your sins, and you shall be stung and bitten with the sense of God's wrath. And when God brings you home to Himself, He will lay you the more low in humiliation and repentance than other men shall be. Therefore remember, O man, that if you allow yourself in sin, in the committing of great and gross enormities, you must expect that God will deal thus with you, to lay you low in the sight and sense of it whenever He brings you to Himself.

(2) But then, second, God casts down most for sin those who fall into the same sins again after they are converted. They thus wound religion, and God will wound their hearts and break their peace. God will surely bring it upon their own heads, and God will lay it on their hearts and trouble their consciences. God will punish them more for that than He does ordinary cases. Before the conversion of David, sins were but as a

little pain in his flesh to him, but after conversion sin was to him as a sword in his bones. He had no quietness in him by reason of his sin. When he speaks of his sin after his conversion, as in the matter of Bathsheba and Uriah, sin was to him as the breaking of his bones (Psalm 51:8), and he prayed to God to "restore unto me the joy of Thy salvation" (verse 12). Before sin might not break his sleep, but sin now broke his heart. Tertullian calls these his "scandalous sins" or "swallowing gulfs," and he who falls foully shall walk heavily and recover hardly. In Psalm 30:9, "Lord," said David, "What profit is there in my blood, when I go down to the pit? Shall the dust praise Thee? Shall it declare Thy truth?" He thought that he was near to the grave, and yet he thought that his soul would not be safe. Therefore take heed of falling into great sins after God has done great things for your soul.

(3) The third sort of men who are cast down for sin are those who are of a melancholy disposition. The devil prevails more against men of this temper than any sort of men in the world, to plunge them into sadder fears, deeper desertions, and greater astonishments than those who are of a more lively, light, and pleasant temper.

(4) Those God casts down for sin most are of a rugged and of a harsh disposition. Now, if God converts them He does more than ordinarily cast them down under the sight and sense of their sins, more than those who are of a soft temper and disposition, who do not need as much humbling as the others do. You know that the hearts of men are compared to stones, and you know that some stones are more easily broken than others are. So some hearts are softer and

The Text Opened and the Doctrine Stated 15

more tender than others are. Some hearts are like large stones that require so many heavy and great and strong blows to break them, whereas other hearts are like smaller and lesser stones that may be broken with a hammer with lesser blows. When God sees stout-hearted sinners who walk on in a course of sin, if He brings them home He must use many blows to break their hearts, to humble and lay them low before Him. It is with sinners as it is with wood: some may be easily hewn and cut; other pieces are more knotty and need more blows to cut it and make it fit for use. So some men's tempers are more rugged and knotty, and need a greater degree and measure of humiliation than others do.

(5) God casts men low for sin who are not converted until old age; when these are converted, God lays them low and keeps them long under the sense of sin. And it is exceedingly just and righteous with God so to do. As they have continued long in the ways of sin, so God will keep them long under the apprehension and feeling of the guilt and burden of sin. You know that if you come to a tree you may cut off a twig with a pen knife, but if you come to the stock of the tree you must take the axe to it. Now all the sons and daughters of men are of the old stock of old Adam, and are grafts of one natural stock, and we are all chips of that old block; but old sinners have spent the greatest part of their days in sin. God will lay more blows upon you to cut you off from your old root, from your vain conversation. God will use many means, and keep you long under the sense of your sin to bring down your proud heart, whereas a young twig, one that God, it may be, converts in youth, God does not usually cast down so

much for sin as He does those who are not converted till their old age.

(6) God casts those down much for sin who harbor and indulge in themselves many known sins in their hearts which may not be known unto the world, and which none in the world can take cognizance of but themselves alone. Such God lays low when He converts them. God will raise a storm and a tempestuous trouble in their consciences for sin. It is as with the wind: all the while it is dispersed in the air it does no hurt, but when it is gathered together into the bowels of the earth, then it overturns hills and houses and all things with it. So it is with sin: all the while that sin (although it is within you) is (like wind in the air) dispersed and scattered by repentance and humiliation, it does not hurt you as much. But when sin is indulged and hugged in your bosom, in your heart, and allowed by you, and concealed by you in thy soul, this will be to your soul as wind in the earth to make heart-quakes and conscience-quakes and cause great trouble of mind unto you. Therefore, O man, whoever you are who go on in a way of sinning against God, and allow yourself in known sins which none can accuse you of but God and your conscience, know that, whatever your professions are, God will make you lie low before Him under the sense and sight of your sins if ever He converts you to Himself.

(7) God most casts down those for sin who backslide and apostatize from religion, those who professed religion and then afterwards backslide and apostatize from that profession. If ever God brings these men back, He will humble them in the dust, and lay them very low in the sight and sense of their sins, according

to that expression of Solomon in Proverbs 14:14: "The backslider in heart shall be filled with his own ways, but a good man shall be satisfied from himself." As the backslider has been filled with the pleasures of sin in time past, so shall he be filled with his own ways; that is, he shall be filled with horror of conscience and with anguish of spirit and trouble of mind, and his own backsliding shall be vexation to him. God will lay such a man very low if ever He brings him back again. Jeremiah 2:19: "Thine own wickedness shall correct thee, and thy backslidings shall reprove thee; know therefore and see that it is an evil thing that thou hast forsaken the Lord thy God." It may be that you have backslidden from religion; now God will make your own wickedness reprove you.

I shall cite that well-known story of Francis Spira. He professed religion and afterwards turned apostate; and though his conscience told him he sinned, yet he sinned so high that he sinned against conscience and the Spirit of God, and wished himself to be in God's place. But read the story and you shall see what fretting, terror, and horror of conscience this wrought upon him. It laid him under the terrors and sense of divine vengeance, and how his soul lay under horror for his apostasy! Now all you, whatever you are, if you fall from the profession of the gospel, and turn apostate from religion, God will meet with you and fill you with terror, and your backslidings shall fill you and your own wickedness shall reprove you.

(8) God lays low under the sense and burden of their sins those whose natures (by reason of their strength of natural parts) are most apt to be lifted up with spiritual pride. God usually brings such persons

very low when He brings them to Himself. He will lay them low under the sight of their sins. The psalmist said concerning evil and ungodly men that they "stand in slippery places," that their ways are like ice who appear in high places, and that they shall not stand long; and what is spoken of outward pride is true of spiritual pride. God brings the proud one to the depth of hell, as you may read in Isaiah 14:11–16. Verse 11: "Thy pomp is brought down to the grave, and the noise of thy viols; the worm is spread under thee, and the worms cover thee." Verses 12–13: "How art thou brought down, O Lucifer, son of the morning! How art thou cut down to the ground, which didst weary nations? For thou hast said in thy heart, 'I will ascend into heaven, I will exalt my throne above the stars of God; I will sit also upon the mount of the congregation, in the sides of the north.'" Verses 14–15: "'I will ascend above the heights of the clouds; I will be like the Most High.' Yet thou shalt be brought down to hell, to the sides of the pit." All this is spoken of the king of Babylon, to bring down his outward pride. They who imagine and think to set their nests on high, God will bring them down to the dust. Now, O man, do you grow spiritually proud by reason of the strength of your natural gifts? Know that if God has purposed to bring you to Himself, He will lay you low before Him in the sense of your own sin. They who are lifted up in the conceit of their own excellence, God will lay them low in the sight of their own sinfulness.

(9) God casts those down low in the sense and sight of their sins whom He intends to make instrumental in His church to the building up and establishing and comforting of souls and perplexed and trou-

bled consciences. These persons God plunges under the sight and sense of their own sins. Regarding the vessels of the sanctuary, there was more filling of them, and more labor bestowed about them, than any ordinary vessels intended for any ordinary use. Now if God intends to make a man a vessel in His church, He will take more pains (if I may so say) to fit him for that use. He shall be exposed to more trials and more temptations, and shall be laid very low so that he may be the more able and fit to comfort and quiet others who are perplexed and troubled in mind. Astronomers who lie low in pits or valleys have the clearest sight of the stars, and those who have been under God's discipline are most fit to comfort others.

It is observable of Luther that there was no man in his age who was so troubled, so tempted, so pestered with temptations from the devil, and so troubled with the sight of sin as he. The devil appeared to him in a bodily shape so that he saw it himself and was fain to fight with him hand to hand. Yet for all this, by this means Luther became the more beneficial to the church of God to administer comforts to those who were afflicted. This suffices for the second question.

Sermon 2

When Are God's People Too Cast Down For Sin?

"Why art thou cast down, O my soul? and why art thou disquieted within me? Hope thou in God, for I shall yet praise Him, who is the health of my countenance, and my God." Psalm 42:11

3. When may God's people be said to be cast down too much for sin? Indeed being cast down for sin and humiliation for sin are good and necessary, but when may it be said that a child of God is too much cast down for sin? David checks himself not that he is humbled for sins, but that he is too much cast down for sin.

A child of God may be said to be cast down too much for sin in these nine particulars.

(1) A man is cast down too much for sin when his humiliation makes him cast off all hopes of pardon, or when he so lies under the burden of his sins that he has no hopes to have it taken off. It is too much humiliation if you say (Jeremiah 2:25) that there is no hope and that you are cut off—this is too much, too great a degree and measure of humiliation. When good men say in discouragement, which wicked men will reinforce scoffingly, that their sins are so great, and their case is so desperate that there is no hope—no help for them in God, no salvation for them to be had, no way for them to get out and escape—this is too much casting down for sin. This is the way to cut off hope. The

hope of the saints in heaven is cut off too—but not in this way. Their hopes are turned to full enjoyment of what they previously hoped for. They have no hope because they are *above* hope. But saints on earth are to carry their hopes still above all discouragements and hope strongly for pardon of sin. Better to have the thread of our lives cut off than the anchor cord of our hope. Despair is the cutting off of hope. But to be so cast down under sin as to have despairing thoughts without hope of mercy is excessive.

(2) A man is cast down for sin too much when he is so cast down for sin that he casts off duty. This is when a man shall thus reason against himself: "What need do I have to pray? And why should I perform holy duties? I know God will not hear me. He will not hear my prayers, let me pray as long as I can and as often as I will. And so for confession of sin. What need do I have to confess sin? I know God will not pardon my sin. And why should I beg for grace? I know God will not give me grace. Why should I hear sermons? I know God will not hear me, nor accept my duties; and I shall not get good by all I do, and by all I hear."

These reasonings, O man, are very sinful, and it argues far too great a humiliation for sin. As despair in any man cuts off hope, so such a sinful frame cuts off endeavors. Fools go on (said Solomon) and are confident, but sometimes fools go on and are careless; for a man to be so cast down for sin as to be careless in discharge of duties argues too much dejection of spirit. Despair is the total eclipse of the mind with the blackest fumes arising from the burning lake of fearful terrors.

(3) Your casting down for sin is too much when

you are so dejected and cast down for sin that it leaves you indisposed for holy duties. Good men have been so, and good men may be so overtaken. You have an instance in Asaph, in Psalm 77:4: "Thou holdest mine eyes waking; I am so troubled that I cannot speak." Asaph prayed, and his soul was so sorely troubled and overwhelmed that he could not speak. It is as if he had said, "I would pray, but I cannot pray." He was so troubled by reason of his sin. Then indeed is your humiliation too much when the sight of your sins shall make you unfit for doing your duty—this is not necessary, but sinful.

Proper composedness of spirit in humiliation for sin is so far from making the soul unfit for duty and prayer that it disposes and fits the soul for prayer to God (Hosea 12:4; Jeremiah 3:21; Nehemiah 9:1, 4.) Therefore it is said that the people of Israel wept and made supplication, and they offered sacrifice (Judges 2:4–5). When the sight and the sense of sin and humiliation for sin fill your heart with matter fit for prayer, that is necessary and good; but when by this the soul is made unfit for prayer and supplication, then it is sinful. In Exodus 6:9 it is said that the people hearkened not unto Moses when he spoke unto them because of the anguish of their spirit, or, as it is in the Hebrew, from their stubbornness of spirit (or shortness of spirit). They were so troubled in mind that they could not hear God's word. In Psalm 77:10 Asaph said, "This is my infirmity." If it hinders, it is not the sacrifice that God commands.

(4) A man is too much cast down for sin where there is an unaptness, an unwillingness in the mind to receive and apply comfortable counsels that are laid

down in the Word, and which pertain to him in that condition. If there is any great aptness in you to entertain such terrible threats and denunciations of judgments against sin rather than to receive any good proofs laid down in the gospel, and clear promises to quiet and comfort your troubled spirit; when you are more apt to trouble yourselves for sin than to comfort yourselves against this disquietness of mind upon and under the sight of sin—in this case, you are cast down too much for sin. In Psalm 77:2, it is said that Asaph refused to be comforted. Bad stomachs in children would rather feed on chalk and dirt than wholesome food. So when comforts are propounded and laid before you by the ministers of the gospel, and comforts are suited to your condition and you do not apply them, but lay them all aside, be confident that you are too much cast down for sin. Proverbs 12:25: "Heaviness in the heart of man maketh it stoop, but a good word maketh it glad." Now when heaviness for sin so oppresses you that all the good words that can be given you out of the gospel do you no good, and administer you no comfort, then is your casting down for sin too much. Mark 9:50: "Have salt in yourselves, and have peace one with another." Maintain good doctrine. "Therefore," said Christ, "ye are the salt of the earth."

If you see a pot boiling, and it boils too fast, salt cast into it will allay the boiling. So if your passions grow so fast that all the doctrines of the gospel, all the precious comforts that are therein, cannot allay this passion and pacify the conscience, comfort the soul, and support the spirit, then is your casting down for sin too much; for there is no spiritual disease so dark to the soul but there is comfort enough in the gospel to support the soul under it. When God shall call to you and say, "Come to me, all ye that are weary, and heavy laden, and I will give you rest" (Matthew 11:28), and you refuse to come to Jesus Christ, and put off comfort from you, you are then too much cast down for sin.

(5) A man is too cast down under the weight, sense, and sight of sin when that sorrow for sin shall be an occasion to wrong, hurt, and disturb the body by diseases. And thus melancholy men are subjected too much to this distemper, and herein they are too much to blame. Many there are who make their tears their meat and drink. They are so filled with tears that they cannot eat their bread with comfort. There are many godly souls so troubled with sorrow for sin that they have no comfort and joy of heart. Job 20:25: "It is drawn and cometh out of the body; the glisttering sword cometh out of his gall, terrors are upon him." Many men lie in the bitterness of their souls so that they cannot eat one morsel of bread with joy (Job 21:25). Now God does not require so much sorrow for sin as to eat out the comforts of a man's life and disturb the comforts of his days, so that he becomes so troubled and disquieted that he cannot sleep by night nor take comfort in the day.

It is said concerning Asaph in Psalm 77:4: "Thou holdest mine eyes waking; I am so troubled that I cannot speak." When it is thus with you, that you are so sorely troubled, so overly cast down, it is excessive. The Lord has bidden you to mourn, not to rack and crucify your body but your lusts. He calls you to weep out your sin's strength and life, not your body's strength and life. God never requires nor expects that any man should kill his body to save his soul through humiliation and sorrow for sin.

(6) A man is cast down for sin too much when he is so far and so much cast down under the sight and sense of sin that he has no mind at all to follow his particular calling. Now this is a sinful sorrow. Sorrow for sin is sinful not only when it takes you off from duties of godliness and religion, but when it takes you off from your calling in the world. And the reason is, as all divines say, that God never requires any duty which belongs to our general calling as Christians if it is inconsistent with our particular callings as men. Therefore, if your trouble of mind for sin has been such that it causes you not to regard your particular calling as men in the world, this is not accounted in Scripture a necessary sorrow of sin, but an immoderate one, and too much casting down for sin.

(7) They are too much cast down for sin when the amiable, admirable, and comforting attributes of God are formidable and terrible to such men; when we so think of sin as not to think on the divine attributes of God—of the mercy of God, the goodness of God, the patience of God, the long-suffering of God, the faithfulness of God—when men shall think so of God as if He were all justice, all wrath without mercy. Good men have been overtaken with this fault. Job was so in Job 23:15: "Therefore am I troubled at His presence; when I consider, I am afraid of Him." Here Job tells you of the trouble of mind that he lay under, that it made him afraid of God and troubled at His presence, and when he thought of Him he was troubled at Him.

One would think that to think on God is a comfort; for a man to think that God is merciful to pardon sin and faithful to keep covenant with His people, that there is a liberality in God to supply His people, and strength and power to defend His people, for He is able to save them to the uttermost—one would think it would comfort men to think so on God. But that presence Moses could not endure to be without, the same presence Job could not endure to see; and the reason was because of his guilt, his fears, and doubting within him which cast him down too much. This was Asaph's case: "I remembered God, and I was troubled" (Psalm 77:3). What! the thought of God to trouble Asaph? Yes, "I remembered God, and I was troubled. I complained, and my spirit was overwhelmed."

He might reason thus to himself: "I think that this God is a glorious and a terrible God, a sin-avenging God. And He sees me and marks all my steps. He knows all my ways and will reward all my doings. Therefore, when I thought on God, I was troubled at Him."

Oh, but the thoughts of God comforted David's soul: "When I thought on Thy name, I was comforted," said holy David, Psalm 94:19. But Asaph said, "When I thought on God, I was troubled." Job said, "When I thought on God, on the Almighty, I was afraid of Him." When the attributes of God trouble men who think of them, and do not encourage and comfort them, then is this sorrow too much casting down for sin.

(8) Your sorrow for sin is too much when under this sorrow for sin you cannot look to God, and bless God for common mercies or special grace. God gives you mercies, great mercies, that you may be rich; and He follows you with mercies and blessings and loving kindnesses daily. His faithfulness is towards you every moment, and He gives you the world at will. Yet, if for all this God does not have glory from you, it shows you

are too cast down for sin.

Trouble and humiliation for sin, if it is moderate and right, administers occasions to serve God, and it occasions you to bless God and give Him glory for common mercies and special grace. It occasions you to glorify God. It draws out the heart to serve God and bless Him for the receipt of mercies. And when mercies do not have this effect upon you, and when sorrow for sin works not in this way, it is immoderate sorrow and too much casting down for sin. When God gives you grace to assist you against manifold temptations, and to keep you from committing manifold sins, and to help you against your corruptions, and to give you grace to establish your heart, and yet not to bring up your heart under your sorrow to bless God, this is a sinful sorrow.

If a man is upon his knees, he may see heaven above and the earth beneath; but when a man lies flat upon his face he can neither see the heaven above nor any creature, but only the earth below him. So when God brings you to your knees for sin, then you can see a gracious God, a faithful God, a merciful God, and a pitying Father. Then you can see those blessings that God bestows upon you, and bless and glorify God. But when you throw yourselves on the ground in a deep sorrow, and lie on your faces for sin so as to be too much humbled under the sight and sense of it, in this case God has neither glory, nor do you have any comfort.

(9) When your sins discourage your souls from laying hold on Jesus Christ, you are cast down too much for sin. That man surely is sick unto death when his disease will not let him send for a physician. Troubled ones often say doubtingly what the wicked say scoffingly: "There is no help for me in God." This is

sinful sorrow.

True sorrow and gospel humiliation for sin is such a measure and degree of sorrow that instead of causing the soul to go away from Christ, it encourages the soul to come to Christ, to lay hold of Christ, and to prize Jesus Christ above all the world. But it is a sinful sorrow when it drives the soul from Christ, and discourages the soul from coming to Him and from setting a high estimation and price upon Him. Nor can the soul in such a condition venture itself upon Him. As we must not with the Antinomians so fix our eyes upon free grace and mercy that we have no eye to look upon sin, so should we not, like doubting and despairing Christians, so look upon sin as never to cast any eye upon Jesus Christ.

And thus I have laid down, in these nine particulars, when it may be said that a man may be too much cast down for sin. Having first looked at what sort of men God casts down for sin, we here looked at when God's people may be said to be cast down for sin too much.

I now come to the uses of comfort and of caution.

USE OF COMFORT. If it is so that God's people may be cast down too much for sin, under the sense and sight of sin, then the first comforting observation for the people of God is that God will never cast *off* His people, though He does and may many times cast *down* His people. Though you are cast down, yet comfort yourself: you shall never be cast off. Psalm 94:14: "The Lord will not cast off His people, neither will He forsake His inheritance." He will cast down His people for sin, but cast off His people He will not. This question made the apostle say, "God forbid." "Hath God cast off His people? God forbid." God has not cast off His people whom He foreknew (Romans 11:1–2).

It is true that God's people may be cast off *seemingly* when they are not cast off *really*. It is with them as it was with Christ when He met the two disciples in the last chapter of Luke. He seemed to go away from them, "as though He would have gone further." But Jesus Christ did not intend to go from them. So may God do to your soul: He may seem to go from your soul, but God will never leave your soul. He may seem to withdraw His face, but He will never really withdraw from your soul. Psalm 74:1: "O God, why hast Thou cast us off forever? Why doth Thine anger smoke against the sheep of Thy pasture?"

Psalm 77:7: "Will the Lord cast us off forever?" See also Psalm 89:38 and Leviticus 26:44. Now this was not really so; it only seemed so. God did not cast His people off, though He cast them down. The church apprehended that God had cast them off, but God did not really.

Augustine had a good observation on John 14:4–5 (" 'Whither I go ye know, and the way ye know.' But Thomas said, 'We know not whither Thou goest; and how can we know the way?' "). Here is a seeming contradiction between Christ and Thomas. They said that they did not know, and Christ said that they did know. How shall this be reconciled? The meaning is this: the disciples and Thomas did not know their own knowledge; they had more grace and knowledge than they knew were in themselves.

It may be so with you. God may cast you off seemingly when you think it is so really; but God does not really cast off His people. Therefore, let this comfort you.

It is not the measure of humiliation for sin, but the truth of humiliation for sin to which grace is annexed. The promises are made to grace not as strong grace, but as true grace; not to humiliation as to the measure and length of it, but as to the truth of it. The Scripture does not entail a promise to faith as strong faith, but to weak faith, to little faith, to faith that is small (if true), even though it is but as a grain of mustard seed. And the greatest promises are entailed to the least measure of faith.

It may be, O Christian, that you have not a great measure of faith, but have you little faith? You may not have strong faith, but have you weak faith? Oh, comfort yourself; all the promises are entailed to the beginnings of faith.

It may be that you have not faith like an ear of wheat, but is it like a grain of mustard seed? There are promises for that.

It may be that you have not rivers of tears, but have you any tears for sin? If you have any sorrow for sin, God accepts that. God holds open His bottle to those whose eyes distill a few drops of tears as well as to those who make their heads fountains of water and their eyes rivers of tears. Though it is wrong for Libertines and Antinomians to say that promises are made to sinners as sinners, so it is false too to hold that they are made only to those sinners who are deeply troubled. For total want of grace many a soul has perished, but never was any man damned for want of degrees. Promises are made to grace, to its truth, and not to a certain degree of grace. True grace, though it is weak, is looked upon by God as having an interest in the promises; therefore this should comfort you.

Let this comfort you also, that God has made promises not only *to* humiliation, but also *for* humiliation. Have you a hard heart? God has made promises that He will break your hard heart. God has promised to take away your heart of stone and give you a heart of flesh. God has promised to take away your old heart and give you a new heart. Both of these promises you have laid down in Ezekiel 36:26: "I will give them one heart, and I will put a new spirit within you, and I will take their stony heart out of their flesh, and I will give them a heart of flesh." So much for comfort. I now come to the use of caution.

USE OF CAUTION. In treating this doctrine, I would not speak as many Libertines do, to lay aside all manner of humiliation for sin. Because other men are cast down too much, these will not be cast down at all for sin. Not to reject such a principle is the way to run into all manner of licentious liberty, and to be all upon the extremes.

Labor to order the affections and passions of your mind so that, whenever you are humbled and in sorrow for sin, you take heed that you do not cast off sorrow for sin. Be sure that you have such a degree of humiliation for sin that it may make you lie at Christ's feet and no lower. Christ would have you be so humble as to lie at His feet in the sight and sense of sin, but the devil would have you be so low in your humiliation for sin as to lie in hell. Christ would have you be sorrowful for sin that you might recover out of it, but the devil would have you lie so low in your humiliation for sin that you might never recover. Oh, take heed of such a sinful sorrow for sin. Do not be humbled so much as the devil and your own evil heart would have you.

Sermon 3

Why Are Wicked Men Not Cast Down for Sin?

"Why art thou cast down, O my soul? and why art thou disquieted within me? Hope thou in God, for I shall yet praise Him, who is the health of my countenance, and my God." Psalm 42:11

4. Seeing that God's people may be cast down too much for sin, and too much humbled under the sight and sense of corruptions, then what may be the reason why wicked and ungodly men are not cast down at all for sin? And seeing that godly men may be cast down for sin here too much, and not cast off for sin hereafter, while wicked men shall be cast into hell for sin when they die, why are they not at all cast down for sin while they live? What reasons may be given for this?

ANSWER. Now for the resolution of this question, I shall lay down these reasons:

REASON 1. The first reason why wicked men, though they shall be cast off, are not at all cast down for sin arises from their ignorance of the dangerous and damnable nature of sin. They have a blind mind and a dumb conscience; they see not such evil as godly men do. Although wicked men know what sin is in general, they have but a vague notion of sin in general; it is but a general notion of sin in the head, and they have no particular, personal, and distinct notion of the evil and dangerous nature of sin upon their hearts and consciences. And therefore it comes to pass that they are not cast down for sin. But this general notion of sin casts them off and does not cast them down; and this is the reason why they do not see sin as exceedingly sinful, and do not take notice of the evil of sin, the damning nature of sin, according to that expression in Jeremiah 2:23: "How canst thou say, 'I am not polluted, I have not gone after Baalim'? See thy way in the valley, know what thou hast done; thou are a swift dromedary traversing her ways." The Jews were great in sin and abounding in wickedness, yet they were ready to say that they were not sinful,or at least they did not know that they were so. It is for want of the knowledge of their ways and the sinfulness of their doings that they are not cast down for sin. Should a man meet a lion in the wilderness, he would be afraid of it because he knows that the lion is harmful; but if a man sees a lion painted on the wall, he is not afraid because he knows it cannot hurt him. When men look upon sin, not as upon a lion in the wilderness that will certainly destroy him if he avoids it not, but as upon a lion painted on the wall that has no power to do them hurt, they are seeing sin only generally and notionally, not particularly and personally.

REASON 2. The second reason arises from a principle of presumption of pardoning grace and mercy. When wicked men hear the thunderings and curses of the law pronounced against sin, and see sinners delivered by the ministers of the gospel to awaken them from the sleep of sin and security; when they hear of the severity of God's justice, and that He is a sin-avenging God, and that He will by no means clear the guilty, but will render to everyone according to his ways and works—now what does a wicked man do in this case? Does this awaken his conscience to see the evil of sin? No, he does quite the contrary. He then, from a principle of presumption of pardoning grace and mercy in God, blesses himself in his own ways, and says, "I shall have peace, though I walk after the imaginations of my own evil heart" (Deuteronomy 29:19).

It is as if they should say, "Let sin trouble them who will, let it cast down them who will be cast down, it shall never cast down me; it shall never trouble me. What shall sin trouble my conscience or disquiet my peace for? Why shall I mourn and trouble myself about that which I need not? That which others seem to break their hearts for shall never break my sleep, for I hope that it shall never damn my soul. But I hope that, though I commit sin, yet God will pardon sin. And though I am sinful, yet I know God is merciful." And thus, from a principle of presumption, they go on in a way of sin without any trouble for it or casting down under the sight and sense of sin at all.

REASON 3. Another reason why wicked men are not cast down for sin at all arises from that obdurateness, from that hardness that is in their hearts, and from that searedness in their consciences. There is a generation of men of whom it may be said concerning sin that they are past feeling, according to that expression of the apostle in Ephesians 4:19: "Who being past feeling have given themselves over unto lasciviousness, to work all uncleanness with greediness." And, as Paul said in 1 Timothy 4:2, "They have their consciences seared with a hot iron." When men have so accustomed themselves to sin that sin shall harden the heart and sear the conscience, then no marvel if they are not at all cast down for sin.

REASON 4. Wicked men are not cast down for sin at all because they stifle the rebukes of conscience when it rebukes them, checks their sin, and casts them down for sin. Men resolve that though they shall be cast off for sin, though they are cast into hell for sin, yet they will not at all be cast down for sin. And rather than cast off their sins to follow the dictates, rebukes, and checks of their consciences, they will aggravate and greaten their sins by stifling their conscience so that it shall not do its office.

Thus did Cain, when he began to be troubled for sin, and conscience began to rebuke him for the evils he had done. What did Cain do then? Did he let his conscience do its office? No, he both heightened and increased his sin, and stifled his conscience. Genesis 4:13: "My punishment is greater than I can bear"; or, as it is in the Hebrew, "my iniquity is greater than may be forgiven." And then he went to stifle his conscience. Verse 16: "And Cain went out from the presence of the Lord, and dwelt in the land of Nod." He went out from God's presence and stifled his conscience by building cities.

And hence it comes to pass that men are not cast down for sin because they stifle the rebukes and checks of conscience. So divines interpret that phrase in the 11th verse of the epistle of Jude: "Woe unto them, for they have gone in the way of Cain." That was when conscience rebuked and troubled him for killing his brother and spilling his blood. And after stifling and stilling his conscience, he went to build cities.

And thus, O man, you who walk in ways of wickedness, and whose conscience rebukes you for your evil course by telling you that your conversation is not good nor upright, and tells you that your ways are unjust and sinful, and yet you, through becoming accustomed to an evil course, stifle the checks and rebukes of your conscience, and delight to go on in a way of wickedness—this is another great reason why wicked men are not cast down in this world for sin.

REASON 5. A fifth reason why wicked men are not cast down for sin in this world is because of their abuse of the long-suffering and patience of God. You have a notable pasage for this in Ecclesiastes 8:11: "Because sentence against an evil work is not speedily executed, therefore the heart of the sons of men is fully set in them to do evil." Because God does not punish wicked men for their wickedness speedily—because a drunkard is not speedily punished for his drunkenness, and because a swearer is not speedily punished for his swearing, and because the adulterer is not speedily punished for his uncleanness—therefore they fully set themselves to work wickedness. When wicked men abuse the patience and long-suffering of God, to presume the more to sin against Him, hence it comes to pass that they are not cast down for sin at all.

REASON 6. A sixth reason is because of the slight thoughts that wicked men have of the omniscience of God. Though wicked men are not usually doctrinal atheists, denying that God sees all things, they most often are practical atheists, living loosely, wickedly, and vainly, as if God did not behold all things and know and see them in their sinful course. Job 22:13–14: "And thou sayest, 'How doth God know?' or, 'What knows God?' 'Can He judge through the dark clouds? Thick clouds are a covering to Him, that He seeth not.' "

It is as much as if they had said that God does not know, and God does not see their wicked and sinful ways, as though the clouds were a covering between God and them so that He could not see their evil ways. And this was the cause why their sins troubled them not. Now I am done with the fourth question, why wicked men are not cast down for sin at all.

5. *Seeing that wicked men are not cast down for sin at all, and yet shall be cast down into hell, and that for these reasons laid down, then what may be the reason why godly men, who shall never be cast off, and shall never be cast down into hell, yet may be cast down for sin in the sight and sense of it?*

ANSWER. In answering this question I shall lay down these seven reasons.

REASON 1. The first is drawn from the nature of sin and the justice of God, considering them together. Sin is, in its own nature, a wrestling and a striving and contending against God, a striving to cast God down and to set itself up. It is the nature of sin to pull God out of heaven from His throne and to place itself there. Now God will, in justice, strive and contend against sin, and show Himself to be too strong for sin and sinners and to cast them down.

You may see that this is the nature of sin in Job 15:25–26: "For he stretcheth out his hand against God, and strengtheneth himself against the Almighty. He runneth upon Him, even on His neck, upon the thick bosses of His buckler." Here Eliphaz describes a sinner in his wicked ways as a soldier coming against his enemy: he strengthens himself against him, and he runs upon him with all his might, so that he might overcome. So a wicked man strengthens himself and runs against God, as it were, with all his might, if it were possible, to overcome and cast Him from His throne where He is. And therefore it is just with God to condemn sin and to humble the sinner. The sinner would cast God's law behind his back; but it is the nature of sin to cast God behind his back. Now God will, in justice, cast away a sinner by condemnation or lay the sinner low by humiliation.

REASON 2. God casts down sinners under the sight and sense of sin so that the children of God might cast away sin with the more indignation. And therefore God casts him down the more by way of humiliation. If a man should fall with his knife in his hand and thereby cut himself with it, he presently flings the knife away from him. Now it is so in the ways of sin and wickedness: when you take sin into your hands, when you go into any unwarranted course, when you fall into sin, you take knives into your hands, and in falling so into sin you cut yourselves. God makes that knife of sin cut your heart, cut your conscience, and so wound your souls. Seeing that sin, like a knife, wounds you in your falling therein, you should with the more indignation cast it from you.

You read in Isaiah 30:19–22 of sorrow for sin: "The people shall dwell in Zion; thou shalt weep no more. He will be very gracious unto thee at the voice of thy cry; when He will hear it, He will answer thee." Here is God's promise upon their humiliation. Then in verse 22: "Ye shall defile also the covering of the graven images of silver, and the ornament of thy molten images of gold; thou shalt cast them away as a menstruous cloth; thou shalt say unto it, 'Get thee hence.' "

God makes His people mourn for sin, and He casts

them down for sin, to humble them under the sight and sense of sin, and to make them have indignation against sin and then cast sin from them as a menstruous cloth. When women are weaning their children, they put some bitter thing upon the breast, like wormwood or gall, to make the child forsake it. So God puts bitter things upon those things which we account sweet. He puts bitter potions upon the breast of our sinful delights so that He might wean His people from sucking any more at those poisonous breasts which we so highly esteem in our corrupt nature.

You read of the prodigal son in Luke 15:16. When he was brought to those great sufferings so that he desired to feed of the husks with the swine, after he came to himself, he desired to eat bread, and be as one of the hired servants in his father's house. God makes His people smart for sin as the prodigal did in his absence from his father's house. When they are laid low for sin under the sense and sight of their sins, as the prodigal was, and when they come to themselves again, then they would be glad with the prodigal to prize their father's house. So when the soul comes to be brought very low for sin, then it sets a high esteem on Jesus Christ. It is very observable that where humiliation for sin is mentioned, there it is joined with a detestation of and separation from sin (James 4:8; Joel 2:12).

REASON 3. God puts sinners under the sight and sense of sin because it causes the soul to throw itself and rely upon Jesus Christ. It is our necessity that puts us first upon the pursuit after and reliance upon Jesus Christ, because we see that we are undone without Him. It is with us as it was with the leprous person we read of in 2 Kings 7:3: "And there were four leprous persons at the entering in of the gate, and they said one to another, 'Why sit we here until we die? If we say, "We will enter into the city," then the famine is in the city, and we shall die there; and if we sit still here, we die also. Now therefore come, and let us fall into the host of the Syrians: if they save us alive, we shall live, and if they kill us, we can but die.' " I apply this passage to our case: If I die in a Christless state, I am gone forever and undone to eternity. And if I rest in confidence in the world, it can afford no safety. I will therefore run to Jesus Christ that there I may have relief, and that there I may ease myself of my burden by resting upon Jesus Christ's promise.

REASON 4. God casts His people down under the sense of sin so that He might suppress our lifting up the pride of our own hearts in the sight and apprehension of our own gifts. When the Lord sees a man become lifted up within himself with pride about his gifts, then God will hide his gifts, show him his sin, lay him low, and make him humble.

So was it with Paul: he was a man of exceedingly great abilities and gifts above other men, even above all other men but Jesus Christ. And yet, for all that, he was apt to be proud, and to be too much lifted up within himself in the apprehension of his own gifts. And for this he had a thorn in his flesh to keep him humble lest he should be exalted above measure (2 Corinthians 12:7). So read in Psalm 9:20: "Put them in fear, O Lord, that the nations may know themselves to be but men."

Men of the greatest gifts have the greatest fears to keep down pride. The swan that has white feathers has black feet. So those who have the greatest excellence shall have some manifest infirmity to keep them down.

Heman was a man of excellent gifts (1 Kings 4:31), yet see how God humbled him in Psalm 88:7, 15. To cure His people of this distemper of spiritual pride, God lays them low and casts them down under the sight and sense of sin.

REASON 5. God casts down His people that thereby He might bring the hearts of His people to a clearer sight and a more sensible and lively feeling of pardoning grace and mercy. The deeper God is pleased to cast His people under the sense and sight of sin, and the lower He lays them under humiliation, the higher will they exalt God in His pardoning grace and mercy. After men are tossed at sea in a tempest, they prize the harbor. God takes the same course with His people as it is reported that astronomers take: they do not lie on the tops of high mountains when they would take a view of the sky, but they lie in the lowest valleys—not in places which are nearest the heavens, but in low places most remote from the heavens. So God does not lift up His people at all times as upon mountains, but lays them low in the valley of humiliation, and casts them low under the sight and sense of sin that thereby their hearts, by faith, might take a more clear view of, and sensibly and lively feel, the free mercy and pardoning grace of God. God casts you into low pits of humiliation, that by that you may see more clearly God's mercy and grace.

God plunges His people under humiliation as you may read in Psalm 44:25–26: "Our soul is bowed down to the dust; our belly cleaveth to the earth. Arise, O Lord, for our help, and redeem us for Thy mercies' sake." Here you see the church complaining of the depth of her sorrow and the greatness of her humiliation; her soul was bowed down even to the dust, a great degree of casting down.

But what was God's end in this great humbling of them? It was to give them a more sensible feeling of God's pardoning mercy and grace, as appears in the words, "Redeem us for Thy mercies' sake." Mercy was precious, and pardoning grace was precious when they lay low under affliction and were deeply humbled. The sense and sight of sin and misery under which they lay made them prize and highly esteem pardoning grace and mercy. And this is another reason why God lays His people low under the sight and sense of sin: that they might esteem pardoning grace.

REASON 6. God brings His people down to make them confess that there is more evil in sin than ever there was seeming pleasure in committing sin. It is a notable instance in Ecclesiastes 7:25–26: "I applied my heart to know, and to search, and to seek out wisdom, and the reason of things, and to know the wickedness of folly, even of foolishness and madness. And I find more bitter than death the woman whose heart is snares and nets, and her hands as bands; whoso pleases God, (or whoso is good before God) shall escape from her, but the sinner shall be taken by her."

Here Solomon applied his heart to find out the deceits of sin. It is as if he had said, "I have studied to know the secret snares and the private nets that sin lays to catch sinners. And in a special manner I labored to know the secret mischief of that sin of adultery." For you read that he had seven hundred wives and three hundred concubines (1 Kings 11:3). And when God made him see the evil of that sin and cast him down under the sense of that sin, so that he could say he found it "a thing more bitter than death, a harlot whose heart is snares and nets," then he could see that it was folly and wickedness and madness.

Now when God casts down His people under the sight and sense of sin, He brings them to see, and to confess with Solomon, that sin is more bitter than death, and to confess that there is more evil in the least sin than there can be seeming pleasure and profit and contentment in the commission of it. The hearts of the people of God have never tasted the bitterness of sin until God lays them low, and casts them down under the weight and sense of sin. And by this means He makes them see how bitter a thing sin is.

REASON 7. God does this to make wicked men afraid to commit sin. And this is done in mercy to them, did they but consider it.

May not wicked men reason thus to themselves? "Why, if God treats His own people so for their sin, what may I expect at God's hands? If God casts down His own people under the sense and sight of sin, what may I expect from His hands who so delights in sin, which His own people suffer so for? Surely if God casts down His own people under the sight and the apprehension of sin, then surely I may expect to be cast off for sin. If they are cast down to the ground for sin, I shall be cast into hell for sin. Does He cast them down in the apprehension of hell? Surely, He may cast me down to the possession of hell. And have I not cause to be cast down for sin who shall be cast off for sin? If His own people shed tears for sin, then I should shed blood for sin. And if they are cast down for sin who shall never be wholly rejected, shall I not be cast down for sin whose sins shall make me be rejected?"

So I say that God, in casting down His own people, does it out of mercy to wicked men that they thereby may beware and not venture to commit sin against God. And thus I have, in those seven particulars, answered this fifth question, why the people of God, those who shall never be cast off, may yet be cast down under the sight and sense of sin.

6. What theological rules may be laid down for the people of God that they may not be overly cast down for sin under the sight and sense and burden of it, nor be too much dejected under it?

ANSWER. Now in answer to this query consider these particulars:

RULE 1. Do not expect so much sorrow and casting down for sin as some other men have had. And the reason why I give you this rule is that some of the people of God will thus reason: "I must be thus and thus cast down for sin, and I must have such a degree and such a measure of humiliation, because I see other men have so. I must have such a sight of sin and lie so low for sin because other men do so. And shall I not do so? Shall I not lie so low? Shall I not be so humbled for sin as I see others are? I have as many sins as they, and I have as great sins as they, and my sins are accompanied with as heinous circumstances as theirs are, and therefore why should I not be humbled as they are?"

Now consider, what if others have been cast down more than you have been? What is this to your humiliation for sin? Other men's degree, manner, or measure of humiliation is not to be a rule for you to humble yourself by. It may be that others who have had such a degree of humiliation and casting down for sin have been more notorious in sin. They may have more rugged natures and be of a more stubborn temper than you are of. It may be that your temper is more flexible, more pliable, more yielding, and more easily wrought upon than others have been. Therefore there is not required such a degree and measure of humiliation as they require.

It may be that you cannot bear that which others can. That ballast which would serve a ship would overload a little boat. Therefore do not compare your casting down for sin with others, lest you cast yourself too low for sin. Other men, it may be, contract more sin than you do, and, it may be, you have not so stifled your conscience as they have. It may be that you have not laid waste your conscience as they have done. It may be that you have not lived so ill as they have. Therefore you do not need so great a measure of humiliation for sin as they. You have an expression therefore in 1 Peter 1:6: "If need be, ye are in heaviness through manifold temptations." God in His wisdom sees that some men stand in need, yea, in more need of a greater measure of affliction and casting down for sin than others. It may be that some men have more spiritual pride in their abilities, gifts, and graces, and more guilt lying upon them than you have.

RULE 2. The second rule is by way of direction: rest satisfied in your conscience. Though you may not find the measure of your humiliation, yet if you find the end of your humiliation, rest satisfied in that. If in your humiliation you desire to be truly humbled for sin; if you desire to lay yourself low in the presence of God; if you desire to abhor yourself in regard to your sinfulness of nature and life; if you desire to amend your ways and your doings that have not been good, and to walk closer to God—if so, though you have not the measure of humiliation and casting down for sin as others have, yet you have the end of humiliation, and you may rest satisfied in your conscience. If that humiliation embitters sin and endears Jesus Christ to your soul, I tell you, O poor soul, though you have not a greater degree of humiliation, you may be dear to Jesus Christ and may go to heaven for all that.

Further, for your comfort, there was never anyone who went to hell and lost heaven for want of *degrees* of grace; but many go to hell and lose heaven for want of *truth* of grace. None ever went to hell for want of such and such a degree of casting down for sin, and for want of such and such a degree of humiliation; but many go to hell for want of humiliation in the least measure and truth of it. If there is faith in you, grace in your soul, though it is but as a grain of mustard seed, a little grace planted in the soul shall spring up to a harvest of glory as your reward. Yea, God rewards the soul with no less a reward than glory for a little grace. Heaven is not promised to the soul upon such and such degrees of grace, or having so much faith and so much repentance, so much humiliation, so much casting down for sin and so much love for Christ (though we are to strive after a strong faith in God, much love for God, etc.); rather heaven is promised to weak faith and a little love. Therefore if you find the ends of humiliation, you may satisfy yourself though you want the degrees. This is the second rule.

RULE 3. Be sure to cast yourself upon Jesus Christ for life and salvation, and then, whatever comes, rest assured that you will not be too much cast down for sin, nor too dejected under it. What is the great reason why so many poor souls are so much cast down for sin, too dejected under the sight and sense of it? It is because they are afraid to cast themselves wholly upon Jesus Christ and roll themselves upon Him for salvation. Though more sin requires more tears for sin upon the thoughts of it, yet Jesus Christ need not shed more blood for sin. Jesus Christ needs no more to die for satisfaction for sin. Christ has paid a full and complete and sufficient ransom for sin, and needs to die no more. But you have not shed all the tears you must for sin, for the body of sin and the remainders of corruption that are within you. It is the nature of wicked men, yea, and good men too, to run to extremes about and concerning sin; therefore observe this rule, for it will be a means to keep you so that you do not cast yourselves down too much for sin.

First, it is natural for wicked men to be so far from being cast down for sin too much that they will not be trouble, nor cast down for sin at all, but will go on from sin to sin, to pass from one degree to another, till they perish everlastingly, and this they do without fear.

Second, on the other hand, good men are very apt to run into the opposite error. While wicked men will not be cast down for sin at all, good men will labor to cast themselves too low for sin under the sight and sense of it. The Scripture makes mention of wicked men as being not at all troubled for sin, as you may read in Job 21:14–15; nothing troubles their consciences when they come to die. See verse 13: "They spend their days in wealth (or, as the Hebrew word is, they spend their days in mirth), and in a moment go down to the grave." But are they at all humbled before God? Read the 14th and 15th verses: "Therefore they say unto God, 'Depart from us: for we do not desire the knowledge of Thy ways. What is the Almighty, that we should serve Him? and what profit should we have, if we pray unto Him?' "Wherefore? Because they lived in mirth and pleasure and at heart's ease; and they never so much as thought of sin, and much less in order to be humbled under the sense of it. And therefore they cared for neither God nor His ways. So you see wicked men are not cast down for sin at all.

But now good men are, on the other hand, very apt to embitter their own condition by being too much cast down for sin. This is possible, and good men are very apt to do it. 2 Corinthians 2:7: "Ye ought to comfort him, lest perhaps such a one should be swallowed up with too much sorrow." This happens when a child of God shall, out of bitterness of soul, cast himself down too much for sin. The church had excommunicated this person for his sin, and when he was under this censure he suffered for his sin; but it was the apostle's fear that he might be weighed down with too much sorrow. Therefore, though wicked men make light of sin who are not humbled under the sight and sense of it at all, take heed that in your mourning for sin you do not cast yourselves down too much for sin.

And thus I have resolved these six questions. I shall now close up this doctrine with a word of use.

USE. Is it so that the children of God may be cast down for sin though they may not be cast off for sin? May a godly man be so cast down for sin that he may cry out with the Psalmist: "Why art thou cast down, O my soul? And why art thou disquieted within me?" While wicked men may live in pleasure all their days and never be troubled or cast down under the sight and

Why Are Wicked Men Not Cast Down for Sin?

sense of sin, I shall direct my speech a little to wicked men.

First, O you who live in a course of ungodliness, in ways of wickedness, delighting to live after the imaginations of your own evil hearts, consider and reason thus with your own souls: "What, are good men cast down who shall never be cast off? Are they dejected who shall never be rejected?" What will you do who heap sin upon sin, and add iniquity to iniquity to multiply your abominations, and never have your hearts be troubled, or your consciences smite you for the evil of your doings? Oh, consider that many may be cast into hell for sin who never have been cast down for sin; and if you go on and continue in this way of sinning, what will become of you!

But you may say, "What may be done, or what means may be used to get the soul into such a frame to be cast down for sin, and to have the soul humbled under the sight and sense of it?"

Now there are three ways that the Lord uses to cast down the souls of sinners and humble them under the sight and sense of sin.

The first is this: God lets in a light into the understanding, and sets at work that great officer of God in man, his conscience, which so smites the heart and convinces the whole soul of the evil of his doings, and makes the man single out sin, yea, single out his master sin, his beloved Delilah, his bosom lust, that has made him most guilty of the breach of the righteous law, and laid him most liable to the wrath of God. He singles out that sin that has been his companion all his days. God not only makes him look upon sin in general (because a general view of sin in the soul works in the soul a general repentance for sin), but God, by the light that He puts in the understanding and conscience, singles out his sin, his dearly beloved sin, and, as it were, brings it to his understanding that he may understand the guilt and weight of it.

Therefore you read of some in their first conversion, in Acts 2:37, who were guilty of many sins, but God, by setting their consciences to work, singled out one sin in a special manner, the sin that they were most guilty of, and that was crucifying the Lord of life. You have it laid down in the 36th verse: "Therefore let all the house of Israel know assuredly, that God hath made that same Jesus, whom ye have crucified, both Lord and Christ."

"Whom ye have crucified"—there was the sin that came home to their hearts. You may read in the 37th verse: "Now when they heard this, they were pricked in their hearts." Here they were taken in the sin that they were most guilty of. God made their consciences bring that sin forward in a most special manner, and this troubled and pricked them at the very heart. Though they stood guilty of many great sins, yet God laid that one great sin to their hearts that they might be humbled for that most of all.

When the woman of Samaria came to Jesus Christ at the well and spoke about her husbands, He told her that was her sin: "He whom thou hast now is not thy husband." Christ told her what her sin was in plain terms. He told her that she was a harlot, and she went and said that He told her all that ever she had done. Christ did not tell her she was a sinner in general, but He singled out what the great sin was for which she was most guilty, and that worked upon her heart and conscience. Her conscience told her, she understood the truth of it, and this made her cast down for it.

So now if God gives you grace to be cast down for sin under the sight and sense of it, He will put a light into your understanding, and set conscience to work to single out your beloved sin, the greatest sin you stand guilty of, your master corruption, so that you may be humbled for it.

The second way God uses to cast a man down under the sight and sense of sin is this: God stirs up the affections of the soul in the remembrance of those aggravations and heinous circumstances with which that sin is clothed. Job 36:9: "He showeth unto men their works, and their transgressions that they have exceeded." He shows men their iniquities, and what follows?—and their transgressions which have been exceedingly great. God not only shows men their sins, and that their sins are great, but also He shows men the aggravations of their sins. And it is not a transient view of the greatness of their iniquities and transgressions, but He causes them to know it. He causes them to know that their sins are clothed with heinous circumstances, that they have sinned against means, sinned against mercies, sinned against love, sinned against light, and sinned against the checks of conscience. And all this is to make you be cast down and humbled for your sins.

The third and last way God uses to cast a man down for sin is this: God puts conscience into office in men not only to single out one particular master sin, but also to bring to remembrance those sins that you stand guilty of before God, and to set them in your sight (especially that master sin, that beloved sin), and to humble you for it, and abase you before God until that sin is mortified in you. Sin must not only be seen, and the affections stirred up in remembrance of those heinous circumstances of it with which it is clothed, and that they are exceedingly great, but also conscience must keep them in remembrance until they are mortified in you, until that sin is subdued and mortified.

And these are the three steps that God takes to cast men down in the sight and sense of sin. And now all you who are strangers to this work, who never yet knew what this casting down for sin meant in any measure, labor to find these three particulars wrought upon your soul so that you may be cast down under the sight and sense of sin. And so I am done with this doctrine concerning casting down for sin.

Sermon 4

Christians Ought to Check Their Own Hearts

"Why art thou cast down, O my soul? and why art thou disquieted within me? Hope thou in God, for I shall yet praise Him, who is the health of my countenance, and my God." Psalm 42:11

Now before I come to the second branch of the words, I shall consider the text in the dialect or form of speech which the psalmist here uses, and then draw out some doctrine that the words will afford. You see that the form of speech here is by way of a soliloquy, which is a form of speech to himself as between two friends: "Why art thou cast down, O my soul?" From this expression or form of speech take this observation:

DOCTRINE 1. Such self-conferences or soliloquies that the psalmist here uses are duties that believers ought to be much conversant about, and ought to busy themselves much in. The Psalms are fraught with these divine soliloquies, as you may read in Psalm 103:1: "Bless the Lord, O my soul, and all that is within me, bless His holy name." Verse 22: "Bless the Lord, O my soul." Psalm 104:1: "Bless the Lord, O my soul." Psalm 34:1: "I will bless the Lord at all times." So likewise Psalm 146:1: "Praise the Lord, O my soul." And there are many places in the Psalms of his praising God.

All these intimate to us those divine soliloquies that the people, the saints and servants of God, have had in themselves to bless God. See not only the divine soliloquies here mentioned, but also the works of Augustine, Bernard, Gerrard, Dr. Hall, and others who have had divine soliloquies between God and their own souls in secret. Therefore let this be your care, yea, make conscience to be much in these divine soliloquies, to have much conference between God and your own souls in secret.

Conferring with others is a duty that Christians are bound to; and this God takes notice of. So also it is a duty to confer with God and your own souls. David sometimes blessed God, and sometimes he checked himself. Sometimes he called to his soul to bless God and raised up his soul to praise God, and sometimes he chided his soul for being cast down: "Why art thou cast down, O my soul?"

Are you at any time troubled in mind? Then use the reasoning of this holy man: "Why art thou cast down, O my soul?" Are you at any time sluggish in duty? Then say to yourself, "It is better to be the servant of God than to be the devil's drudge," and so draw up your soul again to a frame suitable to the duty you go about and the God you serve. It is better to live in peace with God and a good conscience than to live in the service of the devil, which will bring trouble of mind and horror of conscience to thee. And say by conferring with yourself with your soul, "What am I? What is my condition? Am I an elect person or am I a reprobate? Am I an heir of glory or an heir of hell? Am I a child of God or a child of wrath? Am I in the state of grace or the bonds of iniquity?" Such conferences as these with your own heart will be a means to awaken your heart from the sleep of security to consider its own state. This is your duty. Let

Christians Ought to Check Their Own Hearts

this be your practice to enter into a discourse with your own hearts as David did. But I shall not follow this particular point any further.

There is something more in the words to be considered, and that is the manner how David speaks to his own soul, and how he reasons with his own heart and says, "Why art thou cast down, O my soul?" From this manner of speech consider this doctrine:

DOCTRINE 2. A child of God should check his soul for, and use holy reasonings against, excessive casting down for sin. And this I draw from the manner of the psalmist's speech. He checked his own heart and reasoned with his own soul concerning this particular: "Why art thou cast down, O my soul?"

In the handling of this doctrine there are two particulars to be considered. First, a child of God should check his heart for, and use holy reasonings against, excessive sorrow and casting down for sin; second, I will show you in what manner you are to use these holy reasonings against your excessive casting down for sin.

PARTICULAR 1. A child of God should check his heart for, and use holy reasonings against, inordinate and excessive casting down for sin. Why? Because, first, he is the chief actor and principal agent of his own dejections; and he, being the chief agent of his sorrow, is to lay the fault and blame on his own self. I told you, though the words are translated passively, "Why art thou cast down, O my soul?" yet they are to be read actively, according to the original text. "Why, or for what, do you cast yourself down, O my soul?" Therefore, if you are cast down, you are the actor and agent of your own dejection; you cast yourself down. Therefore check your own heart for, and use holy reasonings against, immoderate and excessive dejections for sin. God enjoins His people to believe in Him, to keep up their souls, to lift up their souls to God. Yet sometimes they are subject to cast themselves down, and cast their souls down by immoderate and excessive casting down for sin. When the devil by his temptations does not cast them down, yet will they cast themselves down: "Why dost thou cast thyself down, O my soul?"

This is the readiest and most effectual way to recover himself out of that dejected condition: by checking his own heart for being excessively cast down. Holy and religious arguments with a man's own soul are prevalent arguments to work the soul out of its dejected state, whereas, if he should let himself alone in this dejected state, he would soon plunge himself into such a condition, such excessive and immoderate casting down for sin, such a gulf of misery, that he would not be able to get out again. As it is good for a man to reason with his heart when he is assured of salvation, so it is good to reason with his heart why he doubts it. There is a time to ask "Why am I cast down in sorrow" as well as "Why am I raised up in comfort?".

PARTICULAR 2. After what manner are the people of God to use these holy reasonings against immoderate and excessive casting down of their souls for sin?

ANSWER. There are seven ways how the children of God are to check their hearts for, and to use holy reasonings against, excessive sorrow and casting down for sin.

1. The children of God should reason with themselves after this manner: "O my soul, I am not cast off by God everlastingly by lying low before God; therefore why should I be cast down excessively for sin?" Psalm

94:14: "For the Lord will not cast off His people, neither will He forsake His inheritance." Although God does not say, "I will not cast down My people," yet He does say, "I will not cast them off." So, in Romans 11:2, the apostle repeats the words again: "God hath not cast off His people," and he puts a "God forbid" upon it in the previous verse: "Hath God cast off His people? God forbid." The apostle brings it in as a strong negation: "God hath not cast off His people whom He foreknew." Therefore, seeing that God does not cast off His people, why should we be too much cast down? Let wicked men, let reprobates who shall be eternally cast off, let *them* be excessively cast down; but let not me be excessively cast down for sin, seeing that we shall never be cast off, though we may be cast down for a little moment, according to that expression in Isaiah 54:7–8: "For a small moment have I forsaken thee, but in great mercies will I gather thee. In a little wrath have I hid My face from thee, for a moment; but with everlasting kindness will I have mercy upon thee, saith the Lord, thy Redeemer." This casting down for sin is but momentary, a small time, a little season, but He will not cast off forever.

2. Reason with your own soul against your dejections and say, "Jesus Christ laid down His life for me voluntarily and meritoriously, and laid Himself down very low to be my Savior. Therefore, why, O my soul, should you be cast down excessively for sin? It is true, O my soul, that if you had died, and had purchased your own redemption as your own savior, and if the weight and the extreme burden of your sins had been laid upon your own shoulders, and if you had made perfect satisfaction to divine justice in your own person, if you had

been obliged to have kept the whole law perfectly, and if you had made a full recompense for the wrong and evil that you have done, and you were to offer the fruit of your body for the sin of your soul, yet this would not do, nor procure the least satisfaction, nor make the least compensation and recompense for the evil you have done."

Now if this were your case, to be your own mediator and your own intercessor, and to have your blood spilled for your sins—if this were your case, you would have cause to be excessively cast down for sin. A finite creature can never make satisfaction to infinite justice. "Could I give a thousand rams, ten thousand rivers of oil, yet I could not make an atonement, or give a sufficient ransom for my redemption." But it is far otherwise. Quite the contrary is your portion. Here, O my soul, is your case, which may abundantly administer you comfort: the blood, the precious blood of Jesus Christ, is laid down for sin that you may not be excessively cast down for sin, and you may draw an abundance of comfort and satisfaction from this consideration.

First, consider with yourself: "O my soul, Jesus Christ did not shed His precious blood for Himself, but for me. He did, like a good shepherd, lay down His life for His sheep (John 10:15)."

Second, consider that God the Father accepted the laying down of His life in this behalf. John 10:17: "The Father loves Me, because I lay down My life."

Third, consider and reason with yourself: "O my soul, what if there are great arguments to greaten and heighten sin? So there are many great arguments to greaten the mercy of God in Christ. Are your sins great?

Christians Ought to Check Their Own Hearts

The mercies of God are greater. Do your sins deserve great punishments, even eternal death? The death of Jesus Christ and the merit of Christ are of infinite value to merit life, even eternal life. Are your sins the sins of a man? But the satisfactions of Jesus Christ are the satisfactions of God! Do your sins merit the frowns of God? Oh, but Christ's death merits and purchases the favor of God."

In a word, as Christ's person excels your person, so His obedience infinitely exceeds your disobedience. Therefore, said the Apostle Paul in Romans 5:16: "But the free gift is of many offenses unto justification." Here the apostle intimates that though there is great guilt in sin, yet there is greater mercy and merits in Christ. For as by Adam there came sin and death, so by Jesus Christ there came righteousness and life, for "as the wages of sin is death, so the gift of God is eternal life through Jesus Christ our Lord" (Romans 6:23). There is not so much guilt in sin as there is merit in Christ. There is not so much guilt in sin to condemn as there is merit in Jesus Christ to save. Therefore, "Why should you be cast down, O my soul? Jesus Christ has laid down His life for me, and in laying down His life He has made full satisfaction for sin unto His Father." And though there are required more tears for sin by way of humiliation, yet there is needed no more blood for sin by way of satisfaction. Therefore be not excessively cast down for sin.

3. Reason with your own soul that you may not be too excessively cast down for sin: "O my soul, consider that excessive casting down may hinder you from holy endeavors in suppressing and mortifying sin." It is the policy and sublety of the devil to draw men to run into

extremes. Sometimes the devil draws men to be so possessed with the reigning power of sin that they shall never so much as think of the guilt of sin. And sometimes he possesses them so with the power of sin that they are not able so much as to look at the pardon of sin. I may say to you as God said to Joshua in Joshua 7:10, "Get thee up; why liest thou on thy face?" It was fitting that Joshua should be cast down at the disaster, but not be taken off from pursuing the enemy. Therefore reason and say, "O my soul, it does not become you to be cast down excessively under the guilt of sin, but to lift yourself up against it by resting upon God."

4. Reason thus with your soul: "O my soul, consider, are not these dejections of mind, are not these excessive castings down for sin exceedingly great disparagements of God's free grace and mercy and of Christ's merits?" If a man who is thirsty comes to the sea, the mighty ocean, to seek water, and when he comes there is cast down with the thought that all the water in the sea cannot quench his thirst, this would render the sea to be but an empty thing. So if you are troubled and are exceedingly and excessively cast down for sin, and think that the mercy in God and the merits of Christ cannot comfort and bear up your dejected soul, this exceedingly disparages the mighty ocean of God's mercies and Christ's merits, for you to think that your sins outlast mercy and outstrip free grace.

In the time of the law, the mercy seat wholly covered the ark where the law was kept, to show that if a man violated not only one command, but every command of the law, yet all that might be covered over with mercy and, notwithstanding the violation of the law, they had a mercy seat to go to. Though we violate all the law, all the commands of God, yet this law is covered all over with mercy. The mercy of God is far above your dejections. The Red Sea drowned Pharaoh and all his host with as much ease as it could drown one man. So the red sea of Christ's blood can drown every sin, though they were mountains of transgressions, as well as the least sin. Psalm 25:11: "For Thy name's sake, O Lord, pardon my iniquity, for it is great." It is an emphatic word in the Hebrew. We read it, "for it is great," but it may be read, "though it is great. For the sake of Thy name, O Lord, pardon Thou my iniquities, because (or, although) they are multiplied," or, "therefore Thou wilt pardon them, because they are great."

5. Reason thus with your soul: "Why will you cast yourself down, O my soul, especially considering that the casting down of the soul casts down the body also?" There is such a sympathy between the body and the soul that the one cannot be troubled and cast down but the other is so also. For when the body of Christ was troubled, His soul was troubled also. When the people of God have melancholy and troubled thoughts, it troubles and disturbs the body as well as the mind. It weakens the body and lessens that joy that they should have in God, and puts the whole man out of order. Therefore it is very observable what David said, and I shall lay it down for those who are troubled under the dejections of mind for sin, for those very men who cast themselves down for sin excessively. This also disturbs and troubles the body. Psalm 32:3–4: "I kept silence, and my moisture is turned into the drought of summer.' And it is more fully set forth in Psalm 38:3–5: "There is no soundness in my flesh, by reason of Thine anger; neither is there any rest in my bones, by reason of my

sin. For mine iniquities are gone over my head; as a heavy burden, they are too heavy for me, and I go mourning all the day." Here, too much dejection follows a bodily disease and distemper, as in verse 7: "My loins are filled with a loathsome disease, and there is no soundness in my flesh." And many interpreters hold that his trouble of mind, his being cast down so much under his sin, was the cause of his bodily disease.

So again in Psalm 39:8: "Deliver me from my transgressions." There was his inward dejection, his trouble for sin. And in verse 10: "Remove Thy stroke away from me; I am consumed by the blow (or conflict) of Thy hand." God, with rebukes for sin, makes him see His wrath in the sight of sin that by this means he may not continue in sin. And for you to cast yourself down excessively under the apprehension of sin not only disturbs the mind, but also destroys the body. I would not want any to cast off godly sorrow for sin, provided that it is kept within its due bounds, for sorrow for sin in a due measure neither troubles the mind nor distempers nor afflicts the body; but it is *excessive* sorrow for sin that casts down the soul and causes distempers to arise in the body. Therefore reason with your soul against it.

6. Reason thus with thy own soul: "Consider, O my soul, that opposition against sin rather than excessive casting down for sin is what God accepts and is more pleased with." Christians are very apt to think and believe that if they are thus and thus cast down for sin, and so much humbled and cast down for sin, they have done something great. Yet in the meantime they do not conflict and contest with and against their lusts and constantly oppose their sin, so as to be so far humbled, so far dejected for sin as may encourage the soul to

fight against sin. This is that which is well-pleasing to God. When the men of Israel saw before them the men of Ai, in the seventh chapter of Joshua, Joshua fell upon his face and rent his clothes. Then said God to Joshua, "Get thee up; wherefore fallest thou upon thy face?" (verse 10). So God says to you, to the soul that is dejected and excessively cast down for sin, "Why do you fall down on your face on the ground in a dejected condition for sin? Get up!" So say to your soul, "Why do you fall upon your face? Why do you become dejected? Why do you mourn excessively for sin? Get up!" God would rather see the soul up and fighting against corruption than down on its face in too low a dejection for sin.

It is with your soul as with a soldier: a general would rather see his soldiers up and fighting against their common enemy than lying upon the ground wounded and cast down, crying by reason of their wounds. So God would rather see the souls of His people up and fighting against their corruptions and lusts, their common enemies to their salvation, than down upon their faces on the ground under an excessive casting down for sin.

7. Reason thus with yourself: "O my soul, why are you dejected under the sight and sense of sin?" Consider that it is not the measure of humiliation, nor the degrees of it, but the truth of humiliation that God accepts, and makes promise of acceptance to. Therefore, do not lie so low under so sad a dejection. The Lord make the greatest promises to the least measure and degree of faith. Though your faith is little and your graces are small, yet the least and the weakest measure and degree of grace God accepts. Though there are

many who go to hell for want of truth of grace in the habit, yet never do any go to hell for want of degrees of grace in the act. If there is but the least beginning of grace, God accepts that. If it is but faith as a grain of mustard seed, that is faith. So a little tree may be as truly called a tree as the greatest. Though it lacks the same degree of greatness, yet it is still a tree. So a little grace, a little seed of faith as a grain of mustard seed, may as truly and as properly be called true faith as the strongest faith, though it lacks the degrees of it. God has His bottle for those who shed few tears as well as for those who make their heads a fountain of water. Though your grace is but as a bruised reed and as smoking flax, yet that smoking flax shall not be quenched, nor the bruised reed broken. Isaiah 42:3: "A bruised reed He shall not break, and the smoking flax He shall not quench." Though grace is very weak, and very little and small, as a bruised reed and as smoking flax (or dimly burning, for so the word signifies), yet God will strengthen the one and kindle the other. He will not reject these small beginnings of grace, though they appear to be so dim as scarcely to be discerned.

Though God does not make promises to sinners in that state, yet God does make promises to sinners who have grace, though never so weak and small. Therefore, why should you give way to too much trouble of mind?

USE. The use I shall make is to let you know that the Scripture enjoins you not only to check your hearts for, and to use holy reasonings against, your excessive dejection and casting down for sin, but also to reason yourselves into a way of believing. Many Christians will reason why they should believe, why they should be comforted, and why they should be cast down; but as for why they are excessively cast down they have no reason at all but this: because they must be so, and that you must have the one as well as the other. Now what reason can those Christians give who make conscience of all their ways, and labor to live usefully in all their relations, and to live in the use of ordinances, and to walk close with God in all their ways—what reason have they to be too much cast down for sin?

Therefore, as you will reason for believing and comfort, so also you must reason against excessive casting down for sin. For to do this you have no reason. You must show reasons for your dejections as well as for your assurance and persuasions. Wicked men, if you come and ask them concerning heaven, will tell you that they are sure of heaven. Then ask the reason why they think so, and they can give you no reason at all. Therefore, that is presumption. So good men are apt, under too much dejection of spirit, to say that they shall go to hell and be cast off from heaven. But ask them a good reason and they can give none at all; and this is a sin on the other side.

I would ask those doubting Christians who have such serious thoughts, who are apt to think they shall go to hell: can you say that you have no more reason in you than wicked reprobates have? And can you say that you are guilty of those actual sins that are impossible to stand with a principle of true grace, and that there is that reigning in you that no child of God can have? These would indeed be reasons; but if these are not found you have no cause to be cast down. Though you must check your own hearts for too much casting down for sin, yet you must not cast off all dejection for sin; for to be cast down for sin is a duty, but to be overly and excessively cast down for sin is a sin. There are such duties that you are to put your hearts upon, but not to deject your hearts excessively under.

And if you ask me, "How shall I know that these are duties?" I answer in these four particulars.

1. You are not to check your hearts for dejection under sin when the measure of your dejection is subservient to the ends of dejection. Now, the end of dejection is twofold. First, it is to embitter sin; second, it is to endear Jesus Christ. And when your dejection has these two ends, namely, to make sin bitter to your soul and to make Jesus Christ precious to your soul, then is your dejection right, and you are not to check your heart for it, but to cherish it and embrace it. But when your dejection does not make sin bitter, nor make Christ precious, but troubles your mind and casts down your soul and drives you away from Christ, this is excessive, and not subservient to those two ends, and so becomes sinful.

2. You are to cherish this dejection when with this humiliation and dejection for sin you join with it the sense of God's love and favor, when your heart is brought into this frame so as to see sin with one eye and God's love and free grace and pardoning mercy with another. But when people so pore upon their corruptions and sinful miscarriages so as never to be able to see God's love and free grace and pardoning mercy in the promises of the gospel, this is a sin, and you should check your hearts for it.

3. Your dejections are not excessive when your dejections are more for the evil of fact than for the danger of punishment, when your dejection is more for sin

Christians Ought to Check Their Own Hearts

committed than the state you have endangered. But when your dejections are more in mourning for the state you have endangered than the sin you have committed, that is excessive. When a man commits a sin, and he is dejected and says, "I shall go to hell and lose my happy state in heaven," and fears hell as a punishment more than he mourns for sin as a sin, this is excessive sorrow for sin. When you mourn more for the fear of punishment of sin than for sin as it is a dishonor to God, and that you have committed and aggravated evil, it is excessive. But when your sorrow is more for sin and God's dishonor than for fear of punishment, if this is the trouble of your soul, you are not to check your heart for it.

4. Those dejections and castings down for sin are to be entertained when they make you justify God in all His proceedings and condemn yourself. But when, under dejections of mind, you entertain hard thoughts of God, to murmur and repine and be disquieted, these thoughts are not to be cherished, but you are to check your heart for them. On the other hand, when you can justify God in all His dispensations towards you, these workings of spirit are not to be checked but cherished. Job 40:4–5: "Behold, I am vile; what shall I answer Thee? I will lay my hand upon my mouth. Once have I spoken, but I will not answer; yea, twice, but I will proceed no further." It is as if Job had said, "In my trouble of mind I have spoken often against God, once, and a second time, against God; but I will lay my hand upon my mouth and justify God and condemn myself. I will acknowledge myself to be vile in my own eyes." Thus did Job learn to do.

And so when you can, under your casting down for

sin, justify God, condemn yourselves, and acknowledge God to be just in all His dispensations and yourselves to be vile in your own eyes, then is your casting down for sin not excessive, and you are to cherish it and not to check your hearts for it.

Sermon 5

Why Are the People of God Cast Down?

"Why art thou cast down, O my soul? and why art thou disquieted within me? Hope thou in God, for I shall yet praise Him, who is the health of my countenance, and my God." Psalm 42:11

QUESTION 2. Why are the people of God cast down? It is for want of the apprehension of God's love and favor. In handling this query, I shall take this path:

I will show you why God suffers His people to be cast down under the apprehensions of the want of God's love and favor.

I will show you that, though this is your condition, yet there is no great cause of your dejection and trouble and casting down of soul under this condition.

I will lay down some theological rules as to what a Christian is to do, and what course to take, that he may gain the love and favor of God.

I shall then give the use and application.

First, I shall show you why God suffers His people to be cast down under the apprehensions of the want of God's love and favor. Though God may love them, yet they may not know the love and favor that God bears to them. I shall reduce the reasons into four headings:
- It comes from a man's own self.
- It comes from God.

- It comes from the devil.
- It comes from other men.

These may be the four general causes why God's people are cast down under the want of God's love and favor to their souls.

1. It arises from a man's own self, and that in these five regards.

First, it comes from the prevalence of natural melancholy in a man's body. The prevalence of melancholy in a man darkens the understanding and troubles the fancy. It disturbs the reason, saddens the soul, and clothes it in mourning weeds. And when these meet together, it must cast the man down and suspend the sense of God's favor from him. Melancholy is the mother of discomfort and discontent; it is the nurse of doubts.

Think of the story in Daniel 4 concerning Nebuchadnezzar. He ate grass like an ox, and knew not whether he was a beast or a man. But his fancy was troubled, his understanding was darkened, and his reason was gone. And thus deep melancholy makes a child of God think that he is a child of the devil when he is a child of God. It makes him think he is a brat of Babylon when indeed he is a son of Zion. It is no more wonder, said Baxter, for a melancholy man to doubt, fear, and despair than it is to see a sick man groan and a child cry when he is beaten. The best way to cure this belongs rather to a physician than to a divine.

There is a natural distemper in the body that is the cause of melancholy, yet trouble of conscience, doubtings, and distress of spirit are the companions of it. You may silence a melancholy man when you cannot

Why Are the People of God Cast Down?

comfort him. If you abate his sadness by convincing arguments, yet when he retires alone, through the prevalence of this humor, all is forgotten. His comforts are but a day or two old.

The second cause of the suspension of the favor of God is spiritual security, indulging and harboring in the heart any known sin. There is nothing in the world that will so much hinder him from, and keep the soul from, the assurance of the favor of God as harboring in the soul any known sin. All the while David harbored in his heart and indulged and hid his sin from God, he lost the light of God's countenance. He lost the shining of God's face upon his soul, insomuch that he prayed to God to restore unto him the joy of his salvation. It is true, the salvation of David was not lost, but the joys of his salvation were. The comforts and consolation that he formerly enjoyed were lost; and this he begged God to restore unto him. Psalm 51:12: "Restore unto me the joys of Thy salvation." Although sin cannot make a child of God lose salvation itself, yet sin may cause God to suspend the comforts and former joys of His salvation.

I may say concerning this case as philosophers say of earthquakes: when the wind is in the air, spread abroad and diffused in the air, then it does not throw down either hill or mountain; but when the wind is gathered together and lies in the caverns of the earth, then it causes earthquakes and overturns all that is about it. So while sin is not kept close in the soul, while it is not indulged there, and while it is not hidden and concealed, but confessed and repented of and prayed against, it does not do much hurt; but when that sin is indulged and kept close and not repented of nor prayed against, but indulged in the soul, this will make a heart-quake and a conscience-quake, and will fill your heart with horror and amazement. Psalm 32:3: "When I kept silence, my bones waxed old, through my roaring all the day." When a man conceals his sin, it troubles his soul, wounds his heart, and breaks his peace.

If you will break God's law, it is but just and righteous with God to break your peace. God will not encourage any of His people by giving them peace and comforts and mercies in any sinful course. The Antinomians would make us believe that our comforts have no dependence on our sinful actions, whereas God teaches us no such thing. The prophet Isaiah said, "The work of righteousness shall be peace, and the end thereof is quietness, and assurance forever.'" Here you see that comfort, consolation, joy, peace, and assurance are annexed to the works of righteousness, whereas discomforts and discouragements are annexed unto sin. If you break God's law, God will break your peace. He will break your heart.

The same promises of peace cannot be made to the godly and the wicked, for the former have promises of divine peace; the others have not. Ezekiel 14:4: "Therefore speak unto them, and say unto them, 'Thus saith the Lord God: Every man of the house of Israel, that setteth up his idols in his heart, and putteth the stumbling-block of his iniquities before his face, and cometh to the prophet, I the Lord will answer him that cometh according to the multitude of his idols." When a man comes to the prophets, to the ministers of God, and makes great complaint of inward trouble in his soul, and is much cast down within himself, and yet in the meantime keeps and harbors known sins upon his own heart, God has said He shall not answer that man that He might give him comfort. Rather He says in verse 6: "Thus saith the Lord, 'Repent and turn yourselves from your idols, and turn away your faces from all your abominations,' " and then God will answer him. But those who will not turn from their evil ways, God will answer them with rebuke. God will set His face against that man and make him a sign and a proverb and cut him off. He who keeps sin in his heart, and indulges sin there, shall have no peace in his conscience, nor serenity, nor quietness of soul. He shall not enjoy the smiles of God's face or the light of God's countenance, but the sense of His wrath—much anguish, sorrow, and perplexity of mind for his sin.

The third cause of the soul's suspension and want of God's favor is the defectiveness of the people of God in exercising their graces. Little grace shall have but little evidence; and if you are not abundant in the exercise of grace you will not have the comfort of grace but in a weak measure. John 14:21: "He that hath My commandments and keepeth them, he it is that loveth Me; and he that loveth Me shall be loved of My Father, and I will love him, and will manifest Myself unto him."

You know that all the stars in the firmament have light, but you cannot see the light of the little stars as clearly as the light of the greatest. So though there is truth of grace in the weakest as well as the strongest acts, yet if your graces are weak in the exercise of them, your comforts and evidences will also be weak—hardly discerned and hardly seen. "Peace be multiplied to you," said the Apostle. If you do not multiply your graces, God will not multiply your peace. If you withdraw the exercise of your grace, God will withdraw the comforts of your grace. You cannot see small things. He who sees a small needle, a hair, or a mote has good eyes. In the same way, you cannot see weak grace as easily as you may see strong acts of grace. Therefore your comforts are small. Many men cannot see their graces and their evidences because they are like motes and hairs.

If you do not abound in the exercise of grace, you will not be able to see the evidence of grace and enjoy the comforts of your grace. When a man is in a swoon, you do not know whether he is dead or alive because his breath is not perceived and his pulse is not beating. So when your graces are weak and little, when you do not live in the exercise of grace, you cannot see the evidences of grace.

The fourth cause of the suspension of His love and favor arises from laziness, carelessness, and heedlessness in the performance of holy duties. There is nothing in the world that is a greater bane of your graces and comforts than this is. If you do deny God in your obedience, God in justice will deny you in your peace and comforts. He who will not work shall not eat. As it is true in worldly things, so it is also true in spiritual things. If you do not do your duties towards God, God will suspend the comforts of your graces from you. If you do your duty toward God, you shall eat of the promised land. If you will not let the Spirit of God work and operate in you His sanctifying work, God will not let you enjoy in your souls the comforting work of His Spirit.

You know what Solomon said: "The sluggard shall have poverty enough." So you who are spiritual sluggards, not doing your duties towards God, shall be sure to have spiritual poverty enough in your soul for want of comfort. Remember that expression of Christ in that parable in the gospel, that it is the faithful servant who will enter into the joy of his Lord. If you will not be faithful in your duty, you cannot expect to be filled with inward joy.

Grace, said Baxter, is never apparent and sensible in the soul but when it is in action. The want of action must cause the want of assurance. Though duties do not merit comfort, yet they usually rise and fall with our diligence in duty.

I may illustrate this by a familiar comparison. There is, you know, fire in the flint. But the fire is not seen in the flint. But strike the flint and the steel together and then you may see the fire. So there may be grace in the soul of a man like fire in the flint, but until the Spirit of God comes and strikes upon the soul like a flint to the steel, until the Spirit of God works with the spirit of man in duty, there is no grace seen. And so the soul comes to lie under the dismal workings of soul, under the sense of want of assurance of God's love.

Fifth, it arises because they look more after comfort than they do after grace. This is the cause why they want more comfort than they need. They look more after marks and signs that may tell them what they are than after precepts which tell them what they should do. When Christians are more inquiring after privileges than inquiring after their duty, it is just with God to keep their comfort from them. When Christians labor more to know that they are justified than to know and use the means to be justified, or labor more to know that they are in a state of grace rather than to use those means that are prescribed to get grace, this may be a means why God keeps them from the comforts of the Spirit.

And thus I have given you the first cause why God's people are cast down under the apprehensions of the suspension of the favor of God to the soul.

The second cause why the people of God are cast down under the want of the favor of God may be from God Himself. God may keep you from enjoying His love and favor:

From an act of His sovereignty. Assurance is given out of the goodness of His will and withdrawn to show the absoluteness and liberty of His will. For may not God do what He will with His own people? God has by His power made the day and the night, for God not only gives days of comfort and consolation to His people, but also He gives nights of desertion. As they are acts of God's power and sovereignty over His people to show that, if it is the will and pleasure of God, He can take away the day of comfort and withdraw and suspend His love and favor from the souls of His people, so also, if He wills, He can by act of His sovereignty give us assurance, and give comfort to the souls of His people. God may do what He pleases, and none may say, "Wherefore dost Thou so?"

To manifest His wisdom and goodness to His people. By His withdrawing and suspending comfort, and hiding His face, He hereby keeps His people from being glutted with comforts, joy, and delights. Should God continue the light of His countenance always upon them, should God fill their hearts with full assurance of grace and full assurance of faith always, to let forth the beams of His glorious love into their souls, they would be subject to being glutted, to devalue comfort, and to take little notice of those loving kindnesses of God, those divine favors bestowed upon them. Therefore God in wisdom sees it fitting sometimes to suspend those favors—to withdraw that love, favor, comforts, and joys from them—that they may prize it more and retain it better when they enjoy it.

God may withdraw His love and favor from the souls of His people out of an act of wisdom, that thereby He may let His people see and consider that there is more evil really in sin than ever there appeared seeming good in the commission of sin. A man will commit sin that he may obtain some seeming good, such as to please the lust of the eye or to obtain some other seemingly desirable good. But God lets them see and find, by the withholding of His love and favor and the light of His countenance, that there is more real evil in the loss of God's countenance than ever there appeared seeming good in the commission of sin and the pleasure of it.

God may suspend His favor as an act of wisdom to hide pride and self-conceitedness from men, that they may not be proud of their own gifts and graces, of the strength and degrees of their graces. Job 33:17: "He doth withhold from man His purpose (or, as in the margin, His works) and hide pride from man." Why so? Because a man may be proud in the works that he does and be full of high and vain conceits of himself. Therefore God hides His works that He may hide pride from him; and this is an act of wisdom and goodness in God.

God does it that thereby He might make His people to be more afraid of sinning against Him lest their comforts be again eclipsed. For I must reason, before I commit any sin, that if I do this I break the righteous law of God. And if I break His law, God will break my heart and my peace. And shall I take no care of committing a sin against God, seeing that by committing it I must lie under the sense of God's wrath?

God does it to let a man know and find that assurance is not essential to holiness. Although the people of God have grace, and do believe and have sins pardoned, yet the sense of this pardon, the sense of this faith, and the assurance of this grace are not essential. Though there cannot be peace without grace, yet grace may be where there is not peace. There may be a root where there is no faith, yet there cannot be fruit unless there is a root. God will have men know that the sense of faith and repentance is a gift of mere liberality.

God does it to let men see the difference between heaven and earth. God reserves the best till the last.: God does not think it fitting that men should have constant joy in this inconstant world, nor full joy in this empty earth, nor lasting joy in this transitory world. He reserves that until His people come to heaven. Should the people of God, while they live in this world, have fullness of joy and constant comfort, they would be ready to slight and never look toward that place where is fullness of joy. They would never desire to be in heaven. Therefore God is pleased to mix sorrow with comfort, and suspend and hide His face, to the end that His people might look after heaven, and to let them see the difference between heaven and earth. And thus you see that second reason why God suspends His favor from His people, which is drawn from the wisdom of God.

As an act of His justice. God may suspend His love and favor from His own sovereignty and from His own wisdom, so He may do it from an act of His justice and lay them under the apprehensions of His wrath. God will punish His own people for sin with the suspension of His love and favor. Although He will not punish them with hell and in hell, yet He will and may punish them with the *sense* of hell and lay them under the sense of wrath. And I shall lay down some particulars how God, by an act of justice, punishes His own people for sin with the sense of the want of assurance.

First, God punishes His people for the sin of grieving His Spirit. If you trouble and grieve God's Spirit, He will grieve and trouble your spirits. If you send God's Spirit sad to heaven, God will put sadness into your spirits upon earth; and if you are not comforted, how can you expect to get any comfort when you send Him away sad who should make your souls rejoice? Therefore, when God has withdrawn His countenance, then conclude that you have grieved His Spirit.

Second, God may withdraw His love and punish His people for the sin, for the carelessness and slighting that His people have of God and of His fear. As children are apt to grow saucy and presumptuously impudent and irreverent till the father frowns and majestic austerity takes down their sauciness, so God's people are like wanton children, apt to slight God and His fear. And therefore He sees it as fitting that we should see His frowns as well as His smiles. He will punish His people with the loss of His favor for their sin as well as smile upon them in the light of His countenance. God will sometimes browbeat His own children that they may see the wrinkles of His brows (to speak after the manner of men). Too much familiarity breeds contempt. The Persian kings shunned familiarity, and were seldom seen, that they might be more honored.

Third, God does it to punish that rigidity, unmercifulness, and uncharitableness that men have towards others who are troubled in their minds. There are many Christians who have obtained the assurance of God's favor, the assurance of their salvation. They look upon others who are filled with fear and trouble of mind, and who lie under temptation. They look upon them at a great distance, and carry no more love and compassion towards them than they do for those who have no grace at all. Now God, to care for this distemper, suspends His favor, withdraws the light of His countenance, and lets them lie under doubts and fears that they may learn to pity those who are cast down, and not be so uncharitable to them, not to censure them, not to break those bruised reeds.

I now come to the third reason why God's people are dejected and lie under the apprehensions of the want of God's love and favor toward their souls. It arises from the devil, and may arise from both his malice and his subtlety. Because the devil cannot make the children of God dash their souls in pieces upon the rocks of presumption, therefore he tries to make them drown their souls in the gulf of desperation. Because he cannot hinder a child of God from going into his Master's joy in another world, he labors to hinder their Master's joy from coming into them in this world. The devil will rather play a small game than at no game at all. Seeing that he cannot keep them from going into heaven itself, he will keep heaven from entering into them.

Because he cannot keep you from having grace, he will keep you, as long as he can, from having the sense of grace. And this is the third reason why God's people may lie under the want of the light of God's countenance.

The fourth reason why God may withdraw the light of His countenance arises from other men—partly from good men and partly from bad men.

It arises partly from good men. Good men may slight the society and company of doubting and weak Christians when these weaker ones think to themselves: "I am a trouble to the company and society of good men." And when good men stand at a distance and do not care for the company of weak Christians, it makes the weak ones say, "Surely God will not have good thoughts of me, and surely God will not think well of me, and will Christ have fellowship with me, and not condemn me?"

These reasonings arise in the hearts and spirits of good but weak Christians, occasioned by that strangeness and slightness of spirit in good men towards those who are weak. It is hard to pity much till we have felt much. Women who were never in travail cannot pity them so much who are in travail. Christians who were never tempted cannot pity those so much who lie under great and strong temptations. Those who have not been under strong doubts and fears cannot pity those who are under doubting and fears.

God uses this to make them more experienced in comforting tempted souls. In 2 Corinthians 1:4–6, the apostle lays down one end of their affliction: "whether we be afflicted, it is for your consolation and salvation, which is effectual in the enduring of the same sufferings which we also suffer, or whether we be comforted, it is for your consolation and salvation. God comforteth us in all our tribulation, that we may be able to comfort those that are in trouble, by the comfort wherewith we ourselves are comforted of God."

God's purpose is that they who are under spiritual afflictions may comfort them with the same comforts that they themselves have been comforted by God. A scholar may read much of sufferings, yea, he may read whole volumes of physical sufferings, spiritual sufferings, and of doubts and fears that other Christians have lain under; but for all that reading he may not be able to pity distressed souls because he lacks experience of it himself. A scholar may read books on the art of navigation and yet he may not be a good mariner; but it is experience that makes good mariners. So a man may read books of sufferings, yet not be able so kindly to pity those who are in sufferings because he lacks the experience others have who have been in the same case Those who have been tempted, those whose consciences have been troubled, are the fittest men to succor those who are in that condition. God chooses broken vessels to pour comfort into that they may diffuse it unto others.

It may arise from bad men. Bad men may be the occasion of trouble to dejected souls. Though the Lord leaves and suffers His people to be dejected and cast down, yet the Lord does it:

1. To make wicked men fear their eternal condition. May not wicked men justly reason thus with themselves? "Do I see such a man who follows the ordinances of God, who lives and walks in the ways of God with care, and makes conscience how he lives in his

calling, and labors to keep his heart close to God and maintain communion with Him, and will not nor dares not commit any known sin; who prays in his family, and labors to mortify sin and keeps his body under, and to abound and grow fruitful in the ways of God and in goodness? And do I see such a man lie under fears and doubts and troubles of mind, and so cast down, and even ready to fear that all is in vain, that he shall lose heaven at last? Oh, what then will become of me? What may I think with myself, whose ways are nothing like His ways? He has followed ordinances, but I have not. He has labored to walk in God's way with care and conscience, whereas I never made conscience of any such thing. He has labored to live conscientiously in his calling, which I never did. He dares not commit known sins, whereas, alas, I indulge sin and hug it in my bosom. He labors to mortify sin, whereas sin reigns over me as a lord. He labors to grow fruitful, but I am unfruitful, and never watch my heart or do my duty. I never make conscience to walk holy and humbly with God as he does; and yet behold, he is in trouble and cast down for want of God's favor. What then may I think of myself? Does this man lie under the sense of wrath, and may I not fear that I shall lie under the weight of God's wrath? Does he fear hell, and shall I not surely feel hell?"

And when they see this, it is only to awaken them out of the sleep of security, and to rouse them from those false presumptions and persuasions of their own salvation. And in some sense it is a mercy to wicked men that good men are cast down and troubled, that they may look into their own hearts and ways so as to amend them and repent.

2. God, in a way of judgment to wicked men, lets His own people be cast down under the absence of His divine favor in judgment to the world, that it may be a stumbling block to the world in their way to heaven. They shall say of themselves, "I and my company, there are no such merry men in the world as we are. We can be merry; we can plot and deceive in our trade, and we can do this and that, and yet not be at all troubled in conscience all the year long. And yet behold those who follow ministers, go to ordinances, hear sermons, and love the Bible. See how they hang down their heads and are troubled in mind, are cast down and scarce have any comfort all their lives."

Now what may be the reason that they should go so after their own evil ways and not be troubled, and the people of God in their exact walking be so much cast down? It was so in Calvin's days: Christians' spirits were sad spirits; and this was a stumbling block to many papists, who would not follow a sad religion.

Sermon 6

Why God's People Should Not Be Too Cast Down

"Why art thou cast down, O my soul? and why art thou disquieted within me? Hope thou in God, for I shall yet praise Him, who is the health of my countenance, and my God." Psalm 42:11

I now come to show you why the people of God should not be too cast down when they have a comfortable assurance of God's love. Now in the resolution of this question, consider these nine particulars:

1. Consider that God's withdrawing the sense of His love and favor from the soul is not always an act of justice to punish them for sin, but sometimes an act of sovereignty when it is for sin, as when you grieve God's Spirit. This may make the soul sad; it is neither comfortable nor thankworthy. But when you suffer from God by an act of His power, there is no such trouble nor cause of being cast down but you may take comfort under that state. For God may sometimes withdraw and suspend His love and favor merely upon an act of His power. In peace offerings there was oil mixed, but it is not so in sin-offerings because there is no peace nor comfort in suffering for our faults. As God, to show the goodness of His will, sometimes gives assurance, so to show the absoluteness and liberty of His will He sometimes withdraws it. You read of the desertion of the church in Song of Solomon 5:5–6: "I rose up to open to

my beloved, but my beloved was gone, he had withdrawn himself, my soul failed when he spake; I sought him, but I could not find him, I called him, but he gave me no answer."

Now this was an act of justice in Christ to withdraw Himself. Jesus Christ knocked until His head was filled with the dew and His locks with the drops of the night, yet she would not open to Him. Therefore Christ, as an act of justice, might withdraw Himself to punish them for sin because the spouse would not let Christ come in when He knocked. Then you read of the desertion of the church, not as an act of justice for the punishment of sin, but as an act of His mere power. Song of Solomon 3:1: "By night on my bed I sought him whom my soul loved; I sought him, but I could not find him." Now if your conscience can tell you that you are careful in your duties towards God, and your heart is upright, and to labor to walk exactly, and yet you can not see your comforts appearing, now you may say, peradventure, yea, you may say without all peradventure, "It is not an act of His justice, but an act of power, that He withdraws His favor and the light of His countenance from ny soul."

2. God may withdraw His love and favor from the soul not for any displeasure that He has to them, but out of an act of love to try His own people's love to Him. As a mother, a tender-hearted mother, many times runs behind the door from her child in a corner and hides herself, but it is not because she is angry with her child but to try the strength of her child's love in seeking after the mother, so God may withdraw His love from the souls of His people; but it is not from any anger, but from love to His people, to try the strength of His peo-

ple's graces, and to try their love in seeking Him.

God tries your grace's strength in going after Christ, and your grace's love in looking after Jesus Christ. It was so with Joseph. I allude to Genesis 42:7 where it is said that Joseph spoke roughly to them (or hard things with them), that is, with his brethren, "and he cast them into prison for three days," verse 17. Now all his dealing with his brethren was not for want of love to them, but it was to try the affections of his brethren and cause them to call to mind their former unkindness. Thus God deals many times with His own people: He withdraws His love, suspends His favor, and withholds the light of His countenance to try the strength of His people's graces, and the strength of His people's love to Him. See Luke 24:28. When the two disciples were going to a village and Christ came and walked with them, and when they came nigh unto the village where they were going, Christ seemed as though He would have gone further. But this action of Christ's was to try the love of His two disciples, whether they would press Him to make Him stay with them. So God may withdraw the beams of His love. He may suspend His divine favor to test the love of His people, how they will long after Him and desire His love to their souls.

3. God may suspend His favor because there may be more of God's fatherly love in withdrawing His love than in manifesting His love (in some cases) unto the souls of His people, and that in these two particulars:

(1) When a man enjoys the sense of God's love, and that enjoyment makes him to be spiritually proud, then it is in mercy to withhold His love and favor. When he cannot enjoy the sense of God's love without the sense of spiritual pride, it is, in this case, great love.

Job 33:17: "That He may withdraw man from his purpose, and hide pride from man." It is in the Hebrew, "that He removeth His works from man." Lest men should be proud of God's grace and proud of comforts, God will keep him from the comforts of His grace. And in this case it is great mercy to have the love of God withdrawn when to have it continued God's people would grow proud.

A little boat cannot bear a great sail without sinking, nor a weak vessel strong liquor without breaking. Some of God's people are like little vessels. You know that little boats are like weak vessels. Weak Christians are not able to bear strong comforts. To put strong liquor in weak bottles is the way to break them; so to put strong manifestations—strong comforts—into weak souls would soon break them. God sees that sometimes His people are not able to bear nor able to use comforts and divine manifestations well; and in this case it is great mercy when you cannot bear them then to be without them. For then the want of comfort makes you more eager after Jesus Christ than when you enjoy it. Many times the enjoyment of comfort makes you grow secure and careless, whereas the want of comfort makes you the more eager to look after it. God sometimes forsakes so that He might not be forsaken; and He seemingly forsakes that His people might not forsake Him. As it is cruel mercy for a wicked man to have hopes and presumption of heaven and yet go to hell, so it is merciful cruelty that a godly man should lie under fear of hell and yet go to heaven.

(2) The suspension of God's love and favor is in love when it makes you prize Jesus Christ more in the want of Him than you did in the enjoyment of Him.

The Lord many times brings His own people into great wants and exposes them to great exigencies and straits that they might the more prize mercy, be the more eager in the pursuit after it, and not grow proud when they have it. Deuteronomy 32:13: "He made them to ride on the high places of the earth, that he might eat the fruits of the field; and he made him to suck honey out of the rocks, and oil out of the flinty rock."

God did not give them water, but God gave them honey. It would have been a mercy had God given them water to drink when they were ready to die of thirst; but when Moses came to speak of this he made mention that God gave them honey to suck. Because they saw the want of a lesser mercy, God gave them a greater mercy. So it is in spiritual things: when we in our straits see the want of mercy, a spiritual want of mercy to the soul, O then the soul would be glad for a little mercy; the least crumb of comfort then would refresh the soul! The want of spiritual mercies makes us to see the spiritual worth of mercies; the want of God's favor, the want of the light of God's countenance, makes the soul to prize the enjoyment of it; the want of the love of Jesus Christ shining on the soul makes the soul to see and feel and know that the love of God in Christ is exceedingly precious. Now when the withdrawings of the light of God's countenance from the soul works these gracious effects, it is in great love and mercy to the soul.

4. That you may not be too cast down, consider that the people of God always have a ground of comfort in their souls, though they have not always the sense of comfort. Though the souls of the children of God may be sometimes without the present sense of comfort, yet the people of God are never without the cause of com-

fort in their souls. As a man still has a right to his inheritance though he cannot read the evidences for it, so you who are sanctified by faith in Jesus Christ have a real right to an inheritance, though you may not sensibly enjoy your inheritance. As it was with Hagar, so it is with many doubting Christians. Genesis 21:?: "She flying into the wilderness of Beersheba, her water was spent in the bottle, she casts her child under one of the shrubs, and sat down over against it and wept; and there was a well of water by her (the well was there before) and she knew it not; but when God opened her eyes, then she saw the well of water that was by her."

So it may be with many a poor soul: salvation may be near you, very nigh your soul, yet the soul may not have a sensible knowledge of it, but may be ready to think that it shall perish for want of salvation and want of comfort and consolation from God in Christ. What is spoken concerning Joseph's brethren is very observable: they had so much love from their brother that they had a testimony of his love along with them. They had the money in their sacks and yet they never knew it, nor ever knew him to be their brother. So a poor soul may have the testimony of God's love in the soul, and the sure pledge of God's everlasting and eternal love to the soul, and yet may not know this testimony. You may not know and sensibly feel the lovingkindness of God to your soul.

5. Remember for your support that none of God's people always retain the like sense and manifestation of God's love to their souls, but it fares with the souls of God's people, in reference to comfort, as it is with the sea (sometimes ebbing and sometimes flowing), and as with the air (sometimes cloudy, and sometimes clear),

Why God's People Should Not Be Too Cast Down

and so like the season of the year (sometimes winter and sometimes summer). As it is in nature, so it is in grace: nothing in nature always retains and keeps the same likeness at all times, to keep the like perfection; so it is in grace: no child of God under heaven always, at all times, retains and keeps the same measure of comforts in his own spirit. As Samson had not the same strength at all times, so a Christian has not always the same comforts.

6. If at any time God suspends His love and favor and the light of His countenance, yet consider that God never does this but He sees great reason and need for it. You read in 1 Peter 1:6: "Wherein you greatly rejoice, though now for a season (if need be) ye are in heaviness through manifold temptations." There it refers to the sufferings for the gospel. So I may say to you, if need be, you shall be in heaviness for want of the enjoyment of God's love in Christ. If you need heaviness, you shall have heaviness; if no need of sorrow, you shall have no sorrow. Philoso-phers say there is great need of wind and thunder, as well as of shining of the sun, for thereby the air is kept clear. So when God thunders into your soul, and sometimes blusters like the wind into your soul, God sees some need of that dealing with you to sweep your soul from sin, and the love of the world, and to quell your pride and subdue your lusts and purge away that slightness of spirit wherein you are apt to slight others.

God many times suspends the light of His countenance and holds from your soul the comforts of your graces for this end: that you might not be proud of your measure of grace. And sometimes God may do it to stir up in you a compassionate spirit towards others in affliction, and that you might exercise your grace. God may let you want the comforting work of the Spirit that you might have more of the sanctifying work of the Spirit. Therefore, comfort yourself, for if God did not see need of this afflicting you, He would never let you lie under this sad condition.

7. Consider this for your comfort: Jesus Christ Himself was under spiritual desertion as well as you. Christ Himself cried, "My God, my God, why hast Thou forsaken Me?" Matthew 27:46. Here was the loss of vision, though not the loss of union. And you do no more but cry, "My God, my God," under the absence of the favor of God. Jesus Christ did it to sanctify your death, was buried to make your grave a bed of roses to you, was tempted to sanctify your temptations, and deserted to sanctify your desertions. He drank deep of the cup; you only sip from it. He was under troubles, desertions, and temptations that He might be able "to succor them that are tempted." He was able to succor them before, but now He is made experimentally able to succor His people in the like case.

8. Consider that the seeming loss of God's favor is not simply prejudicial to the state of grace, for it does not hinder your having access to, and having success at, the throne of grace; neither can it hinder you of glory. You may trust and wait upon God in the way of your duties, and though you do not enjoy the light of His countenance, yet this will not hinder your success at the throne of grace. It is the want of Christ, not of comfort, that makes the throne of grace a throne of justice and wrath. For you may want God's face to comfort you, but you shall not want God's hand to help you. God may lend you His ear to your prayers when He may

Why God's People Should Not Be Too Cast Down

deny you the shining of His face. It is the truth of grace, not the sense and sight of grace, that brings the soul to heaven. It is not the measure of grace, nor the sense and sight of grace, but the truth of grace that entitles the soul to glory. Though while you live you may be without your Master's joy, yet you shall be sure to come to your Master's joy when you die. Though you never had a heaven in your soul while you live, yet your soul may come to heaven when you die.

9. Consider, and do not be so cast down for want of comfort; for when you come to heaven you shall have comfort enough. God reserves the fullness of your comfort until the fullness of your glory. This is the time to travel in this world, and you must not expect your reward till you come to your journey's end. Here you have joy and comfort for a time, but in heaven you shall have joy and comfort for evermore. Here in this world joy and comfort enter into you, but in the world to come you shall enter into joy, and that is transcendentally and infinitely more than to have joy to enter into you. Here in this world you have but the beginnings of comfort, but there you shall have enduring lasting comforts; here you have comforts by drops, but there you shall come to enjoy and see an ocean of comfort, and that forever.

OBJECTION 1. There is one objection to be answered, which is this, and it is a practical case of conscience.

I think I hear some poor souls say, "It is true, if I thought that God's hiding His face from my soul, in withdrawing the comforts of His Spirit from me, if the absence of the light of His countenance, was merely an act of His sovereignty and power to try my love, to try the confidence of my heart in trusting in Him, and the strength of my love to Him, and the more to put me forward to look after Jesus Christ, if this was so, I would not be much troubled. But alas, what shall I do? My conscience tells me that it is for sin that God withdraws the light of His countenance, and the comforts of His Spirit, and for this cause He deals with me. My conscience tells me that I have grieved the Spirit of God, and sent that sadness to heaven; and therefore it is just with God to let me live sadly upon earth, and to live in a comfortless condition. I have committed great sins to take away my comforts, and it is for the guilt of sin for which God hides His face." This is the sad objection and reasonings of many a poor soul.

Now there are four particulars why a child of God should not be thus dejected, though he may be cast down under sin.

1. If you cannot retain the sense of God's love, yet if you retain the sense of your own sins for which you have lost the sense of God's love, to be much in the latter, though you have little of the former, to grow downward in humiliation, though you grow but little upward in consolation, it is a great mercy. Hosea 14:5: "I will be as the dew into Israel, he shall grow as a lily (or blossom, or flourish) and cast forth (or strike forth) his root as Lebanon." You who blossom like the lilies, though you may not so much blossom in the enjoyment of comfort, yet if you grow downward, strike your roots downward by the sense and sight of sin, and grow downwar, in humiliation, it is a great mercy. It is better and safer to strike your roots of grace downward in growing in the sap of humiliation than to grow upward

Why God's People Should Not Be Too Cast Down

and flourish in the sense of pardoning grace. The reason is this: because the one is of absolute necessity and necessary to the saving of the soul, but the other is necessary towards the comfort of the soul; and therefore the one is more needful than the other. If I were put to my choice, I would rather want the sense of the pardon of sin than to want the sense of my own sinfulness. The Lord would rather see His people be in mourning weeds than to be in garments of pleasantness. If God does not see your face full of smiles, yet if He sees your eyes full of tears, that is more acceptable to Him. Though you may want the light of God's countenance, yet if you have the sense of your own sinfulness, that eclipses the light of God's favor to your soul, and you have no cause to be too much cast down under sin.

2. If you are cast down for sin, yet if you can love Jesus Christ really you need not be discouraged when you do not know seriously that Jesus Christ loves you. Though you do not know you are beloved, yet if you can love Christ in this time you need not trouble yourself. Though you have not seen Jesus Christ, yet to believe in Him and, by faith, to apply Jesus Christ to your soul, if this has been your work, and you can say so, you may be confident that Christ loves you truly, though it may not be apparently. And the reason is strong: because we can never love Jesus Christ until He first loves us. A man being in trouble of mind, wanting the assurance of God's love, said that he never knew what the testimony of the Spirit of God meant, and what it was to his soul, but yet he *could* say that he rested and believed on the Lord Jesus Christ. Though he knew not that Christ loved him, yet he desired to love Christ. So I say to you, although you cannot sensibly feel the love of Christ to

your soul, yet if you can dearly love Jesus Christ, be confident that Christ loves you.

3. If you want the quieting and comforting work of the Spirit, yet if you have the quickening work of the Spirit, be not too much cast down. You who can act grace, although you want comfort, and although you have not the sight of your graces sensibly to feel and find the comforts of them, yet if you can live in the exercise of grace, in this case you need not be troubled and cast down if it is with your soul as with a well that has two buckets: while one is down, the other is still up; so if one bucket of your soul is down, and you are dejected for want of the sense of God's favor and gracious love to your soul, yet if the other bucket is up in your living and exercising of grace, though you want sensible comforts, yet this is matter of joy and comfort to your spirit. If you are dejected for want of comfort, yet if you abound in grace it is a matter of joy.

Do I speak to any this day who are clouded with sin in want of the sense of the comforting work of the Spirit, and cannot see and cannot feel the sense and manifestations of God's love as others do? Go and pray and mourn and be humbled for your sin; act your grace, and though you go without the manifestation of God's love, yet in this case you are not to be too much cast down. God would rather see and hear your graces than that you should see them yourselves, Song of Solomon 8:13.

4. Though you are cast down for sin, yet do not be troubled if it has this gracious effect upon you, so as to make you to be more watchful against sin than you were before. So when you shall be afraid of sin and hate sin, in this case you have cause to bless God. The

Why God's People Should Not Be Too Cast Down 97

Psalmist said, "My heart is not turned back, neither have we slipped again from Thy ways; all this is come upon us, and yet have we not forgotten Thee, nor dealt falsely against Thy covenant; our hearts have not turned backward, neither have our steppings swerved from Thy path." So when you can say, "Although God has covered me with the shadow of death, and though there is a cloud between God and my soul, yet I am afraid of sinning against Him. I am afraid of offending Him, and I have not gone out of His paths for all this." In this case you may be comforted, though you apprehend that Christ has turned His back upon you. You must say, "I will not for all the world stop living upon Jesus Christ in a way of love and obedience."

OBJECTION. If it is so that many souls may be cast down for sin, and yet you say that it is their sin to be so much cast down, but they are to labor against this trouble and casting down for sin, does not this nourish a principle of presumption in many a man's breast to presume of his salvation and make him bold in sinning against God, seeing you say they are not to be troubled?

ANSWER. It is true, if this doctrine is not well used and wisely handled, it may. As it may comfort one soul, it would cause a hundred to run into a presumptuous condition; for in some cases, God suspends His favor and hides His face from the soul, it being for sin. You have cause for mourning, and that in these five cases:

1. You have cause to hang down your head with sorrow, you who want the sense and manifestations of God's love in Christ to your soul. And yet, at that time you want the sense and sight of sin; you have a troubled

spirit, and yet not a troubled conscience. You want the sense of Christ's love to your soul, and yet you want the sight and sense of your sins against Jesus Christ. Many men are in this case. There are many men who will say that they do not know whether they shall go to heaven or hell, whether they are the children of God or the children of wrath, whether Christ loves them or not, and yet no sin troubles them and no guilt disquiets them; but they presume on grace and presume of pardon when for all they know there is but a step between them and hell. In this case their condition is very sad.

2. You that say that you want the sense of God's love, and yet not at that time want the sense of the loss and absence of that love. You say you once had that man's sad spectacle who grieves for the loss of an estate, but not for the loss of God; when a man shall not know whether God loves him or not, and yet at that time, for all this, to take no care though his state is a lost state. To lose grace and heaven, this case is sad; to be in such danger and yet not to be sensible of that danger.

3. Your case is sad when you lack a sense of Christ's love to your souls, and yet at that time you want acts of love; and to express your love to Jesus Christ you would fain know whether Jesus Christ loves you or not, yet never labor to know and examine whether you love Jesus Christ or not in drawing out your souls in love to Him. But instead of loving Jesus Christ, you draw forth repinings against God, against Jesus Christ, when you shall be so far from trusting in Him as you shall repine against Him, and not say with Job, "Though He kill me, yet will I trust in Him, and though I perish, yet I will perish in trusting in Him." If under the sense of God's love, you also want love to Jesus Christ, your case is sad.

4. At the time when you want the comforting work of the Spirit, and yet at that you want the quickening work of the Spirit, your case is sad. When you shall not only want comfort, but want grace too, this makes your condition to be sad—to be disquieted for want of comfort, and to be disquieted for want of grace. O look into your own hearts! You who want comfort, do you want grace too? Have you no tenderness of conscience? No remorse of Spirit? No love to duties? No zeal for God? No faith to live by? No hopes in Christ to hang upon? No love to Christ in your soul? No repentance for sin? In this case your condition is very sad.

5. When you have been a long time under the loss of comfort, and in trouble of mind and perplexity of spirit, and yet so to live without any inquiry how you may get out of this sad condition, and to get the comforts you want; when it may be your comforting work, and the quickening work is gone too; to want comfort, and to want grace, and yet to live and not to look after it, but to do as Cain did, to pursue the world, to pursue the profits and pleasures of this world, and all for this end, to stifle his conscience, for to take no pains to stir up grace in your soul, and to quicken the heart that you might have the joys of heaven and the comforts of grace, the love of God, the shines of Christ's face, the manifestations of His love, and assurance of your salvation; when you shall not look after any means either of grace or comfort, this renders your case to be very sad.

And thus I have done with this question. The people of God have no cause to doubt, though they may be cast down for sin, or for the absence of the favor of God to their souls.

Sermon 7

Scripture Rules to Recover the Sense of God's Love

"Why art thou cast down, O my soul? and why art thou disquieted within me? Hope thou in God, for I shall yet praise Him, who is the health of my countenance, and my God." Psalm 42:11

    I will now lay down some Scripture rules to help a child of God who is cast down under the want of assurance of God's love to recover the sense of God's love again. And for your help in this matter, I shall proceed in two general directions:
    You are to remove those things which cause a suspension of God's favor and love within you, and which cast you down.
    You must labor to practice those things that may further you in the attainment of this comfortable sense and certain assurance of God's love.
    For the first of these points, here are eight things which are to be removed, which perhaps have occasioned this suspension of the sense of God's love.
    1. Labor to remove natural melancholy. There is such a natural sympathy between the soul and the body that a distemper in the one causes trouble in the other. It is no more wonder for a conscientious man overcome with melancholy to fear and doubt than for a sick man to groan or a child to cry when it is beaten. If there is melancholy on the body, there will be trouble

in the soul, that is, feelings of desertion and trouble of mind. In Christians it sometimes begins from a natural melancholy. Now this must be removed if you would recover a comfortable sense and assurance of the love of God. Physicians say that natural melancholy has sad effects that attend it, such as fear or being subject to fretting, terrible dreams, and sad apprehensions. Why, now, the devil can tell when your apprehension is disturbed, and he can tell how to turn this and make you doubt your salvation. The devil is a powerful spirit, and when the natural temper is thus exorbitant he can make what was a natural evil become a spiritual evil.

2. You must remove spiritual pride. Job 33:17: "That He may withdraw from his purpose, and hide pride from man."

If those swelling humors of pride are in your spirit, God will send a messenger of Satan to buffet you. Men of proud spirits, said [John] Preston, "are exposed to sad desertions, and darkened eclipses of their comforts." It is usual with God, when He sees men who are proud and have a high conception of the measure and degree of their graces, to pull down their pride; He keeps from them the comfort of their own graces.

Pride is not only a bane of grace, but of comfort too. God resists the proud. The Greek word for "resists" signifies that God puts Himself in battle array against him. Beloved, God puts Himself in battle array against a proud man. Therefore, if ever you would regain the certainty and assurance of God's love, remove pride.

3. If you would regain this comfortable assurance, remove dullness and deadness of heart in holy duties. When the vigor and liveliness of our spirits are abated in duty, the comforts of God's Spirit shall be detained.

Little duty and less comfort shall go hand in hand together. When the affections are dead and the heart straitened in duties, evidences will be darkened and comfort will be eclipsed. Careless performances are recompensed by God with frowns, not with smiles.

4. Sensual joys, or delighting in the things of this world, enervate spiritual joy. The sun, when it shines on a fire, hinders it from burning. When you have a sunshine of comforts in this world, it is a hundred to one that your affections have neither light nor heat. Comforts are heated by grace. The more heat is in your affections, the more strength is in your comforts and consolations. Now, sensual delights take away the heart, and, when the heart is gone, comfort is gone. Hosea 4:11: "Whoredom and wine and new wine take away the heart." To be swilling and guzzling at the cup, and to be following wantons, draws away the heart. Sensual joys are very contrary to godly joys. A man will never have joy in the Holy Ghost who is overwhelmed with sensual and vain delights in the things of this world.

5. Take heed of grieving the Spirit if ever you would retain the comfortable assurance of God's love. Isaiah 63:10: "But they rebelled, and vexed His Holy Spirit; therefore He was turned to be their enemy, and fought against them."

If you grieve His Spirit in heaven, He will sadden your spirit on earth. The Spirit of God will handle us as we handle Him: if you grieve God's Spirit, He will grieve yours. He will not pour joy into your spirits when you grieve His. If you vex God's Spirit by resisting the holy motions of the Spirit, He will vex your spirits by holding back the comfortable motions of the Spirit. It is observable that the Spirit of God in Scripture is called not only a Comforter, but the Holy Ghost. Therefore it is in vain to believe that the Spirit shall be a Comforter to you if you withstand the office of the Spirit, as He is the Holy Ghost. Therefore, you who grieve the Spirit by resisting its holy motions, you shall never regain the comforting work of the Spirit.

6. Remove all unmercifulness and uncompassionateness of spirit to others who are troubled in mind. Many Christians are like a herd of deer. When one deer of the herd is wounded by the forester, all the rest leave and forsake him; they put him away from them and let the wounded deer shift for himself alone. There are many such uncompassionate souls who, if a man is in trouble of mind and has the arrows of God's wrath sticking in his soul, run away from him and leave him. Many men are thus wanting in tenderness and compassion towards tempted and troubled souls, but are full of censures, contempt, and rough dealing. Now for this rigidness and lack of compassion, God oftentimes cause eclipses in their souls. If ever you would regain comfort, pity tempted souls; pitying and being compassionate towards disquieted souls is the way to regain your comfort.

7. Remove a wantonness and a fearlessness of the majesty and greatness of God. If the parents dandle a child on the knee, the child, wanting discretion, is apt to grow wanton; therefore the parents are forced sometimes by an austere carriage, to prevent this wantonness. If God should always manifest smiles, it would breed a contempt of God; therefore God, with a majestic sovereignty, carries Himself with a seeming displeasure, with frowns in His brow, and all to correct that

spirit of wantonness that is in His people. The Persian kings shunned familiarity with their subjects, and would be seen but twice a year by them lest their subjects should condemn them if they should often see them. So God hides Himself lest a spirit of wantonness should grow in His people.

8. If you would not be cast down under these desertions, then remove from you all worldly-mindedness, all desire to have your hearts filled with the world. If you are worldly-minded, you will never enjoy a comfortable certainty of God's love. A man who is a worldly-minded man can never be strong in assurance. If you keep your eye at a due distance from the earth you can see far, but if you put your eye to the ground you can see but little. Beloved, keep your hearts at a due distance from the world and you may see far into the sense of God's favor; but let your eye, I mean the soul, be too near the world and you will see nothing. You will not perceive the sense of God's love if you have worldly-mindedness predominant in you.

Put a candle above the ground and it will burn clear and bright, but put the same candle under the ground and it burns but dim; the dampness of the ground hinders the light thereof. Beloved, keep your hearts above the ground and here your candle may burn bright; but if your hearts are buried in the world, your candle will burn dim. You will not have so clear a light and sense of God's love. Philosophers say the reason why the sun is eclipsed is by the interposition of the moon. I may aptly apply this, as the Scripture takes the moon as an emblem of the world. Revelation 12:1: "And there appeared a great wonder in heaven, a woman clothed with the sun, and the moon under her feet, and upon her head a crown of twelve stars."

This moon eclipses the sun. Beloved, if the world is between you and spiritual things—if it is nearer to your hearts than Christ is, than grace is, than heaven is—this moon of the world will eclipse the shining beams of the Sun of Righteousness.

These are eight particulars that must be removed if you expect to regain a comfortable certainty and assurance of the love of God. Next we turn to the things that *should* be done.

Rules for a Christian who would not be cast down under a suspension of God's love

There are nine rules for a Christian to follow if he would not be cast down under a continued suspension of God's love.

1. If you would regain a comfortable assurance of God's love, keep a holy and conscientious care to live in grace throughout the course of your lives; let it be the chiefest of your care to live in grace, and I promise you that it will not be long before you have comfort. 2 Peter 1:5–10: And "besides this, giving all diligence, add to your faith virtue, and to virtue knowledge, and to knowledge temperance, and to temperance patience, and to patience godliness, and to godliness brotherly kindness, and to brotherly kindness charity; for if these things be in you and abound, they make you that you shall neither be barren nor unfruitful in the knowledge of our Lord Jesus Christ. But he that lacketh these things is blind, and cannot see afar off, and hath forgotten that he was purged from his old sins. Wherefore

the rather, brethren, give all diligence to make your calling and election sure; for if you do these things, you shall never fall." These verses tell you how to get assurance of election: add grace to grace. Let it be your care to live in grace and it will be God's work to give you comfort. God will multiply your peace if you increase your grace. You have God's promise for it in Isaiah 32:17: "And the work of righteousness shall be peace, and the effect of righteousness shall be quietness and assurance forever."

Here is the way to gain comfort: do the work of righteousness and comfort shall follow after. Psalm 119:165: "Great peace have they that love Thy law, and nothing shall offend them" (or, "they shall have no stumbling block"). Note also Job 13:18: "Behold now, I have ordered my cause. I know that I shall be justified." "I have ordered my cause," that is, "I have taken care of my life. I have made conscience of my ways. I have labored to exercise grace in all my actions." What follows? "Now I know I shall be justified." Or, "I have now an evidence and a sense of justification." O beloved, the actings of grace are the inlets to inward peace. Many men say they know they shall be justified, but never make conscience of their ways. They never order their cause. Some are as confident as confidence itself, yet as ignorant as ignorance itself, as profane as profaneness itself, as proud as pride itself. O beloved, if you will have a due sense of the knowledge of justification, order your cause well; order your lives well. "To him that orders his conversation aright will I show the salvation of God" (Psalm 50:23).

Beloved, if God inclines your hearts to order your cause and your course aright, then you may and you shall be justified. It is a great fault of Christians that, when they want assurance, they spend more time complaining that they want comfort than acting on grace.

2. Keep conscience pure and clear, and that is the way to keep conscience pacified. Guilt on the conscience concealed and indulged contracts a horror, and causes a hell to arise here. This rule the Scripture gives if you would labor to have assurance in Job 11:14–15: "If iniquity be in thy hand, put it far away, and let not wickedness dwell in thy tabernacles. For then shalt thou lift up thy face without spot; then you shall be steadfast and not fear." That is, if sin is on your conscience, put it far away. What follows? You shall not then be under fear and suspension of God's love, but shall lift up your face and be steadfast. Therefore, if ever you would regain a comfortable certainty of God's love, keep your conscience pure and clean so that you do not indulge the guilt of any allowed sin within you.

3. Call to mind the former experiences, in the days of old, that you have had of God's love. The remembrance of past goodness is very helpful for present encouragement. This rule David followed in Psalm 42:6: "O my God, my soul is cast down within me; therefore will I remember Thee from the land of Jordan."

It is remarkable what course the psalmist took to regain comfort. He remembered three experiences of His goodness: the land of Jordan, the land of the Hermonites, and the hill Mizar. "First, I will remember the land Jordan; that is, I will remember the great goodness of God in drying up the river Jordan that the tribes of Israel might pass over to the promised land. Why, God who *has* been good *will* be good."

Then, "I will remember the land of the Hermonites.

In that land were Sihon, king of the Amorites, and Og, king of Bashan, defeated." That you read of in Joshua 12:1–2: "Now these are the kings of the land, which the children of Israel smote, and possessed the land on the other side of the Jordan toward the rising of the sun, toward the river Arnon, unto mount Hermon." Mizar some think to be a little hill near Mount Sinai, where the law was given.

"I will remember God's goodness in giving a law to His people." Here David called to remembrance the goodness of God of old, so as to regain comfort and quietness in his mind.

Thus, likewise, Psalm 77:10–11: "And I said, 'This is my infirmity,' but I will remember the years of the right hand of the Most High. I will remember the works of the Lord; surely I will remember Thy wonders." Think of old mercies, and old privileges and loving-kindnesses, and that is the way to bear up the heart with present encouragement.

4. Use arguments of faith against present sense and feeling. Abraham would never have believed God's promise if he had not used arguments of faith against present sense and feeling. Divines make old Isaac's behavior applicable to the case of desertion. How did Isaac come to mistake Jacob for Esau? Divines apply that, by sense and feeling, God's people think that they are Esaus, and are rejected and hated by God, when they are the beloved of the Lord. Though sense and feeling tell you that your infirmities are many, your corruptions are strong, your heart is hard, your affections are dead, God knows you cannot believe, and you cannot have comfort, why yet believe this: God is free, God is gracious, God accepts will for work, and He accepts im-

Scripture Rules to Recover a Sense of God's Love

puted righteousness as if it were inherent righteousness. Use arguments of faith against present feelings. If you play the logician, the devil will outdo you. Say, "Though I have not the faith of evidence, yet I will labor for the act of adherence, relying upon Jesus Christ." Use arguments thus.

5. Let your comforts be grounded upon an immutable covenant rather than upon your own feelings and fading affections. This is a rule of great use. Beloved, should Christians build their eternal comforts on their feelings and affections, their comforts would be up and down, ebbing and flowing. Their affections are feelings, sometimes hot as fire, and soon as cold as air. The pulses of the body sometimes beat strongly and sometimes faintly—and so do the affections. Now if you should build your comfort on the affections, you would never have stable comfort, but one that is still up and down. But rather ground your comfort upon a lasting and unchangeable covenant, on such a covenant that accepts will for works, desires for deeds, and endeavors for performances. Building your comforts on an unchangeable covenant rather than on fleeting affections is a way to regain and attain everlasting comforts.

6. In some cases, especially of desertions and temptations, it is safer for you to submit yourself to the judgment of other men about your condition than to your own judgment. Am I deserted? Am I tempted? Am I troubled in mind? Why, it is better for me, if my own judgment cannot suggest comfort to me, and it is my wisest course to submit myself to other men, to those who are experienced Christians, and who, by observing my walking and manner of living, can instill comfort into me. This I am bound to submit to, in case of deser-

tion and temptation. It was reported of a minister of this kingdom (Mr. Frogmorton) that he was for a long time troubled in mind, and could not be comforted till he had the judgments of godly ministers; and by their testimony he got comfort. Mr. Bradford could not be comforted but by the testimony of another martyr, John Careless, assuring Mr. Bradford that he must be a holy and a good man. The testimony of John Careless mightily pacified and quieted the conscience of Mr. Bradford. Thus Nathan's testimony comforted David and Ananias's testimony comforted Paul. Passions of grief and fear blind the judgment and makes it unable to judge. In 2 Kings 5:12–13, when Naaman was under a prejudice and passion, his servants could tell what was best for him to do. Sometimes in cases of desertion or temptation it is a good and a safe rule to trust other men's judgments rather than our own.

7. Never go to wrong ways and means to allay and pacify the troubles of your mind. When Cain was in trouble of mind for his sin and in horror of conscience, he went to allay this trouble by making buildings. Therefore some divines interpret that clause in the epistle of Jude, "They followed the way of Cain," that he allayed and stifled the trouble of conscience by sensual delights and worldly affairs as with Saul playing music. Do not use sinful means to allay trouble of mind.

A man in a fever takes a cold drink, and it cools a little for the present, but afterwards brings more heat. So, when men are heated with God's wrath they run to sin, which increases the heat. If men are stung by a bee, they will run to a bunch of nettles and rub themselves therewith to allay the sting of the bee. Beloved, when men are stung by God's wrath, and then run to sin to heal themselves, it is but like a man rubbing himself with nettles to allay the sting of a bee. They are like a man who has his house falling and will take a firebrand to uphold his building. O beloved, when you are under trouble of mind, to run to merry meetings, to music, to building, to buying, and bargaining, and not to run to God on your knees, is not the way to regain comfort; it is the way to increase your sorrow and cause more anger and anguish in your conscience. I may exemplify it further by a disease which some women have in their breasts, which they call "the wolf." The disease, they say, is fed by flesh, and if flesh is put upon the woman's breast it feeds on that flesh. And if that is consumed, the woman's breast is the more tortured and torn. A merry meeting may allay trouble of mind for a while, but it will recoil on you with more terror than ever it did. Therefore take heed of sinful means to regain quietness and peace of spirit.

8. Be more industrious in doing duty than in getting comfort. It is the fault of many Christians that they spend more time in fruitless complaints that they want comfort than in holy endeavors to perform duties. Now if the people of God would but take this rule, to be more industrious and spend more time in performing duties than in gaining comfort, their comforts might be sooner gotten and their duties better performed. When a house is on fire, it is not our work to inquire how the fire came, but to labor to put out the fire. So when men shall suspect their condition and complain of lacking comforts, their work is not to rest in fruitless complaints, but to engage in holy endeavors after comforts. Psalm 30:7: "Thou didst hide Thy face, and I was

troubled." Then follows verse 8: "I cried to thee, O Lord." David did not spend so much time in fruitless complaints as he did in holy endeavors after duties.

9. Last, spend more time strengthening evidences than weakening evidences. Many men spend more time questioning their evidences than strengthening them. When in trouble of mind, a man will give himself to read dreadful threats, or such places of Scripture and such good books that carry the most dread and terror, and to spurn promises and comforts. This is to strengthen the devil's hands and to weaken your own. Indeed, when you find your heart presuming and deluding itself, then it is good to make application of dread and terror to awaken you. But for a man who is in trouble of mind to shun promises and only to pore over threats in Scripture—I say, this is a course to weaken your comforts rather than strengthen them. If you cannot find your affections up, why run to your inclinations? Why, it may be, you say you cannot mourn, but you would mourn. "I cannot pray, but I would pray. I cannot hear profitably, but I would hear better." It is a rule that divines give that when a believer cannot have comforts from the acts of grace, he is bound then to look for comforts from his general inclination. It may be that you cannot pray well, but for what end do you pray? Is not your end to get more communion with God, and to get more power against sin? When you cannot find evidences strengthened by the acts of grace, you may find evidences by your intention in duty.

Thus I am done with these two great causes of a believer's dejection or being cast down: the greatness of sin and the desertion or divine suspension of God's love.

Sermon 8

Things That Disquiet the Soul of a Child of God

"Why art thou cast down, O my soul? and why art thou disquieted within me? Hope thou in God, for I shall yet praise Him, who is the health of my countenance, and my God." Psalm 42:11

I now come to the second part of the psalmist's distress: "Why art thou disquieted within me?" Arius Montanus, whom [Henry] Ainsworth follows in his translation, reads the words thus: "Why art thou all in a tumult?"— drawing a metaphor from the tumults in the the sea to those in a good man. The manner of the psalmist's dialect is in a way of expostulation. From thence I shall draw this observation.

OBSERVATION. Godly men ought to check their hearts for, and to use holy reasoning against, all inordinate disquietings of soul.

In handling this point in general I shall show you what those things are for which the soul of a child of God is disquieted. That which disquiets the soul of a child of God is either:

First, the prosperity of the wicked or, second, the calamities of the church or, third, outward afflictions on their bodies or, fourth, inward corruption in their hearts.

I shall begin this sermon with the first of these: godly men should check their souls for all disquietings touching the prosperity of wicked men. I do not know any one outward thing in the world that more disquiets the souls of good men than the prosperity of the wicked. Touching this particular, I shall handle it in this method:

First, I shall show you that godly men are apt to be disquieted in soul for the wicked's prosperity.

Second, I will show you why you should reason against and check the soul for all disquietings because of the prosperity of the wicked.

Third, and last, I will lay down some considerations whereby you may reason against disquietings of the soul because of the prosperity of wicked men.

First, godly men have had their souls greatly disquieted because of the prosperity of wicked men.

There are numerous instances of good men in this situation. In David the father and Solomon the son you have examples of great disquietings of soul.

First, we see this in David the father, Psalm 73:3, 12–13: "For I was envious at the foolish, when I saw the prosperity of the wicked; behold these are the ungodly which prosper in the world; they increase in riches. Verily I have cleansed my heart in vain, and washed my hands in innocency." It is as if he should say, "It is in vain for me to be godly, because I see wicked men do so prosper in the world. It is a great stumbling block on good men's way to heaven, to see wicked men prosper; good men have been overtaken with this, and discouraged and disquieted in soul to see wicked men prosper in the world."

Second, Solomon was troubled for the very same thing in Ecclesiastes 10:6–7: "Folly is set in great dignity, and the rich sit in the low place; I have seen servants on horses, and princes walking as servants upon the earth."

To see servants ride on horseback, that is, to see wicked man advanced, prosperous, and successful, and to see the godly in an abject, despicable, and low state, disquieted Solomon.

Third, the prophet Jeremiah was greatly disquieted because of this. Jeremiah 12:1: "Righteous art Thou, O Lord, when I plead with Thee; yet let me talk with Thee of judgments. Wherefore doth the way of the wicked prosper?" He would reason with God, and what did he say? He would fain know of God why the way of wicked men should prosper.

Fourth, you have Job 21:7: "Wherefore do the wicked live, become old, and are mighty in power?"

Thus you see instances in four of the best men, David, Solomon, Jeremiah, and Job.

Fifth, I might give you another instance of a holy prophet in Habakkuk 1:13: "Thou art of purer eyes than to behold iniquity, or canst not look on grievance; wherefore lookest Thou upon them that deal treacherously, and holdest Thy tongue when he devoureth him that is more righteous than he?"

Here the prophet reasons with God why He would do this, that He who was of pure eyes would behold a wicked man prospering in his wicked way.

And thus you see briefly the first point, that good men are apt to be disquieted in soul in seeing the prosperity of wicked men.

The second thing is to show you four reasons why good men should not be disquieted and troubled in soul when they see the wicked prosper in the world:

1. Do not be disquieted because of the prosperity of wicked men, because God gives them prosperity to be a snare to them. Proverbs 1:32: "For the turning away of the simple shall slay them, and the prosperity of fools shall destroy them."

It makes them secure; it proves to be fuel to their lust. Hosea 13:6: "According to their pasture, so were they filled; they were filled, and their hearts were exalted, and therefore they have forgotten me." Their gold, silver, wool and flax did but clothe, enrich, and strengthen sins. Now, beloved, will you envy the prosperity of a wicked man? Would you envy a man to see him have silken halters, and those to hang himself with? God gives prosperity to wicked men to be as silken halters to hang them everlastingly; therefore do not be disquieted, though they prosper in the world.

2. Be not disquieted, because wicked men have the curse of God with their prosperity. This reason appears in Job 5:2-3, which calls those men silly men who envy wicked men's prosperity in the world. Beloved, it is better to have poverty with a blessing than to have increase with a curse. Wicked men have the curse of God with all their prosperity, and this reason Solomon gives why you should not be disquieted in Proverbs 3:31-33: "Envy thou not the oppressor, and choose none of his ways. For the froward is an abomination to the Lord, but His secret is with the righteous; the curse of the Lord is in the house of the wicked, but He blesseth the habitation of the just."

Though you see a wicked man by oppression and grinding the face of the poor become wealthy, do not envy him. Why not? Because the curse of the Lord is in his house. This should be a strong reason not to be troubled at the prosperity of wicked men.

It is promised Esau in Genesis 27:28: "I will give thee the fatness of the earth, and the dews of heaven." This is a large promise, yet you read, "Jacob have I loved, and Esau have I hated." Jacob had but a poor staff and Esau had the fatness of the earth. You may be poor as Jacob with a staff and scrip, and you may be loved with Jacob; and wicked men may have the fatness of the earth with Esau and yet God hates them. Therefore be not disquieted at the prosperity of wicked men. It was spoken of the Chaldeans in Zechariah 1:15 that they were a wealthy nation. God may give you ease in the world and make you abound with wealth. Yet God said, "I am sorely displeased with them." He mingles His wrath and curse with the abundance of wicked men; therefore be not disquieted because wicked men prosper.

3. Their prosperity costs them very dearly. They lose a soul to get a world; they lose heaven's glory for earth's prosperity—it is a dear purchase. Would you envy a man who, to purchase his house, should lose his life? Why, wicked men, to purchase wealth, lose their souls. I have read of a soldier who, when there was a law made by the general that none should rob the country, robbed a vineyard, took away a bunch of grapes, and for example's sake was to be hanged. Some envied the man for the grapes. He said, "Envy me not. I pay dearly for my grapes." I apply it in this way: you may see wicked men about you eating the fat and drinking the sweetness of the land while you eat the bread of affliction and drink your tears. Oh, do not envy them! Their wealth is the price of blood; it has cost them dearly.

4. Do not be disquieted because the wicked prosper,

for this will put you in danger of being as wicked as the wicked are. That man who is troubled because the wicked prosper is likely to be tempted to become wicked that he might prosper as they do. Observe that where the Scripture says that good men should not be troubled because the wicked prosper, it gives this caution: "lest you should be wicked as the wicked are." Observe Proverbs 3:31: "Envy not the oppressor, nor choose none of his ways."

This intimates that if you envy wicked men who gain by oppression, you will become oppressors and will become wealthy as they are. Proverbs 24:1: "Be not envious against evil men, neither desire to be with them."

There is a notable text in which Asaph tells what danger he was in because he was disquieted when wicked men prospered. Psalm 73:2: "My feet had almost slipped." Asaph saw this, he envied them, and he almost fell into the same sin that they fell into.

You have a notable passage in Psalm 37:10: "Yet a little while, and the wicked shall not be; yea, thou shalt consider his place, and it shall not be." Asaph tells of their prosperity in Psalm 73:5, 7: "They are not plagued like other men; they have more than heart can wish." But David says, "It is but a little while, and the wickedness of the wicked shall be at an end." Because they see wicked men prosper, God's own people often go in the same way, and many times act wickedly as they do. Beloved, when you see men who break covenants and deal treacherously be successful in what is before them, if you envy them, you are in great danger of sinning as they do, and of doing wickedly as they do, that you might prosper as they do.

The third question is this: What consideration should a man use to reason against these disquietings of soul because of the prosperity of wicked men?

Beloved, I will give you six considerations to allay those disquietings when you see wicked men prosper in the world.

1. Consider that it is a harder matter for godly men to use prosperity well than adversity. You know it is a harder matter to carry a cup that is full to the brim without spilling than to carry a cup that is half filled. It is harder to carry a prosperous condition well without sin than it is to carry a state of adversity. Therefore, in Scripture, those who have been good in adversity have been bad in prosperity. The men of Israel were good in Egypt, but they were bad in Canaan. In Deuteronomy 32, even when God had delivered them and given them the land of Canaan, even then they rebelled against God. When they waxed fat and plentiful in the promised land, then they spurned God. When David was in a private condition, and hunted by Saul like a partridge over the mountains, David was a good man; but when David came to the throne he became adulterous and murderous, whereas before he was a man of a marvelous strict life. Therefore Scripture says of Jehoshaphat, in 2 Chronicles 17:3, that he followed David's first ways, intimating that David's first ways were his best ways.

I have read Bernard's chapter in *Of Considerations* which treats this theme: it is more dangerous for a good man to be in prosperity than adversity. Cornelius a Lapide commented on Proverbs 1:32 that the same word *(scalvat)* that signifies prosperity in the Hebrew is rendered by the Arabic *investigatio* and by the Septuagint *exetasmos,* that is, an inquisition or examination. The reason is this: prosperity makes known a man's disposition. As we say of magistracy, that when a man comes to be a magistrate it will show what a man is, so I may say that prosperity will show what a man is; it will find a man out. Therefore, said Anselm in his sentences, adversity and trouble try but one grace, your patience, but prosperity will try all your graces. It will try your love, whether you love God or the world. It will try your zeal, whether you will trust in Christ or your estates.

O beloved, will you envy a man who prospers in the world when it is so hard a matter for a good man to use well a prosperous condition? It is said of Pius Quintus that he was called pious because, in their account, when he was a mean man he was thought a good man; and when he came to be a cardinal he doubted his salvation, but when he became a pope he despaired of salvation. Beloved, when you are in a mean condition, you are more holy, pray better, and give God more service than when you have gotten your great livings and much of the world. Bernard made use for this purpose of Psalm 91:7: "A thousand shall fall at thy side, and ten thousand on thy right hand; but it shall not come nigh thee." The genuine sense of that passage is that the godly should not fall in that time by the plague. But, said Bernard, "I may apply this to prosperity: on the left hand there shall ten thousand fall by prosperity when, it may be, not a thousand fall by adversity." Beloved, if adversity slays his thousands, prosperity slays his ten thousands.

2. Consider that the prosperity of wicked men hastens their end and their ruin. Will you envy a man's prosperity when you see prosperity hastening his ruin?

Psalm 37:1–2: "Fret not thyself because of evildoers, neither be thou envious against the workers of iniquity. For they shall soon be cut down like the grass, and wither as a green herb." The more a flower has blossomed, the nearer it is to its withering time. When wicked men flourish and blossom most broadly, they are then nearest to being cut down; therefore fret not yourself against evildoers, for they shall soon be cut off. Proverbs 24:19–20: "Fret not thyself because of evil men, neither be thou envious at the wicked, for there shall be no reward to the evil man; the candle of the wicked shall be put out." Their prosperity shall hasten their ruin, but not their reward. There shall be no reward to evil men. Would not you account it folly in a man who is heir to so many thousand pounds per annum to envy a stageplayer in a cloth of gold in the habit of a king, and yet who is not heir to one foot of land? Why, though he has the form and respect and apparel of a king or nobleman upon the stage, yet he is heir to nothing. Thus wicked men, though they are arrayed gorgeously, and fare deliciously with Dives every day, wanting nothing, having more than heart can wish, are only possessors. You, godly man, are the heir. The laboring ox lives longer than the ox that is put into fatted pastures. Putting him there hastens the slaughter of the ox. When the Lord puts wicked men into fat pastures, He does it to hasten their ruin.

3. Consider that another man's prosperity is neither a hurt nor a prejudice to you. Therefore do not envy their prosperity. Suppose a wicked man has much; by his abundance you have no less. Your portion is not impaired because another's is increased. Leah's fruitfulness was no cause of Rachel's barrenness, yet she en-

vied her. Why do you envy a wicked man when you see him grow rich and prosper? This is an act of folly, because his prosperity is no hurt to you, nor is it any prejudice to you.

4. Consider that in this life you have a prosperity which wicked men have not, and in the life to come you shall have prosperity that they shall never have.

There are two parts in this consideration. The first is that in this life you have a prosperity that wicked men do not have. 3 John 2: "Beloved, I wish (or, I pray) above all things that thou mayest prosper and be in health, as thy soul prospers." When your body does not prosper, when it is diseased, when your estate does not prosper, when you are in debt, and the labor of your hand can neither fill your belly nor clothe your back, even then your soul may prosper. In the Psalmist's language, your soul may flourish as a green herb. Psalm 92:13: "Those that are planted in the house of the Lord shall flourish in the courts of our God." They shall be fat and flourishing.

The graces of the Spirit may thrive in you when nothing prospers nor goes well with you in the world. Now wicked men, though they prosper in their bodies, do not prosper in their soul. They prosper and thrive in wealth and goods, but not in grace. It is a remarkable text in Psalm 106:15: "And He gave them their request, but sent leanness into their souls." He gave them their request, but what follows? "He sent leanness into their souls." The quails were dainty food. It fattened their bodies, but their souls starved. Their souls did not thrive; their graces did not grow; their souls starved. Suppose your estate does not increase, yet do your graces thrive? This should comfort you, and free you from all disquietings in your inward man.

Second, for the life to come, you shall then have prosperity that no wicked man shall have. This consideration should allay all disquieting. Psalm 17:14–15 speaks of men who have their portion in this life—children enough, and money enough to give their children large portions. What does David do to prevent repining and disquieting of soul? Mark the next words: "As for me, I will behold Thy face in righteousness." His meaning is this: "I see them prosper here. They have many children, and they have enough for them all. But as for me, this satisfies me: I shall behold Thy face, that is, when my body shall be raised at the resurrection day, and I shall come to heaven; this will satisfy me." And this quieted the spirit of David.

5. Consider that prosperity makes wicked men worse, and adversity makes good men better. There are two parts in this item likewise:

First, prosperity makes wicked men worse. In the Exodus story, God exalted Pharaoh to a magnificent state to make him worse. All Pharaoh's wealth hardened his heart more. "The prosperity of the wicked slays them" (Proverbs 1:32). And in Hosea 13:6: "As was their pasture, so were they filled; their heart was exalted, and therefore have they forgotten Me." Prosperity makes a wicked man worse. It is a spur to licentiousness; it is fuel to his lust, and a hindrance to his graces.

Second, adversity makes good men better. It weans them from the world; it makes them look after heaven; it embitters sin to them; it makes them spend more time in duty; it thus makes good men better. Themistocles said of himself that he would have perished if he had not perished. Many a good man might say, "If such a disaster had not befallen me, I would have drowned in comforts, and glutted in the world." O beloved, this consideration should greatly allay your disquietings. Prosperity makes wicked men worse and adversity makes good men better.

6. Consider that wicked men do not always have comfort and contentment in their abundance and prosperity in the world. Though wicked men prosper and abound, yet they have a mixture of discontent and vexations and dissatisfaction with their abundance. Would you envy a man to see him have a silken stocking, but a gouty leg? Alas, beloved, wicked men may be clad in silk, but you do not know the pain that may be under a silken garment. It may be that a poor man with a russet coat who gets but his twelve pence per day has more inward contentment of mind than the man who gets his hundreds per week. I have seen many times people wearing a shoe, yet confessing that the shoe pinched them. Beloved, wicked men may be more neatly clad than other men may be, and have more of the world than other men, yet God may pinch them with a galled conscience, that they have gotten their estates by oppression and unjust gain. Oh, will you envy a wicked man? If godly men knew that vexation and horror of conscience which accompany a wicked man's abundance, they would not have their abundance for all the world. They would rather die as beggars than live as rich men. You read of Haman in Esther 5:13: "Yet all this availeth me nothing, so long as I see Mordecai sitting at the king's gate." He was the king's favorite; he had more favor at court with Ahasuerus than all the court besides; yet a trifle ate out all Haman's comfort and contentment, and made him lie down on his bed

with sorrow. He would not be comforted because he could not get a bow of the knee from Mordecai. Why, a little thing will discontent a wicked man, and will make him off the hooks. We read that Ahab had the best kingdom of the world, the kingdom of Israel, yet he could not be content because he could not have Naboth's vineyard. He was sick for it.

You have a notable passage in Ecclesiastes 5:10–12: "He that loveth silver shall not be satisfied with silver; nor he that loveth abundance with increase; this is also vanity." Do you love money? Money shall never satisfy you. Do you love abundance? You shall have abundance. But you shall not be satisfied for all that. "The sleep of a laboring man is sweet, whether he eats little or much; but the abundance of the rich shall not suffer him to sleep."

A poor day-laboring man, whether he eats little or much, can have a sweet night's sleep; but a wicked man, many times, has an abundance that makes him so that he cannot take his rest. What care in the keeping, what fear in the losing, and what thoughts of getting more—these do excruciate and torment the thoughts of many wicked men. So true is that saying of Jesus Christ in Luke 12:15: "Take heed and beware of covetousness; for a man's life consisteth not in the abundance which he possesseth." You may have an abundance, and yet the comfort of your life does not consist in all your abundance. But now good men have more comfort, inward quiet, and contentment of mind with a little than the wicked have with all their abundance. Psalm 37:16: "A little that a righteous man hath is better than the riches of many wicked." Proverbs 15:16: "Better is a little with the fear of the Lord than great treasure and trouble therewith." There may be great treasures and great trouble; there may be little of the world, and yet great peace therewith. Therefore, be not disquieted because wicked men prosper in the world.

Application

I now come to give you a word of application. If it is so that the people of God must check their hearts for, and use reasoning against, disquietings of soul because wicked men prosper, then, by way of inference, first of all, do not so much admire the prosperity of wicked men in the world. Do not think prosperity to be so happy a state for men to be in. It is not worthy of envy; it is not fit to place one troubled thought into a good man's mind. The admiration of a natural thing another man has should not disquiet another man who does not have the same.

Second, if I must not be disquieted because wicked men prosper, then I would infer that I must be far from envying and being disquieted at the graces of good men. If I must not envy a wicked man's growing rich, then I must not envy a good man's growing good. It is the greatest wickedness in the world for you to envy another man's graces. It is a diabolical sin; it transforms a man into a devil; it makes a man into a devil incarnate, because other men's graces outstrip theirs. Another man preaches better than you, and therefore you envy him. Augustine, writing on Psalm 139, calls it a devilish sin because it is properly the sin of the devils in hell.

The devil, out of pure spite and pure envy, envies man's good. Beloved, many men are of this temper, that they envy and are troubled that other men are good—this is the devil's sin. Just as the Philistines envied the good of God's people, so do they. Genesis 26:15-16: "For all the wells which his father's servants had digged, the Philistines had stopped, and filled them with earth."

It is a strange passage. The Philistines would do themselves hurt so that God's children should not get benefit. What did they do? They stopped up all the wells in the country and hindered themselves from having benefit by the water so that God's people should have no water. Why, beloved, wicked men do thus. They envy that other men should get good; they envy God's people not only for their wealth, but for their very graces likewise. Cain envied Abel because his brother's works were righteous and his own were wicked.

Is it so that we must check all envyings and disquietings because wicked men prosper? Then I infer hence that it is just with God to suffer wicked men to envy the prosperity of good men because the godly sometimes envy the prosperity of the wicked. Here you see David envied to see Saul prosper. And God, to recompense David's sin, suffered Saul to envy David. Therefore Saul hunted and pursued David like a partridge over the mountains.

O beloved, God but pays us in our own coin. Isaac envied the prosperity of the Philistines, and the Philistines were suffered by God to envy Isaac, and they stopped up their wells, and would give them no water. The reason was merely out of envy; for, said they, "You have more people than we, and you are more wealthy than we." Therefore they denied them water. It is just with God to suffer wicked men to hate the prosperity of the godly, just as the godly sin sometimes in envying the prosperity of wicked men.

Is it so that we must not be disquieted at the prosperity of wicked men? Then I infer that prosperity is no sign either of a good cause or of good men. I must not envy them. You read in Psalm 73 that the wicked prosper, their houses are safe from fear, they do not come into trouble like other men, yet their cause may not be good nor themselves neither. Indeed, it is a great vanity when men claim their success and prosperity to be a symptom and an infallible sign from heaven that their cause is good. What did we condemn the papists for? If I thought that prosperity were the sign of a good cause and good men, I would concur with papists to make prosperity a sign of the visible church. Beloved, we are even turned papists in our days. They make it a sign of a true church, and some men among us make it a sign that God approves of what they do because they prosper. All our divines have written against popery in that point, and affirm that adversity and persecution is a badge of God's church rather than prosperity.

Sermon 9

A Use of Exhortation

"Why art thou cast down, O my soul? and why art thou disquieted within me? Hope thou in God, for I shall yet praise Him, who is the health of my countenance, and my God." Psalm 42:11

I proceed to a use of exhortation, to persuade you all to labor to check your own hearts for being troubled for the outward prosperity of wicked men. And that I may prevail with you herein, I shall leave with you these three considerations:

First, you have no cause at all to be troubled if you consider what God's ends are in suffering wicked men to prosper in this world.

Second, if you but consider the ends themselves that wicked men have who prosper in the world.

Third, if you but consider why God would not have the godly be troubled and disquieted at the prosperity of the wicked, and what His ends are in not suffering His people so to prosper in this world. And if these three considerations were seriously considered by the people of God, it would take away and allay all murmuring and troubles and disquieting from the hearts and minds of God's people in seeing wicked men prosper in the world.

First, if you would allay trouble of mind in seeing

the wicked prosper, consider God's ends in suffering them to prosper in the world. Now there are seven ends which God has, all of which might allay the troubles of mind in the hearts of God's people when they see wicked men prosper.

1. God suffers wicked men to prosper in the world that they might have more opportunity to display their sin and wickedness, whereas if they were in a poor, low, and afflicted condition they could not have such opportunities to draw forth those acts of sin and wickedness that lie hidden in their own hearts. If these vines of Sodom, and if those fruits of Gomorrah, were not warmed with the sun of prosperity, we would not see the grapes of God and the clusters of bitterness that are in them. Now God is pleased, for ends best known to Himself, to heap the prosperity of the world upon them to draw out that sin and wickedness that lies hidden in the heart, and to make it come to public view. Have we not a pregnant instance of this in Hazael in 2 Kings 8, when he was in power and prosperity? That was an opportunity to reveal and draw forth the wickedness that lay hidden in his heart. Well did the prophet say, "Thou shalt rip up women with child, thou wilt burn their strongholds with fire, and slay the young men with the sword, and dash their children in the streets." But now what did Hazael say to the prophet? "Am I a dog, that I should do such things as these are?" But, said the prophet, "Thou shalt be king, and then thou shalt do it, even all these things." When he was poor and in a low condition, he was not in a capacity to do this villainy; but when the world favored him and he began to prosper and become great in power and in the world, then came the opportunity to draw out this wickedness.

As we see in our days, if there had not been this licentious liberty, and this general toleration among us, we would not have heard of such wickedness. And wicked men would have lacked opportunity to have vented such wickedness, which now is made manifest to the face of the world, and the people of God gain good by all this. For by this means they come to see what is in men's hearts. In Daniel 8:24–25, it is said of Antiochus that "his power shall be mighty, and he shall prosper and practice, and shall destroy the mighty and the holy people (or, according to the Chaldee, the people of the Holy One), and through his policy he shall cause violence to prosper in his hands, and he shall magnify himself in his heart, and by peace (or, prosperity) shall destroy many." If this man had not come to be a king, a great man in power and prosperity, the wickedness of his heart would not have been discovered, but by his being in prosperity he had an opportunity to draw out the mischief that was in his heart to be made manifest to the view of the world.

There is, in Job 12:6, mention made of a tabernacle of robbers who prospered. God let them prosper that people might see the evil that is in their hearts. A shower of rain falling on the ground causes the weeds to appear which otherwise would not. The snake in the fable, when it was frozen, could not sting; but when it was in the bosom, in the warmth, then it could sting. The moral is that, when men are in a low or a poor condition, then they cannot hurt because they have no power in their hand; but when they come to be warm with the prosperity of the world they will hurt and do mischief.

2. God lets wicked men prosper that their mouths

might be stopped, and that they may have nothing to say when God shall proceed in judgment against them. God shall say to them, "I gave you mercies and you never performed your duty towards Me. I gave you prosperity and you returned Me no glory. Such and such a man who had no riches, no prosperity in the world as you had, and yet did his duty and had more grace, and brought Me more glory than ever you have done. I have been bountiful towards you, but you have not been humble before Me. You have had much from Me, and yet returned little to Me." This prosperity will be an argument to stop their mouths so that they shall not be able to speak a word against God.

3. God lets wicked men prosper to the end that He might see whether His people will love Him for Himself and love Christ for His own sake; whether they can love a naked God, a naked Christ, and a naked truth. For their own sakes God does it to try His people whether they will love holiness and grace and the ways of God when they are paved with thorns as well as when they are strewn with roses; to see if His people will love religion when it is a persecuted religion, love holiness and exact walking when it is scorned and the professors thereof reproached, and love religion when it shall have neither power nor success on its side, rather than to love sin and the ways of vanity when prosperity and profit and pleasure and success are all on that side. And this is one end whereby He tries His own servants by letting the men of the world prosper, to see if they will love God for Himself.

4. God lets wicked men prosper that thereby it may hasten and aggravate their ruin. What is the main end of putting oxen into fat pastures but to fatten them up

A Use of Exhortation

for the day of slaughter? So the Lord puts wicked men into fat pastures of prosperity and riches in this world, but it is to fatten them up for the day of slaughter, and to make them be a sweeter morsel not only for worms in the grave, but for devils in hell. God lets wicked men prosper, and lets them have the world at will, but it is that it might carry them with the greater speed into the place of darkness. Psalm 92:7: "The wicked spring up as grass, and all the workers of iniquity flourish, that they might be destroyed forever."

5. God lets wicked men prosper that their prosperity might be a shelter and defense to His own people. What was the reason why Cyrus, a wicked man, should so prosper in strength and power in the world and destroy the Chaldeans and Babylonians? He was a heathen, and God made use of him for His own people's safety. It was by the hand of Cyrus that deliverance came to the poor Jews out of captivity. It was wondered why Egypt must be the fruitful place during the seven years of famine, when all the nations round about them had famine in them. But God's end was that they might have provision to maintain His own people and Jacob's sons. So the land of Canaan was never so fruitful as it was in the very year when the Jews were to inherit it. Now what was the reason? God did not love the Canaanites, but they built houses, and God's people came and lived in them. They planted vineyards, and God's people came and ate the fruit of them. It was for their sakes that He suffered the Canaanites to do this. God did not love Pharaoh, and God did not love the Canaanites, but God did love His own people, and for their sakes He did all this to let them prosper and thrive and grow great in the world, that His own people

might enjoy the lands for their possession.

Now you shall find that there are three texts that particularly intimate and set forth this point. One is Proverbs 13:22: "A good man leaveth an inheritance to his children's children, but the wealth of the sinner is laid up for the just." A wicked man will sell his conscience and engage his soul and everything to the devil, and all to get a little wealth in the world. And God may suffer him to prosper in his ways, and to get wealth by this sinful way. But what then? In the end it shall be laid up for the just; they shall have it. God so orders it many times that that which wicked men get, godly men enjoy.

So likewise Job 27:16–17: "Though they heap up silver as the dust, and prepare raiment as the clay, he may prepare it, but the just shall put it on, and the innocent shall divide the silver." This is the portion of wicked men: to heap up silver as dust and to prepare raiment as clay. This he may do, but the just shall divide it and the innocent put it on. God will not let good men be so far tempted to get the world, but He lets wicked men embrace that temptation. But after they have done all, His own people shall enjoy it.

The third and last verse for this purpose is Proverbs 28:8: "He that by usury and unjust gain increaseth his substance, he shall gather it for him that will pity the poor." Therefore we see how many men may go to hell for getting riches, and leave it to those who are godly and liberal to enjoy that substance. And shall this trouble godly men? It may be that you see wicked men get riches. They run the hazard of losing a soul to get it, and you enjoy the benefit after them. The child who sees his father's shepherd have many sheep, shall the

A Use of Exhortation

child envy him? He but keeps them till his father dies. So wicked men get the world at the hazard of their soul, and do not know who shall enjoy what they have gotten; for godly men have a right to that which God suffers wicked men to enjoy. I do not say they have a civil right, for that they have not; but they have a religious and a spiritual right to that and to all the world, for all the world is given unto you for your good. Though wicked men are suffered to prosper in the world, be not disquieted at them.

6. God does it for the spiritual good of His own people. When God's people see that the wicked prosper in the world, while they themselves do not prosper in the world, this administers an occasion to them to live the life of faith. If God should leave marks of displeasure upon everyone who provokes Him, and marks of favor on everyone who pleases Him, then we would live by sight and not by faith; but when believers see themselves persecuted, holiness derided and scorned at, and the professors thereof live low in the world, while they see wicked men flourish and thrive and grow great in prosperity of the world, not being afflicted as other men, but living in all kinds of pleasure that the world can afford, and having more than heart can wish—now this administers an occasion for the people of God to live by faith.

7. God suffers wicked men to flourish in prosperity in the world because they, living in such power and prosperity, are ordered by God to do God some service in the world. So you read that Jehu did God some service in the world, since he was living in prosperity; and God rewarded him for it, for he and his posterity had the kingdom for the space of four generations. And for

this temporal service God gave him a temporal reward.

Second, as you are to consider God's ends in suffering wicked men to prosper, so you are to consider the wicked's end in living in prosperity. And in the consideration thereof you will not be troubled at their prosperity. That appears in these particulars:

1. Consider that outward prosperity is all the portion that God has allotted that wicked men shall enjoy forever. They have no other, nor shall they ever have any other portion and happiness but in this world. Therefore do not envy their prosperity. Job 9:24: "The earth is given into the hands of the wicked; he covereth the faces of the judges; if not, where, and who is he?" A wicked man enjoys the earth, but he enjoys no more. This is all his heaven, all his happiness, all his portion, all his comfort. He shall have no heaven to reward and receive him, no God, no Christ to smile upon him, no grace to be crowned with glory. Nothing is given to them but the prosperity of this world. So in Psalm 17:14 David prays to God to be delivered from men "who have their part and portion in this life, whose belly Thou fillest with Thy hidden treasure." God gives them their treasure in this world, but God gives them none of the treasure of heaven. They shall never see His face; they shall never have the light of His countenance, no communion with the Father and with His Son, no joys and comforts of the Holy Ghost, no true peace of conscience, neither shall they ever enjoy any part among those who are sanctified by faith in Christ. They have the earth in their hands, but nothing of heaven in their hearts. They hold sway *in* the world who are slaves *to* the world; they rule others at their will, but are slaves

to the will of Satan. They may have the treasure of the world, the portion of slaves, but they shall never have the inheritance of sons. Therefore do not envy them.

2. Do not envy their prosperity, because they have the curse of God that goes along with all that they enjoy in the world. Proverbs 3:31: "Envy not thou the oppressor (or, the man of violence), and choose none of his ways." Why? What is the reason? "Because the Lord's curse is in the house of the wicked" (verse 33). So likewise Job 5:3: "I have seen the foolish taking root, but suddenly I cursed his habitation." God's curse goes along with the prosperity of the wicked. Do not envy that which God curses. Although they may have good things from God, yet they have never a good thought from God—nothing from Him but His curse and anger.

Third, why does God withhold prosperity from His people?

1. God's end is that He might give His people better things than outward prosperity in the world. He gives good things to those who are evil, but better things, spiritual and heavenly riches, to those who are godly. He denies evil things to His people, but He gives them good things. God keeps you empty from the world that He might fill your heart with grace and with Jesus Christ. God lets you enjoy less of the world that He might give you more of Himself. God would not give Moses the land of Canaan, a temporal good, but God gave Moses heaven, a spiritual and an eternal good. So God may deny you outward prosperity to give you inward grace, so that you might have an inheritance among those who are sanctified by faith in Christ. This

He will give you, but He will deny outward inheritances in the world.

He clothes you but meanly with the world that He might richly clothe you with the righteousness of His Son. He has a Benjamin's mess, a rich portion for His children, a portion that lies not in dust and rubbish, but in spiritual blessings in heavenly places. God does not fill your house with lumber, but He will fill your heart with Himself. He gives you little in this world that He might give you pardon of sin, the love of Christ, heaven and glory, and whatever may tend to make you be eternally glorious in heaven.

2. God denies His people prosperity in this world because He sees that they can hardly use prosperity well. David was exceedingly good when he lay under a low condition and under persecution, but when David came to the throne, and when he grew great and rich and in power, then he heaped up more sin than he did before. So it was with Solomon. What abundance of sin did Solomon heap up, not being able to use prosperity so well as he should; his wealth did him more hurt than his wisdom did him good. When God gives you prosperity in the world, it is a hundred to one if you use it well. Should God give you full gales of prosperity and fill you with the world, it would overturn your little vessel. Therefore God denies you that which He will suffer wicked men to have to their own ruin. Prosperity in the world destroys more than troubles and bonds and persecution do. More are slain by prosperity in their chamber than by the sword in the field. Therefore it is a mercy for God to deny His people that which would do them so much hurt.

USE. If it is so that God's people are denied the

A Use of Exhortation

prosperity of the world, oh, then do not censure God's people because they are but mean in the world. There is an aptness in men to run into two extremes. One is to justify men who do prosper in an evil course, and the other is to condemn those who do not prosper in the world in a good way.

First, do not censure those who do not prosper in a good way. It is possible that the church of God, which has God, Christ, the truth, and all on its side, yet may not have victory; if you censure men for this, you may for the same reason censure Christ and the church of old. And for the same reason you might justify the Turk and Pope and condemn Christ, if you should pass your judgment according to who is the victorious and prevailing party; for enemies have much prevailed against the church.

Do not censure because of success, and that you may free yourselves from this unjust censure, take this consideration. It is a metaphor drawn from the trees, the one applied to Christ, the other to Nebuchadnezzar, king of Babylon. In Daniel 4:10–12, mention is made of the vision in which the king saw a tree: "It was in the midst of the earth, and the height thereof was great. The tree grew and was strong, and the height thereof reached to heaven, and the sight thereof unto the end of all the earth. The leaves thereof fair, and the fruit thereof much, and in it was meat for all: the beasts of the field had shadow under it, and the fowls of the heaven did dwell in the shadow of it, and all flesh was fed of it." This is to be understood of Nebuchadnezzar, king of Babylon, and of his kingdom, which spread over all the earth. Now again it is spoken of Christ in Isaiah 53:2: "For He shall grow up before Him as a tender plant, and as a root out of a dry ground. He hath no form nor comeliness in Him, and when we shall see Him, there is no beauty that we should desire Him." This is the testimony of this tree; this is meant of Jesus Christ. And yet, in this tree, there is no form or beauty that we should desire it. This tree was nothing comparable to the kingdom of Nebuchadnezzar for power and greatness and riches in the world, and yet Jesus Christ must be a despised plant. So likewise, when you see the men of the world prosper and live in prosperity in the world, do not censure them who are as low plants in the world, poor and low. If you do, you must condemn Jesus Christ and the church of God and the generation of the just.

Second, do not justify the wicked, though they prosper in the world. You must not therefore judge their cause to be good because they prosper. The papists make their prosperity and successes an argument of the truth of their church, and that they are in the right way. Many men make this to be a standing mark, and upon all occasions will be ready to justify evil actions by asking, "Do you not see them prosper?" They are ready to justify all breaches of covenant, and all wickedness and sinful actions, because they prosper, and there is none to lift up a hand against them because they succeed in all things before them. This is as bad an action as that of the papists. They make prosperity an argument of the goodness of the cause and truth of their church.

When Dionysius had robbed the church and carried away all that it had, he could then say, to justify his action, "Behold how the gods favor us!" He made his prosperity an argument to justify his sacrilege. When men have full gales of wind in the prosperity of the world, and when they prosper in an evil course, and there is none to disturb them, and all is well with them, and they rule the world at will, then can they laugh in their sleeve and think that the God of heaven justifies them in all their actions. They have armies on their side, and strength and powers of the world on their side; but we have truth and God on our side! And though the church and people of God may be in the dust, though they may be trampled underfoot by wicked men, yet the time shall come when the church and people of God shall prevail. Therefore do not justify the wicked in an evil way.

Third, labor to abound in grace as you do in blessings. We read of an altar made by Moses, and also we read of an altar made by Solomon, and that which he made was four times larger than that which Moses made because Solomon had more riches than Moses and more peace. Moses' was made in the wilderness, Solomon's in Canaan. I may allude to this, you upon whom God has bestowed much riches and whom He has caused to prosper in the world, whose estates in the world are four times larger than others' are. Now God requires four times more service from you than He does from others. You whose estates are great and come upon you yearly without pains and labor, God expects that you should employ yourselves to His glory, to bring God glory answerable to what is required of you, more than He expects from handicraft tradesmen in the world, though they must serve God in the performance of those duties which God requires of them. They must sequester so much time from their callings, and rob their back to serve God, and pinch their bellies to do their duties; but this is a good exchange to rob their bodies to save their souls. It was said of the Athenians, the best land with the best laws, that they made use of their land, but neglected their laws. Take heed that your mercies do not make you forget your duties.

In sum, do not admire the prosperity of wicked men, as Augustine wrote, "These good things, that they might not be accounted evil, are given to good men, and, lest they should be thought the only good, are given to wicked men. If there be anything better than another, the worst men shall never have them." Now grace is the best good in all the world; therefore the best men shall have it. Now the riches of the world are the worst riches; therefore wicked men shall prosper therein. Prosperity is not the best good, because it is that which God usually denies His beloved people and His dear children, and bestows it on those who are the worst men. Now when He denies it to His sons and bestows it on slaves, it is an argument that this is not the best good. And thus we have covered the first cause for which God's people are apt to be cast down.

Sermon 10

The Calamitous Condition of the Church

"Why art thou cast down, O my soul? and why art thou disquieted within me? Hope thou in God, for I shall yet praise Him, who is the health of my countenance, and my God." Psalm 42:11

I now come to the second particular for which the people of God are cast down, and that is because of the calamitous condition of the church and the people of God here in the world. However, some would claim that the church of God was never in a more glorious condition than it is at this day. Yet whatever they say, he who but rightly looks at things, and makes but a diligent scrutiny into the church's condition, may easily see and behold the church of God to be very low, and that the glory and the face of the church of God were never so blurred as at this day, and in these times wherein we live; and we may say, "Where has our glory gone?"

We may see our glory even standing on the threshold, and ready to take her wings and fly away as a bird, and our eyes may behold it if God prevents it not; for do we not see a cloud of troubles and sore afflictions hanging over our heads, ready to fall upon us in these parts of the world? And we will certainly fall if God, in His infinite mercy, does not prevent it! Do we not behold profaneness and wickedness, yea, great wickedness abounding among us, and appearing also in the church? And that appears so much the more when the government of the church, which should keep out heresy and profaneness, is cried down, and a toleration of all religions promoted as if that were the true church where the most profaneness and errors abound. Wherever these sins abound, there we may judge that it is the church's swooning, if not the church's dying time.

The erroneous doctrines, doctrines of devils, which so much abound in our days, among those who cast off the assemblies of the true church and seduce the people into sinful practices, laboring to corrupt their judgments by loosening them from the truth and filling them with false opinions—these are the things which most hurt us. This was that which troubled the church of God of old in Revelation 2:15. In verse 13, the term "Satan's seat" is used for the place where such opinions are propogated; and these principles are those which God hates, and for which God has a controversy with the people wherever they are tolerated. These opinions, errors, and heresies are those which disturb the peace and trouble the patience of the church of God—not only when wicked men are in power and place in the state, but when wicked and profane, erroneous, heretical, and heterodox opinions trouble the church. And the Lord knows how soon this land may be overspread with them, causing us to say that the glory of the church has departed and flown away; for these are the church's reproach and not her glory. If things go on as we see they began, the people of God may say they were never in a worse condition.

But in handling this particular, that the people of God may not be too much cast down when they see the calamity of the church:

1. I shall lay down some cautions.

2. I shall show you that the people of God have been afflicted for the calamities of the church.

3. I shall show you the difference between sympathizing with the church in her troubles and having sinful troubles of mind.

4. I shall lay down some rules indicating that, even if the troubles of the church and the people of God are many and great, it is the duty of the people of God not to be too much cast down.

CAUTION 1. When I say that the people of God are not to be too much troubled for the calamities of the church, I do not intend by that to press you to a stoical insensibility and sottish ignorance of the church's miseries. As you are not to be like stoics, not to be troubled for the calamities of the church at all, not to have any concern for your brother's miseries, you must not be of an indifferent, Gallio-like spirit, not to be cast down nor affected by the troubles of the church. But I would have you be affected by and afflicted for the troubles of the church, in measure, in a holy sense and with a holy humbleness of heart.

CAUTION 2. When you find such a sympathizing and sensible concern for the church's miseries, you are to cherish and to stir up that feeling in you, and you are not to check your hearts for it; for this is your duty and not your sin (1 Corinthians 12:26). As it is with the natural body, so it is with the spiritual body, the church. In the body, if the head is in pain, all the body, every member of the body, is sensible of it. So it is with the body of Christ: if one member is in pain and suffers, the rest of the members are in trouble for it.

CAUTION 3. You are to check those castings down and troubles of soul that disanimate and discourage you and lay you under such sorrow of spirit and trouble of mind as to put you in a hopeless condition, and cause you in your sorrow not to retain any hopes concerning the church's future welfare.

And thus, having laid down the cautions, I shall now lay down the second particular to show you that the people of God of old have been greatly sensible of and afflicted for the troubles of the church of God. Under this heading there are two sorts of persons to be considered:
Those who foresaw the troubles of the church, and who feared it and were troubled for it.
Those who felt the troubles of the church when it came, and who were troubled also.
First, as for those who foresaw when the troubles of the church would come and were troubled, one example was Elisha: he foresaw the troubles of the church and fell weeping. And when he was with Hazael he asked, " 'What doth trouble thee, my lord?' And he answered and said, 'Because of the evil and the wickedness that thou wilt do unto the children of Israel, to dash them against the stones; and the strongholds thou wilt set on fire, and their women thou wilt rip up with child.' " The story you may read in 2 Kings 8:12–13. "For, said he, "thou shalt come to be king, and thou shalt do this great wickedness." And the consideration of what this man would do to the church of God made this good man weep.
Likewise we hear the prophet Isaiah say, "Therefore said I, 'Look away from me, I will weep bitterly (or, I will

The Calamitous Condition of the Church 147

be bitter in weeping); labor not to comfort me' " (Isaiah 22:4). Why? What is the reason why this good man will be this heavy and weep? Because of "the spoiling of the daughters of my people." What should the prophet so weep for? There was nothing in his days but quietness, peace, and plenty, and yet in these days the prophet wept bitterly and would not be comforted. The trouble had not yet really come, for it came not until a hundred years after his death; but the prophet foresaw that it would certainly come upon the people of God, and this consideration made him weep. And for this his heart was troubled.

Then you read of Daniel in Daniel 8:27: "And I, Daniel, fainted, and was sick certain days." Now what was the reason why this good prophet was sick and faint for many days? It was trouble of mind, that by his prophetic spirit he foresaw the troubles that were coming upon the church and people of God, and that the church and people of God would deeply and sadly suffer under the reign of Antiochus. For this cause he was sick many days. And this trouble fell not upon the church of God until many years after his death. Daniel 8:11–12: "He magnified himself to the prince of the host, and by him the daily sacrifice was taken away, and the place of his sanctuary was cast down. And a host was given him against the daily sacrifice by reason of transgression, and it cast down the truth to the ground, and it practiced and prospered." And this trouble and sorrow he foresaw would come upon the church two hundred years after, which made him sick and faint, and he was sorely troubled for many days. And thus you have instances of good men who have been troubled for the church's calamities before they came.

Second, you have instances of how good men have been troubled for the church's calamities when they were coming upon them; to see gray hairs upon the head of the church, and sorrows and trouble overtaking them, troubled their spirits. In 2 Samuel 1:11–12, when David heard that the Philistines had defeated and overthrown the people of God, it says that "David took hold of his clothes and rent them, and likewise all the men that were with him; and they mourned and wept, and fasted until evening, for Saul and for Jonathan his son, and for the people of the Lord, and for the house of Israel, because they were fallen by the sword."

Likewise a clear text for this purpose is Nehemiah 1:2–4: when the sad condition of the people of God was brought and told to good Nehemiah, he wept. "Hanani, one of my brethren, came, he and certain men of Judah, and I asked them concerning the Jews that had escaped, which were left of the captivity, and concerning Jerusalem. And they said unto me, 'The remnant that are left of the captivity there in the province are in great affliction and reproach; the wall of Jerusalem also is broken down, and the gates thereof are burnt with fire.' And it came to pass, when I heard these words, that I sat down and wept, and mourned many days, and fasted and prayed before the God of heaven." Here you see how good men have mourned and been exceedingly cast down with sorrow when they have heard of the calamities that have fallen upon the church and people of God.

The third particular is to show you the difference between a gracious sympathizing with the troubles of the church and sinful disquiet because of the calamities of the church. One is a duty, the other is a sin.

First, gracious sympathizing with the church in trouble quickens prayer and supplication for the church's good. You read that the Psalmist, when the people of God were in great trouble, was in sorrow, but his sorrow drove him to the throne of grace to pray for them. Psalm 137:5: "If I forget thee, O Jerusalem, then let my right hand forget her cunning." Though the church's sufferings may make you sad in spirit, yet they must not make you dead in prayer. As they had pity towards God's church in affliction, so they also had prayer in their hearts for them when they were in trouble, that they might have it removed. In contrast, they who have excessive sorrow of mind for the troubles and calamities of the church are apt to complain to men and make men moan of their sorrows; but their sorrow indisposes their hearts to go to God by prayer and supplication to have their sorrow removed. And when people are so pressed down with sorrow as to complain to men and not to God, it is an argument that their sorrow is inordinate and sinful, because moderate sorrow puts the soul to seek God at the throne of grace so that sorrows and troubles might be taken off and removed from the church.

Second, those men who mourn appropriately and moderately for the calamities of the church retain within themselves some good hopes of the church's recovery. Therefore you read in Lamentations 3:31–33: "The Lord will not cast off forever. For though He causeth grief, yet He will have compassion according to the multitude of His mercies. For He doth not afflict willingly (or "from His heart," for so it is in the original) nor grieve the children of men." Here you see that though the church was in great affliction, yet, behold, Jeremiah could sympathize with them and mourn for them, yet so as to have hope in God for all this. He could see and know God's heart towards them, though His hand was seemingly against them. He does not afflict from His heart. It was as if Jeremiah had said, "God afflicts indeed, but it is not willingly; it is for sin which He hates in His own people, and He is, as it were, constrained to strike His children. It is not His wonted work; it is a strange work. It comes not from His heart, but from His hand." Therefore he could sorrow in hope of deliverance out of trouble.

But now sinful dejections cut off hope, as you may read in 2 Kings 7:18–19. Elisha told the people when there was famine in Samaria, and he told them of great evil that should come upon them. And afterwards he told them that by tomorrow this time there should be sold "two measures of barley for a shekel in the gate of Samaria." Here was great plenty spoken of. And a lord answered the man of God and said, "Now behold, if the Lord should make windows in heaven, might such a thing be?" It is as if he had said, "We who are in such deep sorrow, such great trouble today, is it possible that we can have such great plenty tomorrow?" But he said, "Thou shalt see it with thy eyes, but thou shalt not eat thereof." So many men are like this man, so cast down with excessive sorrow for the sufferings of the church; and when the church of God is low and the enemies of the church strong, they are ready to think that they are so low, their wounds so great, and their enemies so strong that it is impossible to be restored.

This is something like the reasonings of the church at another time, Lamentations 3:18–19: "And I said, 'My strength and my hope is perished from the Lord,' remembering my affliction and my misery, the wormwood and the gall." When their sorrow and suffering in Babylon was so long, and they did not see any likelihood of being delivered, no visible means for their restoration, and being brought out of captivity, they were then overcome with sorrow. They said, "Our hopes are cut off from God." This appears in Ezekiel 37:11, when they were as dry bones in the valley, and they thought that it was impossible for dry bones to have flesh and sinews to be put back on them. Again, they thought they were utterly lost, and that they should never be brought out of trouble, and this caused bitter complaints to arise from their spirits.

Third, moderate sorrow differs from immoderate sorrow in this: true sorrow stirs up holy endeavors to act in your place and calling for the deliverance of the church. Thus you read in Jeremiah 51:50: "You that have escaped the sword, go away, stand not still; remember the Lord afar off, and let Jerusalem come into your minds." It is as if the prophet had said, "Jerusalem is in trouble and under great and sore afflictions. Do what you can for her; stand not still, but improve all the interests you can in all places and conditions that it may be for her benefit."

A man who is possessed with a sinful care and a sinful sorrow is so far from improving all his interest for God's people in trouble that he is ready to sit down and say, "I will do no more for religion and for the cause of God," and he is ready to think he has done too much already. He repents of all he has done. This is sinful trouble and sinful sorrow, when they are ready to resolve to do no more, lend no more, and venture no more. If it goes well with the church, then they will own the church and people of God, but if the church is brought into troubles, and if it lies under sorrows, then they will desert it and will not improve any interest for it. They will not do anything for God, His church, or His people, but give all over as lost and gone without any endeavors to relieve them.

Fourth, those who thus mourn graciously mourn more for the church's troubles, and for the people of God's sorrows, than they do for their own particular sorrows and troubles. David's sorrows and troubles regarding his own person were no more to him than a little prick in his flesh; but the sorrows, troubles, and sufferings of the church were to him as a sword in his bones. Psalm 42:10: "As with a sword in my bones my enemies reproach me, while they say unto me daily, 'Where is thy God?' " So likewise you read of Elijah in 1 Kings 19:4–10. When Elijah was sitting under the juniper tree, he said, "O Lord, I beseech Thee, take away my life; for I am not better than my fathers." And he said, "I have been very jealous for the Lord God of Hosts. For the children of Israel have forsaken Thy covenant, thrown down Thine altars, and slain Thy prophets with the sword; and I, even I only, am left, and they seek my life to take it away." Here you see that good man mourned for God's church: "They have slain Thy prophets," and this punished him, and greatly disquieted him and troubled his spirit.

But immoderate sorrow is more let out after particular crosses, troubles, and personal losses. The loss of relations, the loss of your estate, or any other personal affliction upon your body troubles you more than the great troubles that the church of God are under. Now

The Calamitous Condition of the Church

this is a sinful sorrow.

Now to allay this distemper, that you may not sinfully and immoderately mourn for the calamities of the church and people of God, I shall name to you these five considerations (which is the fourth thing propounded) as helps against dejected disquieting and discouragement.

1. Do not immoderately grieve and mourn for the calamities of the church of God, because the church of God grows more numerous by troubles and persecutions. The saints' blood that is shed by persecution is the seed of the church, and many increase and grow from that seed. Cyprian suffered martyrdom, yes, and many were converted by his martyrdom and his sufferings as well as by his preaching. Soul persecutors, by casting one into prison and putting another to death, and banishing another, thereby think they will root out all the rest, both professors and religion too. But God, by an overruling hand, so orders it that it is a means to bring multitudes of the people to God.

If a child comes into a forest and there sees a man cutting off the top of a tree, the child thereby thinks the man is spoiling the tree; but it is otherwise, for by loping and pruning the tree grows more. So wicked men may cut here one tree and there another, and lop off the branches; but God by this means makes the church of God grow more in number and grow better than before. The number of the people of God is more increased, just as it was with the church of the Jews: they went down into Egypt as but a small number, but while in bonds and captivity they grew great in number, and multiplied more in Egypt than ever they did in their own land. For so you read in Exodus 1:7: "And the children of Israel were fruitful, and multiplied, and increased abundantly, and waxed exceeding mighty, and the land was filled with them." If you would find the number who went down to Egypt, you will find that there were seventy souls; but there came out six hundred thousand. Oh, how does the goodness of God in the way of His providence appear for the good and benefit of His own people, that even in the times of persecution He should order it that then it should turn to the good of His own people, to increase and multiply them!

The Jews had the good land of Canaan given to them; and afterward, for their sins and misdoings, they were carried captive into Babylon, as you read in 2 Kings 24:16. There you read of seven thousand who were carried away captive. And in Zedekiah's reign, there were 4,600, making in all not above twelve thousand, and all these were carried away captive into Babylon. One would think that in their captivity they should not increase, but decrease. But it was so ordered by the Lord's overruling power that they exceedingly increased to four times their number, and they returned out of captivity 42,360. Thus they increased in seventy years, and thus the great providence of God caused the persecutions of His people to increase their number. And not only in those former times, but in these latter ages the persecutions of the people of God have been so great and so hot and violent that they thought not to leave the name of a Christian on the earth but he should be persecuted. Yet the more that persecution arose, the more the people of God increased. Therefore, do not be overly cast down, seeing that God makes the sufferings of His people be for

The Calamitous Condition of the Church

their increase and advantage.

2. Even if the number of God's people does not increase, yet consider (and be sure of it) that the graces of God's people shall increase by persecution. The children of Israel were better in the land of Egypt than they were in their own land, and better in a wilderness than in the land of Canaan. It is said of the church of Rome, in the primitive times, that although they had wooden chalices they had golden priests; but now they have golden chalices and wooden priests. So when the church of God is most blessed in outward prosperity, when her people have golden times in the world, yet even then are they most apt to be lowest in their graces and most apt to grow secure and sleepy in the ways of God. Song of Solomon 4:16: "Awake, thou north wind, and come, thou south wind; blow upon my garden, that the spices thereof may flow out." Now you know that the north and the south winds are one against another, and yet these two opposites make the fruit of the garden grow. This north and south wind are compared to, and signify the troubles and the prosperity of, the church. The north wind is affliction, and the south wind is prosperity. But it is the north wind, the cold and sharp persecutions and fiery trials, that make the graces of the church grow most.

The church of God was better, as to the growth of her graces, under the pagan emperors than under Constantine the Christian emperor, because though Constantine was a Christian emperor, and it was much for the comfort of the church and for the good of religion, yet their security made them run into error and heresy. When their bodies prospered, their souls did not prosper, whereas when they were under the pagan emperors, when they were under great and strong persecutions, though their bodies were in trouble yet their graces did exceedingly prosper. So likewise, when popery so prevailed, though the people of God were exposed to great trials, yet their graces thrived and grew green and fresh. As Moulin said, "Men were burned for reading the Bible, but we (speaking of the French Protestants) burn with zeal to be reading." But now Bibles are like old almanacs molding in corners, while play books, the devil's catechisms, are worn out with frequent perusal.

3. Consider that the persecutions and troubles and trials of the church of God at one time and in one place make way for the settlement and establishment of God's church and people in another time and another place. This should comfort you: the destruction of one church is but the building up of many churches. You may read for this purpose in Acts 8:1 of great troubles and persecutions of the church at Jerusalem, so that the believers were all scattered abroad. Now what fruit came by all the troubles and all the persecutions that fell upon the church of Jerusalem? This was the fruit and benefit: it set up a church in Samaria. The persecution caused the gospel to go into those parts of the world and Samaria received the gospel (verses 4–5). Many places which never heard of the gospel came to have it preached in their parts by reason of the hot persecution that was at Jerusalem. So likewise with some kingdoms of the world. The troubles and persecutions of God's people here by the prelates were the great occasion of the transplanting of the gospel into other parts of the world, such as New England and America, which places had never heard of it before. So the seven

Asiatic churches were destroyed by the pagan persecution, but by their destruction it was transplanted into Africa and all Europe, and now since into America. So if God should let the church be persecuted in one place, it still gains by its troubles in going into another place. And though it is persecuted in one kingdom, yet by its transplantation it settles and gains in another. As Christ said in Matthew 21:43, "I will take the gospel from you, and give it to a people and nation that shall bring forth better fruit." That is, Christ would take it from the Jews and give it to the Gentiles. And therefore, said the Apostle, when they would not receive the gospel among them, "Lo, we turn to the Gentiles." This is the great wisdom of God, that the church's troubles and persecutions in one place shall by Him be an occasion to get good in another.

4. Consider that there are such infallible promises made to the church of God for its preservation that it shall never be destroyed by all the rage, fury, and persecution of wicked and ungodly men. They may be persecuted, as the apostle speaks, but they cannot be destroyed; they may be cast down, but not forsaken; they may be perplexed, but not in despair. The church may be in sorrow, but it cannot be annihilated. The church of God shall never be so persecuted as to be cast off, utterly forsaken, and destroyed by wicked men. But the church of God shall continue to the end of the world.

Therefore you read what Christ spoke of Peter in Matthew 16:18: "Thou art Peter, and on this rock will I build my church (that is, on Christ)." And then observe what follows, "The gates of hell shall not prevail against it." The powers of hell, and the policy of all the devils in hell, shall not prevail against the church of

God. Then if hell cannot prevail against the church, the earth and men by persecution shall not prevail to pull it down and destroy it, and to shake it off from the rock on which it is built. It is reported that in the year 1620, when the wars began in Germany, a great brass image of the Apostle Peter stood in St. Peter's church in Rome, having on it, on an embossed roll that hung down, the words of Matthew 16:18–19, on which Rome bases its claim to hold the keys of the church. But then a great stone fell upon it and so shattered it to pieces that not a letter of that sentence, except these five words, "I will build my church," was left intact. God has not made any promises to any kingdom or nation of the world, nor to any commonwealth, that it shall abide and remain forever, but they may be broken and indeed shall be broken. None can stand so sure as to say that this monarchy shall stand forever, and this or that commonwealth shall abide forever. Yet, said God, concerning this kingdom of Jesus Christ, despite the malice of all the devils in hell, and power and policy of all men on earth, it shall stand, and that because it is the Word of God, and the promise of God to preserve His church and people, that "on this rock will I build my church, and the gates of hell shall not prevail against it." Therefore be not overly troubled for the calamities of the church.

5. Consider the end and the results of the church's sufferings. If we would look to the beginning and not to the end of the sufferings of God's people, we might be cast down for it; but do but look to the end of these sufferings and see what the result will be, and then tell me if you have need to be too much cast down. When we see a father and a mother beat their child, the rea-

son is that they would make him better; so when we see God beating His church by a rod of correction, as sweet spices in a mortar, the end of God herein is not to destroy His church, but to make it smell sweeter, and to send forth a more fragrant smell. God is doing a great work in the world, but God's ends are to make His people sweeter, like preserves, and preserve them for a longer time, and make them be more lasting in the world. Therefore be not so overly troubled at the calamities of the church.

We must not judge the works of God before the fifth act, that is, before all the work is done. Had we been alive at the first creation and seen nothing but chaos, we would see no beauty; but what would you have judged of the world, and finally of Adam, when all the world was created in beauty? When all was finished and done, what a glorious fabric was there! So if you look at the beginning of the church's troubles when they fell first into persecutions, you cannot judge them; but if you look at the church in the end of its persecution, when its troubles are done, then you may see it full of glory and full of beauty. Jeremiah 31:16–17: "Thus saith the Lord, 'Refrain thy voice from weeping, and thine eyes from tears; for thy works shall be rewarded,' saith the Lord, 'and they shall come again from the land of the enemy. But there is hope in the end,' saith the Lord." The beginning is bad for the people of God by reason of troubles and persecution, but the end is good. As the martyrs said when they were going to suffer, "Come, we shall have a bad breakfast, but we shall have a good supper; for our end will be good, and our reward great, for we shall go to Jesus Christ." As Joseph said to his brethren, "You intended me hurt, but God intended me good," so I may say concerning wicked and ungodly men who persecute the church of God: you intend evil against the church and people of God, but God intends His people good. You intend to persecute and destroy and root out the church and people of God from under heaven, but God intends to preserve and keep and continue His church on the earth (notwithstanding all persecutors) to the end of the world. Though wicked men may plow upon your backs and make long furrows upon you, yet God's ends are grace, mercy, and peace, to do you good in your latter end.

God's ends and wicked men's ends never fall out alike, for God's ends are one thing and wicked men's are another. A physician lets a man's blood and takes blood from him, and the leech sucks blood from him; but the physician's ends are one thing and the leech's ends are another. The leech draws blood from the man only to satisfy itself, but the physician lets the man bleed to cure his distemper. So it is between God's ends and wicked men's ends in persecuting His own people. God, by suffering His own church and people to be persecuted, purges away their evil distempers of sin and security, or whatever it is that may offend, that thereby God may make His people better by their afflictions. But wicked and ungodly men trouble the church to destroy them and root them out and satisfy their rage and malice upon them their ruin, to accomplish their own wicked designs. But though this is their end, yet God has other ends, namely to do them good in their latter end. And therefore you have no cause to be overly troubled for the calamities of the church.

Sermon 11

Reproof to Three Sorts of Men

"Why art thou cast down, O my soul? and why art thou disquieted within me? Hope thou in God, for I shall yet praise Him, who is the health of my countenance, and my God." Psalm 42:11

If it is so that godly men are disquieted for the calamities of God's church, there are three sorts of men to whom the arrow of my reproof shall be fastened. First, it reproves those who are of a quite contrary temper; who lay nothing of the church's calamities to heart; who let religion sink or swim, the gospel stand or fall, the church of God prosper or not. They care for none of these things. These are the infamy of a church, the brands and blemishes of a church, who enjoy church privileges, and yet cannot be troubled at the church's calamities. It is worth your notice that, when the Holy Ghost reckons up the tribes of Israel for their renown (in the enumeration of the tribes of Israel, Revelation 7:4–9), you read: "And I heard the number of them that were sealed: and there were sealed 144,000 of all the tribes of the children of Israel. Of the tribe of Judah twelve thousand. Of the tribe of Reuben twelve thousand. Of the tribe of Gad twelve thousand. . . . Of the tribe of Asher twelve thousand. . . . Of the tribe of Naphtali twelve thousand," and so on.

Of each tribe there were sealed twelve thousand.

Mark the enumeration and you shall find one tribe left out, the tribe of Dan. Divines make much ado about finding out the reason for the Spirit of God's omission of that tribe. The truest account of the omission is as a sign of disgrace, first because the tribe of Dan defected from the true worship of God and ran to idolatry. Judges 18:30: "The children of Dan set up the graven image."

Another reason is that the tribe of Dan did not lay to heart the calamities of God's church. When the other tribes were hazarding their lives in the high places of the field, the tribe of Dan, it is said, remained in ships. They would let the rest of the tribes shift for themselves; they would follow their trade, their merchandising. Now divines give this reason why God put a brand on that tribe, and the Spirit of God would not reckon that tribe among the other tribes. It is blameworthy, when the calamities of God's church shall be hastening towards it, and you leave that church and are no way available to help, but, like Dan, remain in your ship at your trade. God hates neutral observers.

A second sort who deserve reproof are those who are so far from being excessively troubled and disquieted to see things go ill with the church that they rather rejoice than are grieved and troubled at it. Thus we read of Haman, that monster among men, in Esther 3:15: "Then went up the posts, being hastened by the king's commandment, and the decree was given." There were Esther and Mordecai, her handmaids, and the poor Jews. They were fasting, praying, and mourning for their lives. In this extremity the church of God was then facing, the king and Haman must sit down to drink. They would be merry and jovial when God's church was

Reproof to Three Sorts of Men

in great extremity. Now the Scripture puts this as a brand on Haman and Ahasuerus: "They sat down to eat and drink, but the city of Shushan was perplexed." Thus you read of sensual epicures in Amos 6:7: "Therefore shall they go captive with the first that go captive, and the banquet of them that stretched themselves shall be removed."

A third sort are so far from being disquieted at the church's calamities that they are grieved and disquieted that the church is in no worse a condition; they are troubled that it is no worse with religion and no worse with the church of God. There are many such men nowadays. Psalm 37:12: "The wicked plotteth against the just, and gnasheth upon him with his teeth." Gnashing the teeth is a gesture of revenge. Because they cannot have their will in their plots, they gnash their teeth and fume and fret at good ministers; they are disquieted that it is no worse with good men and no worse with religion. This is vexation of heart to them. A notable text is Nehemiah 2:10: "When Sanballat the Horonite, and Tobiah the servant, the Ammonite, heard of it, it grieved them exceedingly, that there was come a man to seek the welfare of the children of Israel." See what venom and rage are in these men's hearts who were but mongrel Jews. They were exceedingly grieved that a man had come who would seek the welfare of the children of Israel. Many men gnash their teeth, and grieve exceedingly to think that there should be any interest rising up for religion and the church of God. Nothing in the world grieves them more.

I now come to the third thing for which God's people are often greatly disquieted, and that is for outward afflictions. Now when I say afflictions are great causes of disquiet, I shall distinguish the outward sufferings of God's people into two sorts. First, there are private sufferings, that is, some outward good things that the people of God want, and this greatly troubles them. It may be that they are poor and want estates; it may be that they want friends; it may be that they are sick and want help, and are more pinched than other men are. This greatly disquiets them. Or else, second, there are some positive evils of sufferings that they lie under.

I shall speak to the first of these—that God's people should not be disquieted though they lack outward good things—to them not to be disquieted for outward wants. I will leave six considerations with you.

1. Consider that you may be sure you shall want no outward thing the having of which God sees as good for you. If God saw that the thing you want should be good for you to have, you may be sure you should not want it. Are you poor and lack a livelihood? You may be certain God sees the want of wealth to be best for you. Psalm 84:11: "No good thing will He withhold from you." If it is good for you, He will withhold nothing from you; for God, who does not grudge to give you His Son, will not grudge to give you a little piece of the world if He ses it good for you.

2. Consider that God lets His own people want some outward good things that He might give them better things instead of them. I will give you but a few instances. When Job was scraping himself on the dunghill and bemoaning the great loss he had sustained and the wants he was in, you would have thought Job was a very wretched man. Read the catalogue in the

first chapter of Job, how God stripped him naked of all his substance, which was "seven thousand sheep, three thousand camels, five hundred yoke of oxen, and five hundred she-asses, and a very great household," and his sons and his daughters slain, and he himself sorely afflicted and troubled in the want of all outward comforts and accommodations that might make his life comfortable in this world. Now this was an exceedingly great loss to him, and yet all Job wanted and lost was made up double to him. Job lost seven thousand sheep and God gave him fourteen thousand sheep; he lost three thousand camels, and God gave him six thousand camels; he lost five hundred yoke of oxen, and God gave him a thousand yoke of oxen. God gave him double his substance—not double children, but as for outward things God gave him double what he had lost. If God takes away a mercy from a man, or takes away an estate, God may make it double to that man before he dies.

Thus, beloved, does God do us wrong? Surely not. Thus we see it in David when he was likely to lose his son begotten of Bathsheba. He was a sad man for the loss of his son, but God gave him a better mercy in the place of that bastard. God gave him a Solomon; it was a greater mercy to give him Solomon in the place of an illegitimate child. Psalm 71:20: "Thou hast shown me great and sore troubles, but Thou shalt bring me up again." As David tells you here, "Thou wilt increase my greatness." He means the troubles under Saul. David, who was to be king on a throne, was to lie like a hermit in a cave; but though "Thou hast brought me to great and sore troubles, it is but to increase my greatness in a way of mercy."

Oh, then, if God lets you come to great wants of any outward mercies you stand in need of, think that God lets it be thus so that you might have greater mercies in place of them. This consideration greatly quieted the heart of Isaac after the death of Sarah, who was his mother. You read that God gave him his wife Rebecca, and he loved Rebecca and was comforted after his mother's death. Isaac had his mother taken from him, but he had a wife given by God's to him in place of his mother. If God lets you want a mother, want children, or want estates, God will bring in some other mercy to comfort you in the want and absence of them. Let this allay all disquiet and discontent of heart in you.

3. Consider that, though you want outward mercies that are desirable, yet you do not want better mercies, to wit, spiritual mercies. You want crumbs, yet you do not want Christ. You want food, it may be, for your belly; you do not feed on such dainties and delicacies as many epicures of the world do, yet you may feed by faith on Jesus Christ the bread of life. It may be that you do not have such sumptuous apparel as some men have, yet you do not lack the long robe of Christ's righteousness. You lack an inheritance in this world, but you do not lack an inheritance among those who are sanctified in the world to come. It may be you lack health, but you have a healthy soul. Your soul prospers, as John said to Gaius in 3 John 2. You read in Proverbs 14:14: "The backsliders in heart shall be filled with their own ways, and a good man shall be satisfied from himself." It may be that, in outward things, nothing can content you; you take pains in the world; you rise early and eat the bread of carefulness, yet you cannot get enough to feed your belly and clothe your back. Yet if you are a gra-

cious man, reflect thus on yourself: "Though I want these outward things, yet, blessed be God, He is my portion. Though I have no portion in this life, I am heir to the kingdom of heaven even if I am not heir to one foot of land." This should allay these disquietings that might arise in your minds.

4. Consider that if God should give you these outward good things you want, the giving of them would be a greater snare and a curse to you than the want of them would be. It may be that you want wealth; it may be that you have a barren womb and want children. If God should give you the mercy you want, giving it would be a greater snare to you than the want of it.

Let me give you two or three plain instances. One is of Rachel in Genesis 30:1, who was exceedingly impatient for the want of children: "Give me children, or else I die." This passionate desire of hers God gratified, but mark how God punished her for it: she must die in childbirth. Her soul departed from her when she was in labor. Genesis 35:18: "And it came to pass, as her soul was departing, that she called his name Benoni; but his father called him Benjamin." Her children were the instruments of death to kill her. Her child was Benoni, the son of her sorrows. Beloved, this should teach you to take heed of being passionately discontented and disquieted when you want a mercy.

Another instance you read in David. He was passionately eager for the life of a child begotten by Bathsheba, and he wept, mourned, and fasted that it might not die. Now if the child had lived, the life of that child would have been a greater snare to David than the death of it could ever have been; for it would have been a lasting monument of David's shame. Everyone could have pointed and said, "Yonder goes David's bastard." We see even harlots account uncleanness a reproach, and commit a greater wickedness by murdering their children because they would not have their wickedness known. Later, Absalom rose in rebellion against his father and drew the people away by his courteous carriage and by offering the people liberty. By this means he almost took the kingdom from his father. They rose in arms one against another, but, said David, "Deal gently with my son Absalom." But if David had had his request that Absalom should not have been killed, why, Absalom would have been a continual enemy to his father, for he had almost thrown him off his throne. It was a greater mercy to David that Absalom was killed than if he had lived. Herein see the wisdom of God in that, if receiving a mercy might become a snare to us, God will deny it to us.

The children of Israel could not be content with manna that was called angels' food for commendation. They loathed the manna and had to have quails from heaven; but it would have been a thousand times better for them to go without it for while the meat was in their mouths, the wrath of God went down with it. That which they thought the *want* of to be their misery, God made *having* it to be their misery.

5. Lay on the scales your mercies, afflictions, and wants, and see whether what you have received is not more than your wants. Suppose you want a thousand things, yet you have one thing that is of more worth than all the things you want, and that is your life. If you should want your skin and be flayed, and still have your life, it is a greater mercy to you though God should strip you of your skin. You have possessed more mercies

than you have afflictions in that you are on this side of hell and the grave. O beloved, do you want any mercy? Why, think that your blessings are more than your wants, and that will in some measure quiet your discontent.

6. If you would allay disquiet of mind for your wants, then labor to make up all your wants and losses in God. Consider that knowing God is enough to make up for all the wants you have in the world. Thus the church of God did in Psalm 73:26: "My flesh and my heart faileth; but God is the strength of my heart." He was likely to want a kingdom, but he did not want God. God was his portion, and that comforted him.

Oh, look on this: our interest in God makes compensation for a hundred wants. You have a notable passage in Psalm 142:6–7: "Attend unto my cry, for I am brought very low; deliver me from my persecutors, for they are stronger than I. Bring my soul out of trouble, that I may praise Thy name; the righteous shall compass me about, for Thou shalt deal bountifully with me." It is as if he should have said, "I have no friends. I have no strength, but am full of troubles. I cried unto God and said, 'Thou art my portion.' " It should allay a thousand discontents in you if your soul can plead an interest in God, though you want all. It was no wonder that Esau said, when Jacob would have given him an offering, "I have enough." But Jacob could say, "I have all," for he made all things up in his God. He has all things who has the God who has all things. Do you lack health? There is health in God. Do you lack wealth? There is riches in God. Do you lack satisfaction? There is an abundance of contentment in God. There is everything in God.

And thus I am done with the first part, to allay disquietings of soul for all privative afflictions, that is, for the want of outward good things in the world.

I now come to give you some considerations to allay all positive discontent and disquiet.

First, to allay disquiet for worldly crosses in the world, consider that there is nothing that befalls you, no cross nor disaster in all your lifetime, but it is the will of a good, wise, and gracious God that this cross should befall you. If this were thought on and laid to heart, it would allay all bubblings of discontent. Psalm 39:9: "I was dumb, and opened not my mouth, because Thou didst it." 1 Samuel 3:18: "And Samuel told him every whit and hid nothing. And he said, 'It is the Lord, let Him do what seemeth good unto Him.'" Instead of all reasons it is the Lord.

Beloved, it will exasperate and provoke you to passion to look only on instruments, but if you see it is the will of God it will allay discontents. Observe the different responses and behaviors in David. One time you find him a quiet-spirited man—he could bear any injury without any disquiet at all. Another time you see him in a marvelous fury that could not bear a small injury. What was the reason why David was so passionate over Nabal's injury and so patient with Shimei's cursing? When Shimei cursed he called to mind God's hand in it. Therefore that allayed and quieted him.

This allayed discontent in Job: "The Lord gave, and the Lord hath taken away; blessed be the name of the Lord" (Job 1:21). In all this Job sinned not. The messenger told Job that the Sabeans had stolen his oxen, the Chaldeans had taken his camels, and the devil had consumed his children; but Job said, "The Lord hath taken them away; the Lord gave me them, and the Lord took them away; therefore blessed be the name of the Lord."

Genesis 45:5: "Now therefore be not grieved, nor angry with yourselves, that you sold me hither; for God did send me before you to preserve life." When Joseph revealed himself to his brethren who had done him wrong, he said, "I am Joseph that you sold to the Ishmaelites; I am he." And when his brethren heard this, they were all troubled and amazed; but, said Joseph, "Be not troubled, for it was not you, but it was God who brought me here." He saw God's hand in it, and therefore was not angry with them. O beloved, if you saw all afflictions as stones in God's hand, you would never snarl, nor never be disquieted, nor never be troubled; but you see the stone in a man's hand, and therefore you are troubled.

Second, to allay disquietings in you, consider that through the course of your life you have had as many, if not more, mercies from God than you have had afflictions from God. Let that quiet you. This quieted Job, Job 2:10: "But he said unto her, 'Thou speakest as one of the foolish women. Shall we receive good at the hand of God, and shall we not receive evil?' " Ecclesiastes 7:14: "In the day of prosperity be joyful, but in the day of adversity consider; God hath set one against the other." Suppose you are in adversity; has not God set prosperity over against it? Can you not call to mind mercies as well as afflictions? It may be that you have many crosses in the world; you have many mercies in the world too. This would allay disquiet, but here is the misery of it: we look upon our afflictions, but never on our mercies; we remember the wormwood and the gall, but never remember the milk and the honey. Consider your mercies; they will overbalance and weigh down your afflictions.

Third, consider that afflictions which befall you in this world are never without cause and never above cause. God might afflict any of us as an act of His sovereignty. But, beloved, God does not afflict any man in the world but there is a provocation, a cause in man why He afflicts him. Lamentations 3:39: "Wherefore doth a living man complain, a man for the punishment of his sins?" Beloved, if you could stand before God and say, "I am just before Thee. I have not sinned against Thee," it would be something; but you are a sinner before God, and He never afflicts you but there is cause for it. This should stop all complaints and repinings against God.

Again, it is never above cause either; that is, it is not so much as what your sins have deserved here. We may justify God as Ezra does in Ezra 9:13: "And after all that is come upon us for our evil deeds, and for our great trespasses, seeing that Thou art our God, Thou hast punished us less than our sins deserve." And Psalm 103:10: "He has not dealt with us after our sins, nor rewarded us according to our iniquities."

Fourth, consider that impatience and disquiet of soul under sufferings and afflictions provoke God to afflict us more. When a child is corrected by the father, if the child kisses the rod, accepts the punishment, and acknowledges the fault, he has the fewer blows because the father sees the end of his correction. But it is the stout and stubborn-hearted child who has the most blows from the father's hands. But if God sees you fretting and fuming under a cross, this does not lighten your burdens, but rather makes them heavier, lengthens them out longer in time, and makes them heavier in weight and our bands stronger.

Fifth, consider that discontent and disquiet of soul under outward crosses and afflictions embitter to you the enjoyment of your present mercies. A man who is apt to be impatient for one cross loses the enjoyment of a hundred comforts. An impatient man may have a good wife, amiable children, and a rich estate, but if this man is apt to be impatient under one cross, it makes him so that he can take no comfort in anything he has in the world. What a mischievous temper is this! The impatience of one cross eats out the comforts of a hundred mercies.

An impatient and disquieted man may be fitly compared to a hedgehog, and, in fact, some writers make the hedgehog an emblem of an impatient man. They say that the way in which the hedgehod brings provision into its hole is to go after a windy day into an orchard when the fruit is fallen; it turns itself around like a ball, and on its bristles and prickles fills itself full of apples and carries them to its hole. But if, in carrying them to the hole, one falls off it throws all the rest down. So it is with an impatient man. God may load him with many mercies, yet if God takes away one blessing from him, he throws down the comfort of all the rest of the mercies the Lord bestows on him. This is the mischievous effect of those disquietings of soul under outward crosses.

Sermon 12

Uses of Instruction and Trial

"Why art thou cast down, O my soul? and why art thou disquieted within me? Hope thou in God, for I shall yet praise Him, who is the health of my countenance, and my God." Psalm 42:11

I will now finish this third cause of disquiet. There are two uses: the first use of instruction, the second of trial.

By way of instruction, I shall instruct you in ten theological rules that may be laid down to allay all excessive disquiet and discontent of soul under outward afflictions, of whatever kind they be, privative or positive.

RULE 1. Live in continual meditation on the joys and glories of heaven. It is observable of Paul that, though his life was a whole course of affliction, yet when he was taken up into the third heaven, "whether I was in the body I cannot tell." Paul tells you he had many infirmities in his body, in hunger and nakedness, in perils by sea and land, and great troubles in the body; yet when he was taken up in a vision he forgot all the infirmities, sufferings, and sorrows that he met with in the body (2 Corinthians 12:1). So likewise, when Peter saw the transfiguration of Christ in Matthew 17:4, "Then answered Peter, 'Lord, it is good to be here, and let us build three tabernacles.' " A divine observes that Peter begged no tabernacle for himself, but said it was

Uses of Instruction and Trial

good to be there. And yet they were only upon a barren mountain where there was no meat to eat nor house to lodge in. Why, he forgot that there was no house here, nor no food here. Having a view of heaven, he said it was good to be there on a barren mountain.

It is observed by one that those birds of the lowest flight are the most mournful; but those birds of the highest flight are the most noble birds. The dove mourns, the crane chatters, the raven croaks, but the eagle, who is a bird of the highest flight, never makes a lamentable noise. Divines make this use of it, that those who are low-spirited men will croak like ravens and mourn like doves when they are afflicted; but to be as the eagle flying aloft in the joys of heaven in your meditations will keep you from that despondency and mournfulness of spirit. If things go ill with you in the world, there is no better way under heaven to allay disquiet of soul under bodily afflictions than to have your soul transported with the joys of heaven. Jerome gave this counsel to a hermit: "Take but a walk or two in heaven, and then you will not think you are in a wilderness." Could you but take a turn or two in heaven, then you would not be troubled for the afflictions here upon earth.

The apostle has an expression in 2 Corinthians 4:17: "For our light affliction, which is but for a moment, worketh for us a far more exceeding and eternal weight of glory." The weight of glory made the apostle look on heavy afflictions as but light; therefore he called them light afflictions. An eternal glory made the apostle look on long afflictions as but short afflictions. If you would not then account afflictions as burdensome, think what a weight there is in glory. And if you would not think afflictions to be long, why, think what eternity there is in glory.

RULE 2. If you would not be inordinately disquieted for afflictions in this world, labor to get your hearts more troubled and disquieted for sin. When a man bleeds too much in his nose or any one part of the body, physicians open a vein in another part to make a diversion of the blood. Beloved, when you grieve too much for worldly crosses, do as physicians do with the blood, make a diversion. Make a diversion of your sorrows; open the sluices of your tears for sin; pour them out for sin, and then you will grieve less for the world. The reason why men are so troubled for afflictions is that they are troubled too little for sin and corruption. It is a true rule that religious fear banishes a slavish fear and yields spiritual joy, eternal joy. So spiritual trouble expels worldly trouble. Those who are much troubled for sin are not much troubled for anything in the world besides sin.

RULE 3. Be sure you do not place an excessive love on any worldly comforts you enjoy. if you would keep your trouble within bounds, keep your love ordinate. It is observable of Jacob, Genesis 37:34–35: "And Jacob rent his clothes, and put sackcloth on his loins, and mourned for his son many days. And all his sons and all his daughters rose up to comfort him, but he refused to be comforted, and he said, 'I will go down into the grave unto my son, mourning.' " What was the reason why the good old man was so excessively grieved for his son? Genesis 37:3: "Israel loved Joseph more than all his brethren, because he was the son of his old age." Now Jacob's loving Joseph more than all his children made him grieve more for Joseph than all his children;

if he had not loved Joseph so much when he had him, he would not have grieved too much for him when he thought he had lost him. Oh, labor to keep an ordinate love for worldly comforts. A man who can part with his fingernail cannot part with his finger. Why? Because he looks on the nail as superfluous. Look on the world as but a fingernail: it is but a superfluity. You can go to heaven without the abundant comforts of it; you would not grieve so much if God takes some comforts away from you. Men use the world as the skin of their hands, and not as gloves that they can easily pull off. Therefore, when God tears it from them, it is irksome and tedious to them. If a picture is in a frame you may hang it on a wall and take it down again and not hurt the picture, but if it is pasted to the wall you cannot take it down without tearing the picture. If your hearts are in frame, God may take you from the world and not disquiet you; but if you are glued and pasted to the world, it will cause an inordinate disquiet in you when the world is taken from you.

RULE 4. Look on the comforts of the world as unnecessary and, at best, as uncertain. Luke 10:42: "One thing is needful." Christ tells you that one thing, grace, is the only thing necessary. Grace is necessary for a Christian; other things are but inconveniences. If God takes away inconveniences from you and does not take away necessary things from you, if He leaves you grace, if He leaves you Christ and leaves you heaven—why, you should not be disquieted. You must look on the comforts of this world as mutable, not as the anchor at the bottom of the sea, but as the vane on the top of the mast of a ship which turns with every blast of wind. Socrates did not mourn when his child was dead: "I know he was mortal." That is the reason why men are troubled by worldly crosses and losses: they do not look on the world as mutable.

RULE 5. Consider that disquiet under afflictions can do you no good, but it may do you much hurt. It can do you no good, as Christ tells you that you cannot add one cubit to your stature. By all your thoughts, you add no comfort to your life; all your troubles do not ease you, but rather make your affliction more heavy. You may get much hurt by disquiet, and, beloved, the hurt of disquiet under afflictions is twofold. First, it makes afflictions heavier; second, it makes them longer than they would otherwise be.

First, it makes them heavier in weight, and more in number, than else they would be. A child who is patient under his father's correction has the fewest and gentlest strokes, but the stubborn child has most. When God sees men fume and fret and be disquieted under afflictions, they bring more blows upon themselves. Proverbs 27:3: "A stone is heavy, and the sand weighty; but a fool's wrath is heavier than them both." It is not meant only for another man, as if others should fear my anger and wrath when I am passionate, but the meaning is that it is heavy to himself. Afflictions shall be laid more heavily on him than a heap of stones or sand. A bundle of folly causes a bundle of rods. A man under a burden, if he goes gently, may carry his burden with some ease; but the more the man stirs and struggles under his burden the more he tires himself. When God lays burdens on us, we strive, fume, fret, and are impatient; this makes the burden heavier.

Second, we make our afflictions longer by being disquieted under them. The father gives longer whip-

Uses of Instruction and Trial

pings to the child whom he cannot make to kiss the rod and confess the fault than another child. Beloved, we lengthen the day of our calamity by impatience and disquiet under the afflicting hand of God.

RULE 6. Compare the present mercies you enjoy with the present sufferings you endure. Ecclesiastes 7:14: "In the day of prosperity be joyful; but in the day of adversity consider." When you are prosperous, think thus: "God has set adversity over against prosperity that I might not be sensual." Then, in adversity, be not discouraged because God has set prosperity over against adversity. It may be that you have lost one child; have you not another? It may be that you have lost your estate; have you not health in body, comfort in your relations? Thus, when facing any cross in the world that befalls you, presently reflect upon your mercies.

RULE 7. See God's hand in all the afflictions that befall you in this world. Psalm 39:9: "I was dumb, I opened not my mouth, because Thou didst it." Remember that God's ear hears all the murmurings of your tongue, and you will not complain in your disquiet against God. This is an effectual remedy. See God's hand in all that befalls you here in the world.

RULE 8. If you would not be disquieted because of afflictions, do nothing that may renew your grief or call to remembrance your afflictions. There are many people who aggravate their own sorrow and cause their wounds to bleed afresh, putting themselves in mind of their own crosses and losses. It is said of Rachel in Genesis 35:17–18: "When she was in hard labor, the midwife said unto her, 'Fear not, thou shalt have this son also.' And it came to pass, as her soul was in departing, that she called his name Benoni, 'the son of my sorrow.' " But observe that Jacob would not have the child called Benoni, but he would have his name be Benjamin, "the son of my right-hand, and of my joy, and of my strength." Why would not Jacob have it be Benoni? If he had, the child's name would have put him in remembrance that his wife died in childbirth; therefore despite the mother's naming him Benoni, "the son of my sorrow," Jacob called him Benjamin, "the son of my right hand." Therefore it is a painful fondness in those who look at the pictures and clothes of dead friends. All these are but provocations to more sorrows and more griefs.

RULE 9. Consider the end that God aims at in your affliction as well as the measure and the degree of how much you are afflicted. This is the great ground of impatience, that people consider the measure and the time they are afflicted, but they do not call to mind *why* they are afflicted. I may exemplify this rule by this: A physician and an enemy may do the same act to a man, yet you know a man will bear with a physician to let him bleed, but he will not endure an enemy to let him bleed. The reason is that he knows the physician's end is to cure him, but the enemy does it to kill him—yet both let bleed. Why, beloved, do you consider that God's end for your soul in sending afflictions upon you is to cure you, to purge you of sinful maladies in your soul? Why, let the end countervail the measure (how much) and the time (how long) you are afflicted, and this will allay all unquietness and inordinate trouble in thy mind.

RULE 10. Last, consider that God in His wisdom will proportion all afflictions that befall you in this world according to the strength that you have to bear them. 1 Corinthians 10:13: "There hath no temptation taken you but such as is common to man. But God is faithful, who will not suffer you to be tempted above what you are able." If the Lord lays heavy burdens on you, He will give you strong shoulders. Seneca said, "If afflictions are heavy they shall be short, but if afflictions are long they shall be light." Heavy afflictions shall be short afflictions, and long afflictions shall be light afflictions. God will proportion them. Job 14:1: "Man that is born of a woman is but of few days, and full of trouble." Troublesome days are made short days. Why, now, if they are full of trouble they are but few; how sad would it be if perpetuity and misery, a multitude of troubles and a multitude of days, met? God will proportion your afflictions according to your strength. Isaiah 28:27: "For the fitches are not threshed with a threshing instrument, neither is a cart wheel turned about upon the cummin, but the fitches are beaten with a staff and the cummin with a rod." The meaning is that God will not exercise weak people with great afflictions. There shall be afflictions proportional to their strength; this God has promised in Isaiah 27:8: "In measure, when it shooteth forth, thou wilt debate with it; He stayeth His rough winds in the day of His east wind." If men are not able to bear a boisterous storm, He will stay His rough wind. He will abate the measure of His afflictions. Let this quiet your soul, that God proportions all His dealings with you according to your strength. Thus I have laid down ten rules how to bear afflictions without inordinate disquiet of soul.

QUESTION. But since we must not be stoics, insensible of God's afflicting hand, and seeing that some kind of trouble and sorrow for afflictions is allowed by

God, how shall we know whether we are inordinately disquieted over outward afflictions?

ANSWER. When outward afflictions swallow up the comforts and enjoyments of present mercies, then you are excessive. This we see in Ahab: he had a flourishing kingdom and stately palaces, yet could take no comfort in them because he could not get poor Naboth's vineyard from him. That argued too much disquiet in him. We read of Rebekah in Genesis 27:46: "And Rebekah said to Isaac, 'I am weary of my life, because of the daughters of Heth.' " This was a very impatient speech, as when a present affliction shall make you say, "I have no joy in my life." Many people, when they are crossed in their wills, will say, "I have no joy in my life," though they have many mercies. Such speeches as these are but the issues of disquiet. Let not one cross make you fly off from all your comforts in the world. Thus we read of Jacob: he was too much disquieted in that one loss, which made him so that he could not take joy in all his comfort, in all his mercies. Read the story in Genesis 37:35: "And all his sons and his daughters rose up to comfort him; but he would not be comforted." Jacob had eleven sons living whom he knew, and many daughters, and all came about him to comfort him, but he refused to be comforted. Why, beloved, men are so overborne and overwhelmed with troubles upon a cross that if they lose one child, all the other children shall not affect them. Certainly this kind of sorrow is an excessive sorrow.

Second, disquiet of soul for worldly afflictions is inordinate when afflictions in the world so disquiet a man's mind that it makes a man weary of life and makes him wish for death merely because of afflictions.

This was the failing of Jonah in Jonah 4:8: "It is better for me to die than to live," because God took away the gourd. The same you read of in Job 7:15: "So my soul chooseth strangling, and death rather than life."

Job was in a distemper and wished death rather than life. This was a sin in him, for affliction so to disquiet his mind that he wished, "Would to God I were out of the world." All these are but the flowings and impatience of a disturbed heart. And so again in Job 10:1: "My soul is weary of my life. I will leave my complaint upon myself." This was his trouble. You who have drunk deeply of a bitter cup, either by trouble with children, or in estates, or reproach in your names, and all this has made you inordinately upset and cry out, "I am weary of my life," you are sinfully disquieted. You have a passage in Isaiah 32:2: "And a man shall be as a hiding place from the wind; as rivers of water in a dry place; as the shadow of a great rock in a weary land." As it speaks of Christ, the land cannot be weary; but it also refers to the inhabitants of the land. Here is a rock in a weary land; the inhabitants of the land were weary in the land because they were so scorched with the heat of afflictions. When afflictions press so hard upon you that they shall make you unwilling to live, this argues that the disquiet of soul is very inordinate.

When a man is disquieted for afflictions that lie upon him, yet he is not at all troubled for all the afflictions that befall the church of God, and never lays them near his heart; when disquiet for personal sufferings jostles out all compassion for the sufferings of God's church—this argues that your trouble is excessive.

When a man is so disquieted for outward afflictions

that it indisposes him for duty, then a man is too disquieted. Thus in Exodus 6:9. The poor Israelites were in so much anguish and trouble because they were held as vassals in Egypt that it is said they could not hearken to God's Word because of the grief and anguish of their spirits. When afflictions make you unfit to hear sermons, and make you unfit to pray, as in Psalm 77:3 ("I remembered God, and I was troubled; I complained, and my spirit was overwhelmed"), this is a sinful disquiet.

Disquiet under afflictions is inordinate when a man dares to venture on any sinful shifts or means to get rid of his afflictions. Suppose you are poor, and dare to venture on deceitfulness to get an estate; suppose you are in a low place, and you dare to sin against conscience to get a place of preferment here in this world—this is a sinful disquiet. Thus we read of Saul. An evil spirit from the Lord troubled him; the Philistines were upon him, and he was in distress in his spirit. 1 Samuel 28:7–8: "And Saul said unto his servants, 'Seek me a woman that hath a familiar spirit, that I may inquire of her.' And his servants said unto him, 'Behold, there is a woman that hath a familiar spirit at Endor.' " What does he do in his afflictions? Why, he goes to a witch and uses sinful means, and all to see what he might do to prevent the prevailing of the Philistines over him. Oh, you who dare to venture on any sinful shift to avoid any affliction, this is an argument that you are inordinately disquieted under afflictions.

A man is excessively disquieted under afflictions when he is so troubled for bodily afflictions that he distempers his own body. You read this of Job, who was so troubled that his spirits were dried up, his bones were consumed, and his strength was wasted. Psalm 38:2–3: "Thine arrows stick fast in me, and Thine hand presseth me sore." What follows? "There is no soundness in my flesh." Here the psalmist so grieved for God's hand upon him as to weaken his own body and consume his strength. This, then, is an argument that sorrow is too inordinate, when disquiet and trouble of mind for afflictions dismember the body.

Thus I am done with the third cause of soul disquieting, that is, for outward afflictions.

Sermon 13

Differences Between a Natural Conscience in a Wicked Man and the Conscience of a Godly Man Who Is Troubled for Sin

"Why art thou cast down, O my soul? and why art thou disquieted within me? Hope thou in God, for I shall yet praise Him, who is the health of my countenance, and my God." Psalm 42:11

I am on the second part of David's trouble. I have shown you three causes for which the souls of God's people are troubled and disquieted:
1. For the prosperity of the wicked.
2. For the calamities of the church.
3. For the personal afflictions of the body.

I now come to the fourth: Godly men are disquieted in their souls because of guilt of sin on the conscience. The guilt and the power of sin on the conscience of all things in the world troubles the soul of a godly man. To handle this point, there are several particulars to be considered.

First, I shall show you how it appears that God's people are disquieted in conscience for sin.

Second, I shall show in what seasons and cases the people of God may be most troubled and cast down for sin.

Third, I shall show the difference between sorrow

Differences Between the Consciences

and disquiet of soul in those who are godly, and disquiet of soul in those who are ungodly and reprobate men.

Fourth, I shall show how it comes to pass that they are so much disquieted for sins.

Fifth, I shall show when God's people are said to be too much disquieted for sin.

Sixth, if the godly are disquieted so much, what is the reason why the wicked are not disquieted at all?

First, as for how it appears that the souls of God's people are apt for to be disquieted in their souls under the guilt of sin, I shall begin with David in Psalm 38:3: "There is no peace in my bones by reason of my sins," that is, "I am exceedingly troubled." Psalm 6:2: "Have mercy on me, for my bones are vexed." Now the Scripture, by a trouble in his bones, means an exceedingly great measure of trouble, that is, "I am in such great and sore troubles that it even vexes my soul and trouble my body."

So likewise again in Lamentations 1:13: "From above He hath sent fire into my bones." Now when a man is in so great trouble of spirit and so afflicted in body by reason of sin that there is no quietness in his bones, when he is in so great affliction for sin as to disturb soul and body, this is immoderate sorrow and too much disquiet. So the psalmist cries out in Psalm 51:8: "Make me hear the voice of joy and gladness, that the bones which Thou hast broken may rejoice." That is as if he had said, "I have lost, by reason of my sin, the light of Thy face, and I have broken my peace. Now let the light of Thy countenance come into my soul, and let the peace of conscience come to my soul which I have lost; let this come to me again."

So again the psalmist said, "I go mourning all the day, by reason of my sin; and I am sorely troubled, and I roar, because of the troubles of my heart" (Psalm 38:6–8). So again in Psalm 77:3–4: "When I remembered God, I was troubled. I complained, and my spirit was overwhelmed. Thou holdest mine eyes waking; I am so troubled that I cannot speak." So in Psalm 88:3, Heman says, "My soul is full of troubles, and my life draweth nigh to the grave." And in verse 7: "Thy wrath lieth hard upon me. Thou hast afflicted me with all Thy waves." And so in verse 16: "Thy fierce wrath goeth over me; Thy terrors have cut me off." See how this man multiplies his complaints by reason of his sore troubles, and the great afflictions that lay upon his body and spirit.

So likewise you read of Job's troubles, how he was sorely disquieted by reason of his personal troubles. In Job 23, Job was troubled and afraid of God. His presence was terrible to him, and he complained that the Almighty troubled him (verse 16). All this makes it appear that the people of God are apt to be disquieted for their troubles and sins.

Second, in what seasons are the people of God most apt to be troubled and disquieted for sin? A man is not always disquieted and troubled for the guilt of sin, but there are some special seasons wherein God lets men's consciences be more troubled and disquieted for sin than ordinarily.

Now there are seven special seasons wherein the conscience is most troubled and disquieted for sin.

1. The first case is upon the consideration of the

threat and pronouncement of some great judgment. The apprehension of some great judgment brings the guilt of sin to remembrance, and then conscience is sorely troubled. And thus we read that wicked men are troubled in conscience in 1 Kings 21:27. When Ahab was told that he would be destroyed, then guilt of sin came to mind, and conscience was troubled, and his mind perplexed; and then he went and humbled himself: "And it came to pass, when Ahab heard those words, that he rent his clothes, and put sackcloth upon his flesh, and lay in sackcloth, and went softly." When he heard the warning of judgment threatened by the prophet, then he went and humbled himself before the Lord. So likewise Jehoshaphat and Hezekiah's hearts and consciences were troubled at such a time as this was.

2. A second case is when the Lord lays them under some great affliction—when it is not just nigh them, but when it is already upon them. An example is Manasseh in 2 Chronicles 33:10–12: "And the Lord spoke to Manasseh, and to his people, but they would not answer nor hearken. Wherefore the Lord brought upon them the captains of the host of the kings of Assyria, and took Manasseh among the thorns, and bound him with chains, and carried him to Babylon. And when he was in affliction, then he besought the Lord his God, and humbled himself greatly before the Lord God of his fathers." When Manasseh was in his prosperity, then God called to him and he hearkened not; but when the Lord brought him into the thorns, into troubles and afflictions, when he was in captivity, then he thought to himself and sought God.

So likewise you read of Joseph's brethren. They

endeavored to destroy their brother, and, during all the time of their prosperity their consciences never troubled and checked them for this sin; but when they went down into Egypt for corn and were put in prison, then they remembered their sin concerning their brother, and then they began to say (their consciences being in perplexity), "Verily we are guilty of our brother's blood" (Genesis 42:21). So likewise it may be that some men may live seven, ten, or twenty years under the guilt of sin and not repent of it; but when they come to lie under some great affliction, and under some sore trouble, then conscience is awakened and they are exceedingly troubled for sin. And now this is the season that God takes to trouble the soul and conscience for sin. So you read in Judges 1:7 of Adonibezek, what cruelty he used to threescore and ten kings in cutting off their thumbs. Now this did not trouble his conscience in his prosperity, but when he was in trouble and taken captive, then he remembered his sin and could say, "As I have done, so God hath requited me."

3. The third season is in that time when a man is under a reproving and sin-searching ministry, and has his particular sins reproved in the ministry of the Word. That is a time when God troubles the conscience for sin against God. When a man comes to a sermon, and there lets the Word take hold of him, and meets with his beloved sin, this is a time when God stirs up conscience to trouble the soul. Thus you read of the unconverted Gentiles in 1 Corinthians 14:25, and of one who may come into the church, and after he comes in he falls down on his face, will worship God, and the secrets of his heart shall be made known. That is, he shall confess his faults and acknowledge his guilt. So

likewise you read in the Acts of the Apostles about Paul. When he was "preaching of temperance, righteousness, and judgment to come, Felix trembled" (Acts 24:25). It seems that Felix's sin was intemperance, drunkenness, and unrighteousness. Now by the ministry of the Word Paul touched his sin, that sin he met with of which he was most guilty, and that made his heart to tremble.

So likewise Peter preached the gospel to the Jews, and told them that they were the men who crucified the Lord of life. You read what follows in Acts 2:37: "And when they heard this, they were pricked in their hearts (or cut to their hearts)." This was a fit season for conscience to work and tell them that they were guilty of such a sin.

4. A fourth season is when God awakens conscience to rebuke and check them for some greatly indulged and bosom sin, which may have been indulged and let lie in their hearts for many years, unrepented of. Now whenever God comes to awaken this man's conscience, this is the nick of time when he will be most apt to be disquieted for sin. You read in Judges 16:20 that Delilah told Samson that the Philistines were upon him, but he had lost his strength and God had departed from him. So when you are lulled asleep, and enticed to yield to a sin and allow yourself in some known lust; when you are secure and asleep in this pleasant sin—time will come, as Delilah told Samson, "the Philistines are upon thee." So conscience will tell thee, "Arise, O man, for the devil is upon you, and hell is near you, and destruction approaches you.' And thus conscience will terrify and disquiet you for the sin you have committed. As Eliphaz said to Job in Job 22:9–10: "Thou hast sent widows away empty. Therefore snares are round about thee,

and sudden fear troubleth thee." It was true in the doctrine, though false in the application to Job.

5. A fifth season is when a man, for fear of loss and in hopes of any gain, shall be drawn to do anything against the dictates of his own conscience. Now if men belong to God, He will disquiet them for this great evil. We have many instances of this. It is observable of Bilney in King Henry VIII's days, as being condemned to die, to save his life he subscribed to popish articles; but the story is that for that sin he was troubled in conscience two years together, and never enjoyed one comfortable merry day in peace and quietness until he renounced his subscription, preached the truth, and was burned. So likewise Dr. Cranmer, through fear to save his life, subscribed to a recantation; but he soon broke his promise and recanted of what he had formerly done, and could never be quiet in his conscience until he had made a recantation for his recantation. And when he came to suffer, he first burned the hand which for fear subscribed to save his life against his conscience. So Baynham, a lawyer, subscribed to popish articles, but had no peace in his conscience till he owned the truth. O beloved, take heed that you do not do anything or subscribe in any case against your conscience to save your life or estate.

6. A sixth season is when a man falls from the true principles of religion to apostatize to any evil way, and conscience troubles and rebukes him for his backsliding. Proverbs 14:14: "The backslider in heart shall be filled with his own ways, but a good man shall be satisfied from himself." As a good man shall be satisfied within with peace of conscience and quietness of mind by his upright walking, so, on the contrary, the back-

slider shall be filled with trouble of conscience and disquiet of soul for the evil of his ways. Likewise in Jeremiah 2:19: "Thine own wickedness shall correct thee, and thy backslidings shall reprove thee; know therefore and consider, that it is an evil thing and bitter, that thou hast departed from the Lord thy God, and that My fear is not in thee, saith the Lord of hosts."

The sin of backsliding, of all sins, shall most rebuke the sinner, trouble his conscience, break his peace, and disquiet his soul. And if God ever brings you back, He will make conscience be like a mastiff dog flying in your face for your backsliding from God. Conscience will tell you what you have done in your wicked departure from God; and then your own conscience will be worse than the snarling of a dog to you. Then shall conscience use this season to tell you of your sins against God.

7. A seventh season is when a man comes to lie on a sickbed or on his deathbed; that is the last season that God takes to rouse the sleepy sinner and lets conscience awake, and disquiets him for the sin he has done. Perhaps you can be living drunkards and living adulterers, and not be troubled; but when you lie upon a sickbed or deathbed, when conscience shall be awakened, can you then be a dying drunkard and a dying adulterer and not be troubled? Take heed of these sins.

There is a caution in Proverbs 5:8: "Remove thy way far from her, and come not nigh the door of her house." Here is a caution for young men laid down by Solomon, to take heed of a whorish woman lest you become mourners at last. This is the season for conscience to disquiet you for sin, and if you belong to God He will make you mourn at last for the evils you have done. Job 21:25: "Another dieth in the bitterness of his soul, and never eateth with pleasure." Oh, the bitter pangs that are in many a man's soul when he dies, and another may think he goes away in peace. And thus we have answered the second question: What are those seasons that God takes to trouble men's consciences and disquiet them for sin?

I now come to the third question: What is the difference between the disquiet for sin that is in the godly and the disquiet that is in the wicked and reprobate man? For it is possible that wicked and ungodly men may have trouble in conscience for the sins they have done, because God has put natural conscience in wicked men to rebuke and check and trouble and disquiet them for some sins, sometimes.
Now in resolving this question, I will note thirteen differences between the one and the other.
1. Wicked and ungodly men are troubled for sins, but their trouble and their disquiet are only for great and gross sins, and not for small and secret sins. Before conversion, Paul was never troubled and disquieted for concupiscence, for secret corruption and heart lusts. Therefore Paul said, "I had not known lust, if the law had not said, 'Thou shalt not covet' " (Romans 7:7). That is, he would not have known the inward part of lust, that the inward and secret desires of the heart were sin. He was alive then without the law, and he thought himself to be in a very good condition, and kept himself from great and gross enormities, but never made any reckoning and account of smaller enormities and lesser evils.
Unconverted men see sins as we see stars in the

night. We may see the stars of the first magnitude only, but we cannot see the lesser stars. So wicked men, by the light of natural conscience, can see sins of the first magnitude, gross and infamous sins, but they never take notice of lesser crimes, smaller sins, secret sinful lusts and desires, so as to check their hearts for them. These the light of nature (as it was with Paul) never takes notice of.

But now look upon godly men, and there you find a great difference. Their disquiet of conscience differs much, for their conscience disquiets them not only for sins as big as camels, but for sins as small as gnats; not only for mountains of sins, but for molehills of corruption. Small sins are the trouble and disquieting of good men's spirits. Hezekiah greatly humbled himself, though it was but for an inward sore, "for the lifting up of his heart in pride." This is an argument of true grace, when the soul shall be humbled for inward, secret, and heart sins. So David's heart smote him after he had numbered the people. It is questionable what was the particular sin, because for a king to number his people is in itself lawful; but it was some secret evil or heart sin, pride or some other sin, for which this his heart smote him. Those sins that will not trouble wicked men's sleep will break a godly man's heart. That which may be to a wicked man as dust in the finger of his glove, not any trouble to him, to a godly man is as gravel in his kidneys, greatly to trouble and disturb him.

2. The second difference is that wicked men may be disquieted for some outward acts of sin, but they are never troubled for the inward habit of sin, for the sinful nature, that depraved disposition of heart to sin. We

read that many times wicked men have been troubled for the reigning acts of sin, but never troubled at all for the sin of their nature. Cain was troubled for murdering his brother and Balaam for witchcraft. Ahab was troubled for the sinful act of idolatry, Judas for his treachery, and Saul for his cruelty; but none of these, nor any wicked man in the world, was troubled for original sin, for the depravity of their natures.

But now godly men's disquiet for sin not only reaches to the acts, but also to the habits of sin, to the natural depravity which is the foundation and fountain from whence all these corrupt actions flow. This is that which doth greatly trouble them. You read of Paul in Romans 7:24: "O wretched man that I am, who shall deliver me from the body of this death (or this body of death)?" He was alluding to those sins wherein men were wont, in a way of punishment, to tie a dead body to a living body. He speaks here of his body of sinful and depraved nature that was to him as a dead man tied to a living man, whereas before conversion he never complained of any inward corruption, nor once made mention of corrupt nature.

Are you troubled for sin? But can your conscience bear you witness that your disquiet of soul is for the sin and depravity of your nature as well as for the sins of your life? Are you troubled for the nature of sin as well as for the acts of sin? Are you troubled for the corrupt fountain as well as for the corrupt streams that flow from thence? If you are thus troubled and disquieted for sin, all your conflicts with sin shall end in conquest over sin another day.

3. The third difference is that wicked men may be troubled for sin, but their disquiet for sin is more for

Differences Between the Consciences

the evil of punishment (which is the effect of sin) than it is for the evil that is in the nature of sin. They are disquieted for sin, but it is because sin destroys the soul and not because sin defiles the soul. It is because God pursues sin, not because He hates sin; more because God's justice is provoked because the holiness of God is dishonored. Wicked men are troubled and disquieted because God threatens sin, not because God forbids sin; because of the hell *for* sin, not because of the hell *in* sin.

But now godly men hate and loathe sin more because it is against the nature of God, and because God loathes and hates it; more because it is against God's commands than because God punishes sin.

It is as with a child who forbears to touch a coal not because it will blacken his hand, but because it will burn his fingers. So it is with godly men: they will not touch sin because it is of a smiting and defiling nature. But wicked men are like the child: they will not touch sin, but only because it will burn them. Now if you can say that you hate sin because God hates it, and you hate sin not because of the punishment of sin, but because of the evil of sin; not because of the damning power of sin, but because of the defiling power of sin—in this case your disquiet for sin shall never hurt you.

4. The fourth difference is that although wicked men may be troubled and disquieted for sin, yet that disquiet does not make them leave sin, but when their pangs of sorrow are over they will run to their sin again. They may be disquieted for sin sometimes, but only for the time that the trouble lasts and no longer. Read Jeremiah 18:12: "They said, 'There is no hope, but we will walk after the imaginations of our own hearts.' "

Their consciences smote them a little for sin, but they would follow sin still for all that.

But godly men reason with themselves thus: "Do such sins trouble my soul, disturb my conscience, hinder my communion with God, and break my peace, and shall I yet touch them? No, I will cast them away as a menstruous cloth and break off from them. I will say to them, 'Get you hence.' " This is another difference: godly men break off from sin, but wicked men, though they may be disquieted, yet continue still in the same sin as soon as the trouble is over.

5. Wicked men may be troubled for sin for the present, yet this only lays a bare cessation on the act of sin; it does not put the soul in a way of detesting sin. It is possible that there may (by reason of natural conscience) be such a cessation of sin that for a long time he may not commit the same sin again, but yet this does not breed in the soul a detestation of sin. But when the trouble is over, then the cessation is ended, and he goes to the same way of sinning again.

You have an instance of this in Pharaoh, in Exodus 8:15: "When Pharaoh saw that there was respite, he hardened his heart, and hearkened not unto them, as the Lord had said." When he had a pang upon him, and was in great trouble, then his sin was abated and he saw a cessation of it; but when the trouble was gone, then his heart hardened again. So when conscience flies into the face of ungodly and wicked men, and tells them what they have done, then they will try to stifle conscience and say they will leave their wicked ways and do so no more. And when trouble of conscience is over, then they will go their old sinful ways again. This is the condition of wicked and ungodly men.

Differences Between the Consciences

2 Peter 2:22: "It is happened to them according to the true proverb, 'The dog is turned to his own vomit again, and the sow that is washed to wallowing in the mire.' " Wicked men are like dogs: while they have a pang in their stomach they are troubled and vomit it up, but when the pang is over they return to the vomit again. So it is with wicked men when conscience grips them, troubles them, and punishes them: then they will vomit up their sins and say they will do so no more, but when pain and trouble are gone they go to their sin again.

Trouble of soul, to a wicked man, is like a prison to a thief. A prison restrains a thief's practice, and keeps him from committing acts of robbery which he would be apt to do were he at liberty; but it does not change his thievish disposition and inclination toward that sin. Just so it is with a wicked man's conscience: it may check and control and restrain him from those exorbitant practices, and keep him from gross acts of sin, but it cannot change his sinful inclination and take away that wicked habit of sin that is within him, or stir up indignation against sin.

2 Peter 2:15 tells of those who "have forsaken the right way, and are gone astray, following the way of Balaam the son of Bosor, who loved the wages of unrighteousness." He loved profit, and the pangs of natural conscience were so great upon him that they restrained him from receiving this sinful gain and profit; but when Peter referred to the sin of Balaam, you find that he said that he loved the wages of unrighteousness though he did not receive them. His love and desire went out after it, though he did not (by reason of the trouble of his natural conscience) receive it. He would

fain have had it. It is no thanks to you, O wicked man, if you do not commit sin. You, it may be, cannot do it because of the checks of conscience, but have you not a love for it and a desire to commit it? It is charged upon you as if you had done it. Have you a desire to commit adultery? Though you have no opportunity, yet if you love it and delight to contemplate it, this is looked upon by God as your sin. And so, if you have a desire to be drunk, and love strong drink, and have no opportunity to do it, it is no thanks to you. Yet your love for the sin renders you guilty, and God will judge you according to that.

But godly men are disquieted for sin, and they desire to take not only away the act, but the habit of sin. Psalm 119:104: "Through Thy precepts I get understanding; therefore I hate every false way." The Psalmist, by considering the sweet precepts of God, came to understand the nature and the evil of sin; and therefore he hated sin and every false way—not only false ways in the outward acts of sin, but false ways with regard to the secret acts of sin in his own heart, and sin in the habit and nature of it.

6. When a wicked man is disquieted for sin, he does not go to God's Word for comfort and consolation, and to allay the sorrow and trouble of mind he lies under, but he has recourse to sinful and sensual pastimes and delights in the world to allay the troubles of his soul and conscience. So you read in Genesis 4:13–17 that Cain lay under sore troubles of mind for his sin, even to despair, insomuch that he said that his sins were greater than can be forgiven. But under this disquieted condition, what did he do? What course did he take? Did he take to God for satisfaction, and to allay his

Differences Between the Consciences 201

troubles? No, he took a wrong course, for it is said, "And Cain went out from the presence of Jehovah," and then after he was gone from God, then he went to build cities. His going out from the presence of the Lord means that he went out from the ordinances of God and the church of God to sensual delights in the world. It does not mean that Cain could go out from the essential presence of God; no man can do that. [Henry] Ainsworth intimates that this verse means his going away from the place of God's Word and public worship. And so to come into God's presence is the greatest joy for a godly man in this life, to come into God's presence in His ordinances in His church. This joy Cain now was deprived of, whereas he should have had recourse to these to allay his trouble of mind, and should not have gone to build cities in the world to stifle his conscience.

But godly men know that when they are disquieted for sin, to have recourse to pleasures, profits, pastimes, and sensual delights in the world can administer no true comfort, no true joy, no true peace of conscience, no more than a silken stocking will administer comfort to a broken leg. What can the stocking do? It may cover the broken leg, but it cannot cure it. So delights may cover the wound of conscience for a time, but they cannot give any real comfort. Godly men know they must hear and pray and seek God in public and in private in His own way, according to His own will, in ways which He has sanctified, to the end of easing troubled consciences.

You read that Jonah was troubled for sin in going from God's presence and not obeying His voice; under his trouble for sin his soul fainted within him. But did

Jonah go to worldly, sinful, and sensual delights to allay his troubled soul? No, the text says, "I remembered the Lord, and my prayer came in unto Thee, in Thine holy temple" (Jonah 2:7). He saw no other comfort was available to ease his spirit and pacify conscience, but only God's ways which He had sanctified for that very end.

Godly men will present their supplications to God, and address themselves to Him in the way of His worship to cure their distempered souls and labor to find God's love in Christ and in His promise. Godly men may see sin in their hearts, and guilt upon their spirits may make them sad. But they labor to find a smile from the face of God to make their souls glad; to call their sins dead; to speak peace to their consciences, joy to their heart, satisfaction to the soul, and delight in the spirit which makes the soul rejoice and be glad in God's presence.

Sermon 14

More Differences Between a Natural Conscience in a Wicked Man and the Conscience of a Godly Man Who Is Troubled for Sin

"Why art thou cast down, O my soul? and why art thou disquieted within me? Hope thou in God, for I shall yet praise Him, who is the health of my countenance, and my God." Psalm 42:11

I have already laid down six differences between that disquiet which arises from a natural conscience in wicked men under the guilt of conscience for sin and that holy disquiet of soul for sin found in the godly.

7. The seventh difference is this: wicked men are disquieted for sin because it causes outward afflictions rather than because it causes inward and spiritual withdrawings of God's face. Job 41:25: "When he raiseth up himself, the mighty are afraid: by reasons of breakings they purify themselves." When God breaks them by outward afflictions, then they think to themselves what evil they have done, and how they must amend and better their days; but it is more because of danger of death than out of love of purity. This makes men say, "I must purify myself, not because sin is impure, but because it breaks my body and takes my outward comforts from me." If sin did not afflict the body, it would never afflict the soul of a wicked man by his will.

Wicked men are like that man who had tuberculosis in his lungs, and complained to a physician of a sliver in his finger. Men are troubled at afflictions that are but trivial and toys, but when they reject grace and are near unto an eternal death, sin and the rejection of grace does not trouble them. Men who are thus disquieted more because of affliction than due to the inward withdrawings of God's face from them are fitly set out by ducks in a pond of water. Let a little pebble stone be cast into the water and the ducks will dive, but let it thunder in the heavens and the ducks are not afraid. Wicked men are like ducks: let God but give them a blow on their outward man or afflict their bodies and this will make them dive, crouch, tremble, and be afraid. But let the heavens be lowering, let God's face be eclipsed, if sin did not trouble the body it would never trouble the conscience. A godly man is troubled at affliction for sin's sake, but a wicked man is troubled at sin for affliction's sake. It is affliction that makes him troubled at sin. But now a godly man is of a far different temper: he is disquieted at sin more because of the inward withdrawings of God's face than because of the outward afflictions of the body. Psalm 30:7: "Lord by Thy favor Thou hast made my mountain stand strong; Thou didst hide Thy face, and I was troubled." David had trouble in the kingdom at that time; he had troubles on his person; but all this did not go so near his heart as the hiding of God's face. The heaviest stroke of God's hand did not so much disquiet David as the eclipse of God's countenance. Outward troubles were to David but as a scratch with a pin in the flesh, but the withdrawings of God's face troubled him as a sword in his bones.

8. The eighth difference is this: wicked men under disquiet for sin complain more *of* God than they complain *to* God. But good men complain more *to* God than *of* God when they are disquieted for sin. It is the usual behavior of the wicked to complain wretchedly against God, but not humbly to God when they are in horror of conscience under the disquiet of sin.

Revelation 16:9: "And men were scorched with great heat, and blasphemed the name of God." When God lets the fire of His wrath scorch the consciences of men with rage against the church, this but makes them blaspheme God, as in Isaiah 8:21: "It shall come to pass that when they shall be hungry, they shall fret themselves, and curse their king and their God, and look upward." They cursed their God and their king.

Wicked men complain that God is a hard master, that He loves to inflict cruel and severe judgments upon His creatures. The horror of conscience makes them expostulate with the Most High as if He were unrighteous. They complain that His decrees are partial, that His mercy is defective, that His justice is severe; but they never humbly complain to God under the trouble and disquiet of the soul. A notable text to characterize a wicked man is in Job 15:24–26: "Trouble and anguish shall make him afraid; they shall prevail against him as a king ready to battle. For he stretcheth out his hand against God, and strengtheneth himself against the Almighty. He runneth upon Him, even upon His neck, upon the thick bosses of His buckler." It is spoken by Eliphaz in a warlike sense. When a man is angry, he will run at another man to do him a mischief. A wicked man, in the horror and trouble of his soul, will arm himself against God, even in complaints. This is the temper of wicked men, who, even in horror of conscience will think ill of God, to complain *of* Him, but not *to* Him. But as for a godly man, when God lets him be troubled for sin, his temper is to complain *to* God. Lamentations 1:18: "The Lord is righteous, for I have rebelled against Him. Hear, I pray you, all people, and behold my sorrow; my virgins and my young men are gone into captivity." There is a complaining to God but not of Him. "Thou art righteous, but I have sinned." Psalm 51:4: "Against Thee only have I sinned, and done this evil in Thy sight, that Thou mayest be justified when Thou speakest, and be clear when Thou judgest." It is as if he had said, "I will blame myself, and I will judge myself now that my conscience flies in my face, but I will clear God, and will not judge God." This is the temper of a gracious man under trouble of mind for sin: he complains *to* God, but never *of* Him.

9. Wicked men in disquiet of soul for sin are more apt to complain to men of their trouble than to God. When Judas had betrayed Jesus Christ, his master, it is said that he came to the high priest and the scribes and Pharisees, and said unto them, "I have sinned in betraying innocent blood." But we never read that Judas went to the Lord and said, "I have betrayed Thy Son; I have sinned in betraying innocent blood."

Haman was troubled when he could not get Mordecai's knee. He told his wife and friends what befell him, but he never went to God. When Saul was troubled and vexed in spirit, it is said that Saul told his servants an evil spirit troubled him; but we never read that Saul went to God to allay the trouble and disquiet of his heart. This is the character of a wicked man: sin dogs him and conscience flies in his face, and to men he can complain, but he never goes to God to complain and say, "My soul is troubled and my conscience is galled." He can never go to God and pour out his complaints.

But godly men complain more to God than to men. They may experience doubts that need to be satisfied, but God shall hear their moans and complaints in private. The psalmist expresses this notably in Psalm 61:2: "From the end of the earth will I cry unto Thee, when my heart is overwhelmed; lead me to the rock that is higher than I." Jonah 2:7: "When my soul fainted within me, then I remembered the Lord, and my prayer came in unto Thee, into Thine holy temple." There was Jonah's trouble for his sin: "My soul fainted within me"; but when he was under soul trouble, why, said he, "I remembered the Lord." He would complain more to God than to man when he was under trouble.

10. The wicked are disquieted for sin, but it does not put them upon conscientious and effectual endeavors to effectually mortify those sins they are troubled for. They are more troubled about the guilt of sin than about the power of sin. If they can remove the guilt, they never care about the power and dominion of sin. This is the character of a wicked man. Thus it was with Pharaoh: he might feel guilty that God punished him, but the power of his hard heart never troubled him. Thus it is in wicked men: their disquiet of sin never makes them undertake effectual endeavors to subdue and mortify sin. But godly men are of a different temper: they work more to mortify sin than to pacify conscience, more to subdue the power of sin than to remove the guilt of sin. The godly man knows he must either kill or be killed. If he does not kill sin, sin will kill

him. Therefore his work is to purify as well as pacify the conscience, to remove the power as well as the guilt.

11. Wicked men, in disquiet of soul for sin, are prodigal and free in promising to leave sin while trouble is upon them, but when trouble is over they run into those sins for which they were troubled with more vehement eagerness and desire. This is expressed in Deuteronomy 5:27-28: " 'Go thou near, and hear all that the Lord our God shall say, and speak thou unto us; and all that the Lord our God shall say unto thee, we will hear, and do it.' And the Lord heard the voice of your words, and the Lord said unto me, 'I have heard the voice of the words of this people, they have well said all that which they have spoken.' "

When the people heard the terrible manner of God's delivering the law, in thunder and lightning, they made Moses a large promise: "Whatever God commands us by you, we will observe to do it."

But God said in Deuteronomy 5:29, "Oh, that there were such a heart in them, that they would fear Me, and keep all My commandments always, that it might be well with them and their children forever." And it is observable that when their trouble was barely over, the people were worse than ever they were before. They fell to murmuring afterwards, and murmured ten times against that God who had delivered them.

This is the character of wicked men, that when trouble of conscience disquiets them their sins remain on them. Oh, how they will promise what men they will be! They say they will begin a new life and never will be as they have been; and yet let their trouble be allayed and you shall see that this restraint of their consciences shall put them on to more eagerness to commit sin than ever they did in all their lifetime before! Men's sins are compared to an oven in Hosea 7. Fire dispersed into the air does not burn so fiercely, but in an oven it burns fiercely. When sin is kept in wicked men's hearts, through disquiet of soul for sin, once this fire has vent it will burn with more fierceness and more rage. When conscience dams up a sin, once that trouble is over and conscience has gotten over the dam, sin prevails on the soul with more eagerness and more prevalence.

In a godly man it is otherwise. When disquiet of soul is over for sin, a godly man retains an awe of running into that sin again. Though trouble is over, yet he remembers how he was troubled: "I confess I remember what it is to lie under the weight, burden, and guilt of sin." Therefore this puts an awe upon the conscience so that he dares not venture on sin as in former times.

12. The wicked, when under disquiet of soul for sin, are more apt to apply the comforting part of the Word than to apply the threatening and commanding part of the Word. When they were troubled by the ministry of the word, Deuteronomy 29:19 warns of a time when it would "come to pass, when he heareth the words of this curse, that he bless himself in his heart, saying, 'I shall have peace, though I walk after the imagination of mine heart, to add drunkenness to thirst.' " Say they, "We shall have peace, though we do according to the imaginations of our own hearts, to add drunkenness to thirst." They could apply words of peace, but they would not apply threats though they walked in the imaginations of their own heart.

Wicked men under horror of conscience are more apt to apply comforts, though groundless, than to apply threats, though that is their portion. Jeremiah 3:4–5: "Wilt thou not from this time cry unto me, My father, thou art the guide of my youth? Will He reserve His anger forever, will He keep it unto the end? Behold, thou hast spoken and done evil things as thou couldest." They did evil as much as they could, yet they would presume to say that God was their father. They claimed interest in God. It is the character of a wicked man to apply the comforting part of the Word, not the threatening part of the Word. But good men are more apt to apply the threatening part of the Word than the promising part of the Word. Psalm 77:2: "In the day of my trouble, I sought the Lord; my sore ran in the night, and ceased not; my soul refused to be comforted." Asaph could apply terror, but he would refuse comfort. Thus by daily experience, look upon a conscientious man under the disquiet of soul for sin and you shall see that man take to heart all the threats, all the terrible parts of the Scripture that may work against him—he will remember them all, but apply no promise that may allay disquiet of soul for sin.

13. Wicked men under trouble of mind for sin go to sinful shifts and means to allay and pacify the disquiet of their souls due to conscience; they use four sinful shifts which godly men dare not do.

First of all, they shun a soul-searching and sin-reproving ministry. This you see in Felix in Acts 24:25: "And as he reasoned of righteousness, temperance, and judgment to come, Felix trembled and answered, 'Go thy way for this time; when I have a convenient season, I will send for thee.' " Paul told him of two sins that he was most guilty of, drunkenness and injustice. When he had thus dealt with him roundly, and made his conscience tremble and troubled the heart of Felix, Felix said, "Get thee gone; I will hear thee some other time." Paul had galled him and troubled him, and Felix shuns the continuance of the rebuke and reproof of the word.

But a godly man dares not do this. A godly man loves that word which most alarms his conscience, and he loves that man who shall awaken a secure conscience. Observe the difference between Felix in Acts and the converts in Acts. Felix bade Paul go from him and shunned the reproof of the word when it galled his conscience, but the converts were troubled for sin and were pricked in the heart for killing Jesus Christ. They loved the apostles and cleaved to them, and laid their possessions at the apostles' feet. The apostles might command all they had, they loved them so well. Good men dare not do as wicked men do in that particular.

Second, wicked men, to allay disquiet of conscience, allay it by running into a crowd of secular employments. This you read of Cain in Genesis 4:17. After Cain had gone out from the presence of the Lord by reason of his sin, he, to stifle his conscience, went and built a city. God's people dare not do this; they dare not go to the world to allay disquiet of conscience. But they go to God's Word; they retire into a corner and search the Word to see what God says to them in the day of their trouble. Proverbs 12:25: "Heaviness in the heart of man maketh it stoop; but a good word maketh it glad." I stoop under heaviness and trouble, but only a good word only from God can comfort me.

Third, wicked men under trouble turn to carnal pleasure and sensuality to allay disquiet of mind. Saul called for instruments of music in 1 Samuel 16:16 to allay the troubles of his spirit, as the Israelites who offered their children to Molech drowned the cry of their children with a noise of drums and tabrets. So wicked men do with their consciences. God's people dare not do this; they know that sensual pleasures can no more pacify a disquieted conscience than a silken stocking can cure a gouty leg. They dare not wallow and swim in sinful pleasures, but they go to the promise, and in that they take their delight.

Fourth, wicked men go to bad company, to merry company, to see if that can make them forget their troubles. This Herod did. Mark 6:18: "For John said unto Herod, 'It is not lawful for thee to have thy brother's wife.' " Immediately after John had troubled his conscience for having his brother Philip's wife, then, to allay this trouble of John's reproof, Herod called for his merry company, his nobles and his soldiers about him, so that he might forget the disquiet of spirit. But godly men go to good men and to God in a corner. Psalm 61:2: "From the end of the earth will I cry unto Thee, when my heart is overwhelmed; lead me to the rock that is higher than I." This is the carriage and behavior of ungodly men.

14. Wicked men look more after comfort than after duty. If God gives them ease and peace they never care for grace. But God's people look after duty more than comfort when in disquiet of conscience. When the converts were troubled in mind they cried not after comfort, but after duty. They cried, "Men and brethren, what shall we do? What shall we do to be saved?"

Thus I have dispatched to you the third query, the differences in these fourteen particulars between the disquiet of soul for sin that may be found in wicked men and that evangelical, holy trouble of soul for sin which is found in the godly.

QUESTION 4. Why are God's people so disquieted for sin that they are more troubled for sin than they are comforted in the sight of their graces? Sin shall not damn their souls. Why, then, does sin so much disquiet their consciences?
There are five reasons.
REASON 1. It arises partly from that softness of heart and tenderness of conscience that is implanted in God's people by God. The eye is troubled at a mote when the hand is not troubled at a greater thing; the eye is the tenderest part of the body. Why, beloved, God's people have tender consciences. Sin on their consciences is as a mote in their eye that greatly troubles them. It is worth your notice that God makes a promise that He will keep His people as the apple of His eye. Deuteronomy 32:10: "He found him in the desert land, and in a waste howling wilderness. He led him about, He instructed him, He kept him as the apple of His eye." So God's people are said to keep His law as the apple of their eye in Proverbs 7:2: "Keep my commandments and live, and my law as the apple of Thy eye." Beloved, a blow on your eye offends the eye, and you must keep the law as the apple of your eye. The apple of your eye is the tenderest part of the eye. One breach of the law by sin will disquiet you as much as a blow on your eye, if you keep the law as the apple of your eye.
REASON 2. God's people are troubled for sin because God's people see that they sin against God more than they obey God. Therefore sin troubles and disquiets them more. Grace is as the gleaning of the vintage,

and sin is as the full harvest. Job 15:16: "How much more abominable and filthy is man which drinketh iniquity like water." God's people see their sins to like mountains and their graces like molehills: "My lusts burn like a flame, but my graces like a glowing coal; my sins are at full tide, but my graces are at a low ebb." That makes God's people be so troubled for sin. Disquiet of soul is more incident to the godly, as the moth is ordinarily in the finest cloth and the worm in the rose sooner than in the briar.

REASON 3. Sin is more visible and manifest to the soul than their graces are; therefore they are more troubled for sin. You read in Galatians 5:19–20: "Now the works of the flesh are manifest, which are these: adultery, fornication, uncleanness, lasciviousness, idolatry, witchcraft, hatred, variance, emulations, wrath, strife." But when the Apostle gives you the list of the graces of the Spirit, he does not say that the fruits of the Spirit are manifest, as he said the fruits of the flesh are manifest. This shows, as one observes well, that a man may more easily discern and have a sight of his sin than a godly man can have the sight of his grace.

REASON 4. A fourth reason is drawn from a consideration that Christ's soul was troubled for sin. Christ's soul was troubled for sin as imputed to Him, though He had no sin inherent in Him. "Now is My soul troubled," said Christ. Christ not only suffered in His body upon the cross, but likewise in His soul in the garden (John 13:21). His soul was not troubled for His own sin, for there was no guile found in His mouth; but it was for our sins that He was troubled. Now, beloved, note that Christ was troubled for your wounds, for your sins; and this makes a godly man reflect, "Shall Christ's soul be

More Differences Between Consciences

troubled for my sin that was imputed to him, and shall not I be troubled for sin that is inherent in me?"

REASON 5. The people of God might taste and see the evil and the bitterness of sin more in the course of their lives, and may be more put in fear of committing sin in the future. Solomon gives this reason why godly men are troubled in mind for sin. Ecclesiastes 7:25–26: "I applied mine heart to know, and to search, and to seek out wisdom, and the reason of things, and to know the wickedness of folly, even of foolishness and madness. And I find more bitter than death the woman whose heart is snares and nets." That is, by "knowing the evil of sin, folly, and madness" is meant sin, in Solomon's dialect. Said he, "I find it to be more bitter than death."

Solomon by experience speaks this: "I find sin to be worse to me than death." Beloved, this is why God will make a man discover the wickedness of sin and troubled in conscience for sin, so that he might find sin to be more bitter to him than death, and so that he might avoid those sins, and shun them for which he has smarted so much.

Sermon 15

When Are God's People Too Disquieted for Sin?

"Why art thou cast down, O my soul? and why art thou disquieted within me? Hope thou in God, for I shall yet praise Him, who is the health of my countenance, and my God." Psalm 42:11

QUESTION 5. When may God's people be said to be excessively or too much disquieted in soul for sin?

There are seven answers to this question. Four of them I shall gather from one Psalm, Psalm 77:2–4: "In the day of my trouble, I sought the Lord; my sore ran in the night, and ceased not; my soul refused to be comforted. I remembered God, and was troubled; I complained, and my spirit was overwhelmed. Thou holdest my eyes waking; I am so troubled that I cannot speak."

Here are four discoveries to show when a man's trouble of soul for sin is immoderate and excessive.

First, a man's disquiet and trouble of soul for sin is immoderate and excessive when a man is so disquieted under the guilt of sin that he is not only unable to receive comfort, but unwilling to receive that comfort that belongs to him. Verse 2: "My soul refused to be comforted." This was his sin. I prove it by the 10th verse: "And I said, 'This is mine infirmity.' " It was an infirmity in Asaph, when he was under trouble of mind, to refuse comfort. God intends trouble for sin to be an exercise of grace, not to obliterate the evidence of our graces. When trouble for sin proves to be an eclipse of grace, not a spur to grace, it is excessive.

Second, a man's disquiet and trouble of soul for sin is immoderate and excessive when the amiable and glorious attributes of God are represented unto the soul of a godly man under a formidable and a dreadful notion. This is laid down in verse 3: "I remembered God, and was troubled; I complained, and my spirit was overwhelmed." The thoughts of God should comfort a soul in trouble of mind, but when a man in trouble of mind makes the attributes of God trouble him, then it is excessive. Job 23:15: "Therefore am I troubled at His presence; when I consider, I am afraid of Him."

After Adam fell, what did he do? He went and hid himself from the presence of God. Genesis 3:8–10: "And they heard the voice of the Lord walking in the garden, in the cool of the day; and they hid themselves, for they were afraid." Beloved, when you cannot think of God without the thought of God troubling you, this is excessive trouble in a godly man.

Third, a man's disquiet and trouble of soul for sin is immoderate and excessive when a man is so disquieted in soul for sin that he denies himself the use of those natural comforts that God allows him to enjoy—when he cannot eat, drink, or sleep. This is laid down in the fourth verse of this psalm: "Thou holdest mine eyes waking; I am so troubled that I cannot sleep." His meaning is, "I am so troubled in conscience under the guilt of my sin that I cannot sleep at night when I lie down on my bed. I cannot eat nor sleep. I cannot enjoy those natural comforts and sleep which the Lord allows me to enjoy." Worldly care is described in covetous men in Ecclesiastes 5:12: "The sleep of a laboring man is sweet, whether he eat little or much; but the abundance of the rich will not suffer him to sleep." It is an argument of excessive worldly care and trouble in a man when he is so puzzled and glutted with the world that he cannot take his rest at night.

Fourth, a man's disquiet and trouble of soul for sin is immoderate and excessive when disquiet of soul under the guilt of sin either discourages a man or makes him unfit for religious duties. Then they are excessive and inordinate. This is laid down in verse 4: "I am so troubled I cannot speak. He was so overwhelmed with fears and troubles in his spirit that it either discouraged him from praying or made him unfit for the use of prayer. To show this further, note verse 10: "I said, 'This is mine infirmity.' " It follows that all those troubles that are so inordinate as to make him refuse comfort and be troubled at the thoughts of God, and to make him likewise that he could not sleep or pray—all this was his infirmity. These are the four discoveries taken from that one psalm.

Fifth, it is inordinate when a man is so disquieted under the sight of sin that he has no mind to follow his particular calling wherein God has set him in the world, so that he can take no comfort in wife or children, estate or comforts. When a man shall be so perplexed that he cannot follow his trade, then it is sinful. God enjoins no duty belonging to our general calling as Christians that should clash with or jostle out our particular callings as men. And herein the devil's policy lies, that if he, in trouble of mind, can keep a man out of his calling, he has the better way to work upon an idle man.

Sixth, a man's disquiet and trouble of soul for sin is

When Are God's People Too Disquieted for Sin?

immoderate and excessive when trouble and disquiet of soul for sin is prejudicial to the health of our bodies. It is not God's sacrifice that is prejudicial to bodily health. This infirmity appeared in Heman, one troubled deeply in mind. Psalm 88:3: "My soul is full of troubles, and my life draweth nigh to the grave." Heman's trouble of soul was so great that it weakened his body and brought him to nothing but skin and bones. You read of trouble in Psalm 31:9–10: "Have mercy upon me, Lord, for I am in trouble; my eye is consumed with grief. For my life is spent with grief, and my years with sighing; my strength faileth because of my iniquity." Here was a mixture of weakness in this, though it was for sin; yet as for consuming the bones and spending the strength, God does not require that.

Last, a man's disquiet and trouble of soul for sin is immoderate and excessive when a man is so disquieted under the guilt of sin as to be utterly discouraged from venturing to lay hold on Jesus Christ. When one says doubtingly what the enemies say scoffingly, "There is no help for him in God," when the kind or degree of trouble of mind is so much that it conceals the of it, it is then excessive. What is the end of trouble of mind for sin? The end is to embitter sin, and to provoke a soul to look out after Jesus Christ.

QUESTION. You will ask me, "If it is so that godly men are so disquieted in soul under the guilt of sin, then what is the reason why wicked men can live so jocundly under such heavy loads of guilt, yet never have a troubled thought or disquieted heart all their days? Why do they not come into trouble as other men? What is the reason for all this?"

It is a very fruitful question, and well to be considered. There are ten general causes.

1. It proceeds partly from the malice and subtlety of the devil, that those souls he hopes to damn when they die he does not disquiet for sin while they are alive. This is hinted to you in Luke 11:21: "When a strong man armed keepeth his palace, his goods are in peace." The strong man signifies the devil; the palace represents the heart of a wicked man; the goods being at peace means that the thoughts of a wicked man are at peace, and nothing troubles him. When the devil possesses a wicked man's heart, he labors to keep all his thoughts quiet and calm and at peace with him.

Stella, although a popish author, yet has a good point regarding the great cunning of the devil. The soul that he has possession of, he would not have him trouble his conscience. It is his labor that such a man should not endure one prick of conscience. The devil does with wicked men as the Babylonians did with the Jews in captivity: they made them sing songs. When the devil has wicked men captive, he would fain have them sing songs and be secure, and have nothing to trouble them all their days.

2. It proceeds from the gross ignorance that is in a wicked man's mind or understanding, whereby he does not see the evil nature and aggravation of sin. A blind mind and a dumb conscience go hand in hand. If the understanding of a man lacks an eye to see the evil of a sin distinctly, the conscience will lack a hand to smite for sin effectually. If sin were more in men's eyes, sorrow for sin would be more in men's hearts.

It is worth comparing two scriptures together. Psalm 51:3: "I acknowledge my transgression, and my sin is ever before me." And Psalm 38:17: "For I am ready to halt, and my sorrow is ever before me." How came the Psalmist to have sorrow for sin continually but by having the sight of sin continually? He had the sight of sin continually before him; he had then the sorrow of sin before him. The sight of sin is an inlet to sorrow and trouble of mind for sin. What is the reason why a man who sees a lion in the wilderness is afraid, but if that man sees a lion painted on the wall he is not troubled? The reason is that he knows the lion in the wilderness is of a fierce and cruel nature; therefore he fears it. But he knows no such evil in a painted lion; therefore he is not troubled at that.

Beloved, if wicked men could look upon sin as a loose lion in the wilderness, that would fly in their faces. Why, the sight of sin would make them afraid then. But they look upon sin as a painted lion; they do not see sin to be so odious and aggravated. This is the great cause why wicked men are so little disquieted in soul under the guilt of sin.

3. It proceeds from a judicial hardness in the heart and a cauterized or seared conscience. Romans 2:5: "But after thy hard and impenitent heart, treasurest up unto thyself wrath against the day of wrath and revelation of the righteous judgment of God." This is to let you know that it is from hardness of heart and searedness of conscience that a man cannot repent, confess, and be troubled for the evils he has done, and the guilt he lies under. Seared flesh is sensible of no touch with a pin; it is your raw flesh that is sensible. Men's consciences are cauterized and seared, and that makes their sin not function as a sword in the flesh.

4. It proceeds from a continued custom of sinning, which hardens the heart and sears the conscience. It is

in this case as with a man when he first comes to be an apprentice to an artificer or craftsman: he comes with a tender hand to the work, and when he begins to work with hard instruments he cannot work, but he galls and blisters his hand. But when he has been many years at work, by continual labor, his hand hardens so that he can use it and never blister. It is just thus with a sinner: before a man becomes accustomed to an evil way, conscience is tender and full of remorse; but a continued custom and making a trade of sin makes the conscience grow hard and brawny and feel nothing. In a smith's house, a dog that comes newly in cannot endure having the fiery sparks fly about his ears; but when the dog is used to it he sleeps quietly. Let wicked men be long used to sin, to the devil's workshop, to being slaves and vassals to sin, the sparks of hellfire may fly about their ears and never trouble them. And all this arises from a continued custom of doing evil.

5. That a wicked man is not disquieted for sin arises from a wicked man's stifling the checks and rebukes of his own conscience. As quenching the Spirit in its holy motions to do good causes God to withdraw the holy motions of His Spirit, so stifling the conscience provokes God so that conscience shall not trouble you more, but shall be given up to a sottish and senseless stupidity of conscience.

6. It arises from a mistake and misapprehension that wicked men maintain, that trouble of conscience for sin it is an utter enemy to all worldly joy, and if a man comes once to be troubled in conscience for sin he shall never have a merry day more, but must hang down his head in pensiveness and lead a melancholy, sad life. Beloved, wicked men's veiling holy disquiet

with these prejudices is a special reason why they are no more troubled for sin than they are. This is hinted to us in the saying of Solomon in Ecclesiastes 7:4: "The heart of the wise is in the house of mourning, but the heart of the fool is in the house of mirth." The wicked are afraid to be in the house of mourning, to mourn and grieve for evils they have done, lest they should never have glad and comfortable days in the world. Thus the papists entertained this prejudice against the Protestant religion, that the spirit of Calvin is a melancholy spirit. Beloved, the way to have a well-composed and ordered joy and comfort in the world is to have a gracious sorrow and an evangelical grief for the evils you have done in the world.

7. It proceeds from a groundless and a presumptuous persuasion that wicked men have of pardoning grace. "Tush," said a wicked man, "if I have hopes of heaven when I die, why should sin trouble me? I hope it shall not damn my soul, and therefore it shall not disquiet me. I will not lay sin to my heart, for God will not lay sin to my charge. I shall go to heaven when I die; why should I break my peace while I live?" This was the great reason given by those who were no more troubled for sin. Deuteronomy 29:19: "And it may come to pass when he hears the words of this curse, that he bless himself in his heart, and say, 'I shall have peace, though I walk in the imaginations of my heart.' " God did not bless them, but they blessed themselves. They presumed of mercy, and they presumed of heaven. They will presume of blessing; why, this makes them so that they are not troubled for adding drunkenness to thirst. They can add sin to sin, but not add sorrow to sorrow for sin.

8. Men content themselves under a pleasant and a flattering ministry. Men who, under pretense of preaching free grace, the love of God, and the merits of Christ, make all their sermons comfortable strains, are indeed but making the way to heaven wider than God makes it. This reason is given by God Himself in Isaiah 8:11: "For the Lord spake thus to me with a strong hand, and instructed me that I should not walk in the way of this people." They speak peace when indeed they were in trouble. Jeremiah 23:13–14: "And I have seen folly in the prophets of Samaria; they prophesied in Baal, and caused my people to err. I have seen also in the prophets of Jerusalem a horrible thing: they have committed adultery, and walk in lies; they strengthen also the hands of evildoers, that none doth return from his wickedness; they are all of them unto me as Sodom, and the inhabitants thereof as Gomorrah."

9. They have a fullness of outward prosperity and blessing in the world. This may refer to soul trouble as well as body trouble, in that prosperity in the world mightily keeps a man from having his soul trouble him under the guilt of sin. Hosea 12:8: "And Ephraim said, 'Yet I am become rich, I have found me out substance; in all my labors they shall find no iniquity in me that were sin.' " They were a wicked people, and yet their prosperity in an evil way hardened their hearts in a way of sin. Take the instance of Pharaoh: there was nothing in the world that more hardened his heart than his prosperity. God, lifting him up to be a king, hardened his heart. When men are glutted with prosperity, they do not have an open ear to the shrieks of conscience. 2 Chronicles 33:10: "And the Lord spake to Manasseh, and to his people; but they would not hearken." In

prosperity he would not hearken to the checks of conscience till God laid him in fetters; then he hearkened.

10. Men are not disquieted in soul for sin. Why not? Because they do not consider the omnipotence and all-seeing eye of God. Though men are not doctrinal atheists to hold the opinion that God does not see all things, yet they are practical atheists who live and continue in so evil a way as if God did not see them. Job 22:13-14: "And thou sayest, 'How can the Lord know? Can He judge through the dark clouds? Thick clouds are a covering to Him, that He seeth not, and He walketh in the circuit of heaven.'" They act as if the Lord does not see, nor does the holy One regard: "Is there not a cloud between Him and us?" The wicked make a "tush" of sin, "Tush," say they, "the Lord regards it not." But what is the reason why men make a "tush" of sin? Why, they do not think that God regards sin. Sin does not trouble or disquiet them because they think God does not behold them. They are inconsiderate of the omnipotence of God.

I shall now only give you a short use of what you have heard regarding godly men's disquiet under the guilt of sin. It shall be by way of trial or examination. You have heard much concerning that trouble and disquiet of soul that may be found in reprobates. Now the use shall be to put you upon trial how you may be satisfied in your conscience that the disquiet of soul that is in you under the guilt of sin is an evangelical and a gracious trouble for sin, and not such a trouble that arises from a natural conscience in wicked men. And to satisfy you herein, I shall name six particulars.

1. Do you find within you that your trouble of soul is

more for the evil of what you have done than for the danger you may incur? My meaning is this: when you are troubled more for the sin than you are troubled for the penalty of the sin you have incurred by the commission of it, when you are troubled for sin more because it robs God of His glory than because it will keep you from glory, this is an evangelical grace.

2. Yours is an evangelical trouble for sin when you are more troubled for the sin of nature than for the sins that break out in your life; when the sin of nature disquiets you as well as the sins of your practice. We never find in all the Scripture that a wicked man has any remorse of spirit at all for the sin of nature. If you can say that sins of nature trouble you as well as sins of practice, this is an argument of evangelical trouble of soul for sin. David discovered grace herein when he wrote that penitential Psalm 51 for the sin of adultery with Bathsheba. David not only bewailed the unclean act, but he bewailed also the unclean nature.

3. You may be satisfied if you are as much disquieted in soul at the sight and apprehension of the power of sin as of the guilt of sin. "I am troubled not only that sin is so dangerous, but also that sin is so strong within me."

4. The disquiet for sin is evangelical when the measure and degree of your trouble of mind for sin is subservient to, and promotes, the purpose of the trouble of mind. The end of trouble of mind, I told you, was to embitter sin and endear Christ to you. When you have so much of the measure and degree of trouble of mind as to embitter sin to you, and to endear Jesus Christ to you, this is the true evangelical humiliation that the gospel calls for.

5. You may be sure that it is an evangelical trouble of mind when you are troubled for sin because it is against a good God as much as because it is against a just God. A wicked man may be troubled for sin against a just God because justice will be avenged on sin and on the sinner; but now a godly man says, "God loads me with mercies." When you can grieve and be troubled for sin, this is evangelical. "They shall fear the Lord, and His goodness in the latter days" (Hosea 3:5). I may apply that fable that Plutarch tells in his *Morals,* of the sun and the mind contending which should make a traveler put off his cloak. O beloved, storms and blustering tempests of God's wrath may make a wicked man leave sin and be troubled for sin; but when the sun of God's love shall melt the heart and sweetly insinuate into your soul, and make you unclothe yourself of the rags of sin, that is an argument of evangelical trouble.

6. It is an evangelical sorrow and trouble of soul for sin when you can be as truly troubled for sin committed, when you know it is pardoned, as if you had not known your sin to be pardoned. To be a troubled and a pardoned Christian is evangelical trouble. A pardoned sin shall fill your heart with trouble when you are of such a temper that you will bathe that sin in your tears in a way of contrition even though you know it to be bathed in Christ's blood in a way of remission. In this case you have a gracious temper of heart engraved upon you.

Sermon 16

Practical Instruction

"Why art thou cast down, O my soul? and why art thou disquieted within me? Hope thou in God, for I shall yet praise Him, who is the health of my countenance, and my God." Psalm 42:11

    I now come to give you some practical instructions by way of rules. My work shall be to prescribe some theological rules to those who are greatly troubled and disquieted in soul under the guilt of sin. These rules are of two sorts: there are rules by way of direction and rules by way of consolation.

    I begin with the first sort, directive rules. There are eight rules to allay trouble and disquiet of conscience when it is excessive and inordinate.

    RULE 1. When you are excessively troubled under the guilt of sin, take this rule: what troubled thoughts you have about the guilt of sin, spend them upon the power of sin within you. This is a holy diversion, to be always conversant about the power of sin; it is an evangelical and a gracious temper. If Christians were more troubled about the power of sin, they would be less troubled about the guilt of sin. The devil does not care if professors of religion are terrified Christians, so long as they are not mortified Christians.

    RULE 2. Keep conscience clear so that you do not add guilt to guilt. Adding guilt to guilt is the way to add horror to horror and terror to terror upon the conscience. Guilt in the conscience contracts dismal fear, amazement, and consternation of soul. If conscience does not shut sin out of doors, sin will shut peace of conscience out of doors. This is a rule that Bernard gives: conscience is to be comforted, but first it is to be purified and made clean. This rule is laid down by Eliphaz in Job 11:14: "If iniquity be in thine hand, put it far away, and let not wickedness dwell in thy tabernacles."

Beloved, that is the way to keep out fear, to keep out guilt. If conscience is not a swept and cleansed room, it will gall, disquiet, and vex your soul. To have conscience pacified when it is not purified is but to skin over an old sore, which before it is healed will break out again. "Peace," said Bernard, "in many men is worse than a spiritual conflict." What kind of peace is it for a man to have peace in his conscience when he indulges guilt in his conscience? Expect not trouble of conscience to be allayed if your conscience is not purified. Proverbs 29:6: "In the transgression of an evil man there is a snare, but the righteous doth sing and rejoice." By "snare" Solomon there means horror of conscience, as is shown by the opposition. Interpreters give this rule, that in the Proverbs of Solomon one opposition explains the other. Why, here the righteous shall sing and rejoice in his grace, but the wicked shall have a snare in his sin. He shall have horror and dread of conscience in the sight of sin (Proverbs 15:15).

A good and a clear conscience keeps holiday every day of his life, though he has hardly anything else to feed upon. Guilt on the conscience is the way to cause a resurrection of your fears and doubts, and to bring all your spiritual hopes to the grave.

RULE 3. Take heed that you do not go about to allay the disquiet of your soul for sin by sin. To run to vain pleasures and to sensual delights so as to stop and quell the voice of conscience—what is this but to go to the devil for a plaster to heal the wounds of your soul? Beloved, these men who go to allay trouble of mind for sin by sin go the way that will make conscience recoil and turn upon them with more fierceness and savage cruelty. It is just like a man who is thirsty: he will drink a cup of poison to quench his thirst. Oh! when you are scorched with God's wrath, and to allay this you drink a cup of sin, what do you do but drink so much poison! Many men, when they are under trouble of mind, will go to sin for a shelter, and there a serpent puts them to more pain.

RULE 4. Fix your thoughts on the evidences of your graces when your hearts are overly disquieted in the sight of sin. As trouble of conscience in the sight of sin will keep a man so that he shall not be proud in the sight of his grace, so the evidence or sight of grace will keep a man so that he shall not be excessively troubled in the sight of sin.

RULE 5. In your meditations, ponder the comfortable promises of the gospel rather than the threats of the law. If I were to speak to a secure sinner I would give him a quite contrary rule, that he should rather ponder the threats of the law than the promises of the gospel; but a sinner greatly pressed under the weight of God's wrath must rather ponder the promising part of the Word than the threatening part of the Word. Proverbs 25:12: "As an earring of gold, and as an ornament of fine gold, so is a wise reprover to an obedient ear." The good word of a promise makes glad a poor soul that stoops in heaviness under the guilt of sin. When a pot boils over the fire, and boils too fast, cast a handful of salt and it will allay the boiling of the pot. When your soul boils and is restless in disquiet for trouble of sin, and is boiling too fast, cast in a handful of salt, a handful of the promises of the gospel, and this will allay the excessive trouble and disquiet of your soul. The promises are called by one "the instruments of a Christian's peace." They are called God's proclamations of pardon to a poor creature. They are the writing wherein he may read all his privileges. Oh, study them well!

RULE 6. Compare the guilt of your sin with the merits of Christ's righteousness, and you will find that there is more in Christ's righteousness to save than is in sin to damn. Christ's righteousness is imputed to a believer so that the guilt of sin might not be charged on him. As Christ's person is above your person, so Christ's righteousness is above your righteousness. This the apostle lays down in Romans 5:15: "The gift by grace hath abounded to many." The gift exceeds the sin and exceeds the offense. Compare them in your thoughts, and that will be a means to allay the trouble of your heart.

RULE 7. Disclose and reveal that sin, the guilt whereof so disquiets your soul, unto some judicious, compassionate, and experienced Christian. Giving vent to your own sorrows by complaints is a great way to ease the mind. If God thought it fit that Adam in innocence should not be alone, but should have a helper, much more now in a state of defection since the fall do we need others' help as well as our own. If God thought it fit to send an angel to comfort Jesus Christ when He was in agony, oh, then, do not believers need much more when they are in their spiritual agony, conflicts, and temptations, someone to comfort them? It is on this ground that the apostle bids Christians to comfort one another. 1 Thessalonians 4:18: "Comfort one another." 1 Thessalonians 5:14: "Comfort the feebleminded, support the weak, be patient toward all men." God enjoins Christians to this mutual act of love: "comfort ye one another." An arch is built so that though the stones of the arch all hang downwards, yet one stone supports another so that they do not fall. O beloved, Christians who are lively stones in Christ's spiritual building should be as the stones of an arch, that though one stone hangs downward, yet the stones next to it should bear it up. This makes Solomon say that two are better than one, for if one falls the other should help him up.

In this there are three cautions to be observed:

First, you are not to reveal that sin for which your conscience troubles you to everyone, but to a man who is experienced. When Judas was troubled in conscience for betraying Jesus Christ, it is said that he went to the high priest and to the Pharisees, and confessed to them, "I have sinned in betraying innocent blood." Why, they were not compassionate with him. So, should you go to some men and complain to them, they would jeer at you and send you away with a flout and a scoff. Go to those who are most compassionate, most judicious, most acquainted with the spiritual state of a Christian.

Beloved, in our bodily infirmities, when a man is sick he does not tell every neighbor he is sick and reveal his infirmity to all, but to a doctor. It is not for a man in trouble of mind to go to everyone, to men who lack compassion, experience, and wisdom to speak a word in due season to a wearied heart. Many men are like a company of deer: when one deer is shot all the rest of the herd run away from the wounded deer and leave it to shift for its life. When a man is wounded in conscience, the arrows of the Almighty sticking in him, they think it is a melancholy wound in him, and they are shy of him and run away from him. Oh, go to those who can show the deepest compassion towards you.

Second, you must not disclose your particular sin on every slight trouble unless your trouble is very urgent and vexatious in the soul. Beloved, you do not go to the surgeon for every aching finger and every slight wound. You do not need, upon every slight trouble of mind, to disclose your particular sins. Confession to another man should never be but when of all means you have used by yourself nothing can comfort you, when your spirit is troubled with great bitterness. Only in a case of urgent necessity must you open yourselves to another man.

Third, take heed, when you reveal your mind to any, not to deal doubly with that man. Men will come sometimes to a minister and tell him they are troubled in mind, but they will not tell him what it is that puts a sting into their conscience. They will share some other thing that is slight and trivial, but not the real thing that troubles them. The lapwing will not cry near her nest, but afar off. Many men carry themselves so that you shall not find out their nests; their beloved sins they will not reveal and disclose.

RULE 8. When you are disquieted for sin, then go to God through Christ in prayer to pacify your conscience and speak peace to your soul when you are troubled. We can speak peace, but it is God that gives peace. This is one prerogative ascribed to God, that He is a God who comforts those who are cast down. 2 Corinthians 7:6: "Nevertheless, God, that comforteth those that are cast down, comforted us by the coming of Titus." He is a God who creates peace out of nothing. It is very observable in Isaiah 8:11: "For the Lord spake thus to me with a strong hand, and instructed me that I should not walk in the way of this people." When God would comfort the prophets against the accusations and combinations of the enemies against the church of God, He spoke to them with a strong hand. The tongue is the instrument of speech, not the hand. We speak with our tongues. We can speak to a man comfortable words, but we cannot make him believe them; but the Scripture says that God speaks with His hand because He can do what he speaks. His word is like Christ's word in the sixth chapter of Mark: Christ spoke to the winds and, lo, they were still and there was a great calm. Beloved, God's Word has a great hand in it; it can do what it speaks. Oh, then, go to God through Christ in prayer and, having recourse to God, there are two things you are to beg of God in prayer if you would have the trouble of soul allayed. First, beg God to grant a share in the blood of Christ that merits your peace, and, second, to grant a share in the Spirit of Christ that works your peace. These are the two main things in prayer to allay the trouble of soul for the guilt of sin.

Beg a share in the blood of Christ that merits your peace. Colossians 1:20: "And (having made peace through the blood of His cross) by Him to reconcile all things to Himself, whether things in earth or things in heaven." There is peace with God and a peace in your conscience. Peace with God and peace in your conscience are the certain results of Christ's personal treaty with God the Father in heaven. It was exemplified under the law, in Exodus 12:23: "For the Lord will pass through to smite the Egyptians; and when He seeth the blood upon the lintel, and on the two side posts, the Lord will pass over the door, and not suffer the destroyer to smite you." The blood of the paschal lamb that sprinkled the posts of the door of any house was a pledge that there was peace and safety in that house. If you have the blood of this paschal lamb, Jesus Christ, sprinkled on the doorposts of your conscience, this will be a sign that there shall be peace and safety in your house. The destroying angel shall pass over.

Along with this, beg a share in the Spirit of Christ that works your peace. Therefore it is that the Spirit is called the Comforter as well as the Holy Ghost. He is called the Holy Ghost to show that it is one part of His office to work holiness in us, and He is called the Comforter to show that it is one part of His office to comfort His people.

And thus I have hastily gone over the directive rules to allay excessive disquiet of soul under the guilt of sin.

I now come to lay down some consolatory rules which may be given to comfort a godly man who is grievously vexed and disquieted under the guilt of sin. There are six such rules to comfort a godly man who is disquieted in soul under the guilt of sin.

RULE 1. Take this rule to comfort you: if the power

of your sin does not prevail over you, you may be sure the guilt of your sin shall never damn you. Why, then, if sin does not have a domineering power in the filth of it, it shall never have a damning power in the guilt of it. O you mortified Christian, it may be that you are troubled at what you have done when you were a child; but have you mortified those sins? Then I can assure you that those sins you have destroyed shall never damn you. It may be you are troubled about the guilt when you have destroyed the power. Oh, lift up your head; the guilt shall never damn you when the power does not prevail over you.

RULE 2. It is better for a Christian to have a soul troubled too much for sin than too little or not at all for sin. It is better to have a troubled and a terrified conscience than to have a stupefied conscience, better to have a sore than a seared conscience, better to have the conscience raw and galled than to have it numbed and in no way sensible of the evil of sin. Why, beloved, there is more hope for a soul in a spiritual fever who is in disquiet, who is raging by reason of the accusation of conscience, who is lying under trouble and disquiet of his own apprehension, than for him who lies under a spiritual lethargy, sleeping and snorting in his sins which never trouble him.

A wound that has raw and quick flesh in it will more easily be healed than a wound that has proud and dead flesh in it. If your conscience is dead flesh, you are not so near healing as when your conscience is raw and galled flesh. It was one mark of leprosy that was unclean if there was dead flesh in the sore. A numb and stupefied conscience argues an unclean leper, one in a state of nature. It is better to have God's officer, the conscience, be overly busy, and too much checking and curbing you, than to have no office of conscience stirring in you. This is another consideration for the comfort of an afflicted soul.

RULE 3. Consider that God's mercy and Christ's merits in pardoning the guilt of the sin you have committed are far greater than the greatness of your own guilt. Romans 5:15: "But not as the offense, so is the free gift. For if through the offense of one, many be dead, much more the grace of God, and the gift by grace, by one man Jesus Christ hath abounded to many." The meaning is that the gift of Jesus Christ, the value and worth of man, far exceeded the guilt and evil of sin. Psalm 32:10: "He that trusteth on the Lord, mercy shall compass him round about." My own fault is very great, but God's grace and mercy are far greater. When God is said to pardon sin in Micah 7:18, we read, "Who is a God like unto Thee, that pardoneth iniquity, and passeth by the transgressions of His people? He retaineth not anger, because He delighteth in mercy." He is said to throw them into the bottom of the sea. The Red Sea could as easily drown Pharaoh and his host as it could drown a single man. Beloved, the red sea of Christ's blood can as well cover an army, a host of sins, as it can a single sin. The sea can cover the whale as well as lesser fishes. The sea of Christ's blood can cover great sins as well as small. David makes it an argument in Psalm 25:11: "For Thy name's sake, O Lord, pardon mine iniquity, for it is great." "Pardon my sin, for it is great," that is, "although it is great." And so you have often the particle used in Scripture. The Lord would not punish man, "for the imagination of his heart is evil"; that is, *though* his heart is evil. It is observed regarding the ark, wherein the moral law was kept, that the mercy-seat covered the whole ark, to denote, beloved, that Jesus Christ, the mercy of God and merits of Christ, provides a propitiation, a covering of all the breaches of the law. The mercy-seat is broad and large enough to cover all. Therefore let this be of great comfort.

RULE 4. Observe that the more trouble of mind you lie under for the present in the sense of sin, the less trouble you shall have in the future. God does with His people as landlords do with their tenants: if a landlord takes a great payment at the renter's first coming into the house, he takes less yearly rent in the future. God takes from you a great payment at first. He makes sin cost you many a tear, many a night's trouble, and many a day's disquiet. The greater payment God takes from you, the less yearly rent He expects of you. The more you are troubled for the present, the less fear and torment shall be your portion hereafter. Am I troubled now? It is that I might have more peace when I come to die, that in the residue of my days I might have joy and peace in believing. Oh, think, then, that if God upon your first coming into Christ makes you pay dearly for your sin, and makes you smart for it, why, there is less sorrow and trouble for you in time to come.

RULE 5. Are you troubled in soul for sin? Take this comfort: the more you are troubled for sin, the nearer you are to getting away from the devil. When the devil makes conscience howl, it is an argument that the devil and sin are thrown out. When the devil stayed for a long time in the child, the devil did not trouble the child so much. Mark 9:26: "And the spirit cried, and rent him sore, and came out of him, and he was as one

Practical Instruction 239

dead, insomuch that many said, 'He is dead.' " It is said that when the devil came out of the child, then the devil rent him sorely and laid him down for dead. O beloved, when the devil is in a man, when the strong man has full possession of a man, the devil does not trouble him then. As Stella said, "The devil would not have him suffer one touch of conscience then; but when the devil is going out, and sin is thrown out, then the devil rends a man, and lays a man for dead; this is the property of the devil." Gregory, in his comment upon the book of Job, has a notable saying, "Therefore the devil more vehemently stirs up fears and doubts in the heart, because sin is thrown out of the heart." Oh, let this comfort you: Does the devil trouble you more than ordinarily? Does your conscience terrify you that you are a burden to yourself? Beloved, it is an argument that the devil is casting off and sin is being cast out. Oh, comfort yourself thus: "I hear the noise of conscience every day. I hear my conscience suggest this guilt to me and that guilt to me. Oh, blessed be God, I hear my conscience roar and howl, and I have more hopes that the devil is being thrown out and sin is being cast out." That is a fifth consideration.

RULE 6. Lastly, take this for your comfort: there are more promises of the gospel made to men in this condition than to any other sort of men in the world. I could give you multitudes of promises to men in this case. Matthew 11:28: "Come unto Me, all ye that labor and are heavy laden, and I will give you rest." So in Isaiah 54:10–11; 35:4; 57:15. Many other texts I could give you where God makes abundant promises to men under disquiet of soul, under the guilt of sin. When children are well, they shall have, it may be, but pebbles to play with; but if there is one sick child in the house, the mother goes to the cabinet and looks for fine things to quiet the child. O beloved, it may be that healthy Christians shall go on comfortably, and shall have now and then smiles of God's face towards them; but God's rich cabinet of promises is open to them when they are sick. When a poor sinner suspects that he is not pardoned, then God comes with a promise to comfort him that he *is* pardoned. The healthy children in the house are beloved by the parents, but the sick child is dandled on the knees. The well child may have bread and butter, but the sick child has the comfortable things to comfort it.

Beloved, when God's children are sick with sin and greatly troubled in conscience, God provides for them the promises to allay and pacify the troubled spirit. Oh, let these words of comfort sink into your hearts!

Sermon 17

Further Rules

"Why art thou cast down, O my soul? and why art thou disquieted within me? Hope thou in God, for I shall yet praise Him, who is the health of my countenance, and my God." Psalm 42:11

I now come to give you some other rules, for those who complain and say, "The Lord help me. I am so far from being overly disquieted that I do not find my heart to be disquieted at all. I do not find my soul to be so much as troubled under the guilt of many evils that I am guilty of." Touching this I shall proceed to give you rules of direction and consolation.

How does a child of God, who does not find his soul sensibly touched and evangelically disquieted under the sense of sin committed, come to have his soul evangelically troubled under the guilt of sin?

RULE 1. Do not rest satisfied with a general and a confused sight of sin, but labor to single out the chiefest of your corruptions, to have a particular and distinct view thereof. This is the course that God's people have taken. Acts 2:37: "Now when they heard this, they were pricked in their hearts, and said unto Peter and the rest of the apostles, 'Men and brethren, what shall we do?' " Peter does not tell them that they were sinners in general, but of all sins he singles out one: "you have crucified the Lord of glory." And when they heard that, they were pricked to the heart. They singled out that sin to have their hearts brought to brokenness and to contrition. When Christ would bring the woman of Samaria to remorse and trouble for sin, He singled out one sin of all and told her, "Thou art a harlot." And the Scripture gives you this hint, that the singling out of that one sin made her see all her other sins, for, said the woman, "Lo! behold the man that hath told me of all that ever I have done." And yet Christ told her only of her adultery.

Do this yourself. What is that Delilah that you play with in your bosom? Single out that sin, and that is the way to have a distinct view of all the evil. General and confused apprehensions of sin do but bring in a general humiliation. It has been the undoing of a great many souls to rest satisfied with general apprehensions of their guilt. They have lived and died without any saving remorse on their consciences. He who writes of Bellarmine said of him that when he came to die, such was the innocence of that man that he could not tell one sin in him that he was to make confession for. It did not arise from the innocence of the man, but it arose from an indistinct sight and observation of his ways.

Beloved, this makes a man hard-hearted when he comes to die, that he does not have evangelical remorse in him because he has but a confused and general view of sin. You read of Ahimaaz, who was running posthaste to bring news of what had happened. David asked him, "What news?" Ahimaaz said, "I saw the battle, and I heard a great tumult, but I know not what it was" (2 Samuel 18:29). Thus many men do with their sins as he did with his intelligence: they are troubled for sin, but they know nothing but in general. They know not what the sin is, just like Nebuchadnezzar. He called his magicians and enchanters together and said, "Tell me the interpretation of my dream, for I have dreamed, and I know not what it is." Some men say they have sinned, but they do not know what sin they have committed, what particular sin they have done.

RULE 2. Look upon small sins clothed with great aggravations. Beloved, this is the reason why men are not troubled: they look on their small sins as small, but do not look on them as clothed with many heinous circumstances. Suppose your sin is a small sin, invisible to the world, yet clothe this sin with aggravated circumstances. It may be a sin against conscience, a sin against much mercy; it may be a sin committed after many purposes and vows. This course Justin took in the second book of his confessions, chapter 4, about his robbing the orchard. "I did it," said he, "compelled neither by hunger nor poverty, but even through a cloyedness of well-doing, and a pamperedness of iniquity; for I stole that of which I had enough of my own, and much better." And so he aggravates his sin.

Beloved, when you find your souls not troubled for sin, clothe it with many heinous circumstances. And this we read of one who would aggravate his sin. Said he, "It is true, the devils have sinned, but they never sinned against a Savior as I have done. Adam sinned, but he never sinned against a Christ as I have done." Do thus aggravate a small sin and this will bring humiliation.

RULE 3. Live in meditation on pardoning mercy. It is true, wicked men make pardoning grace a means of presumption; but pardoning grace rightly applied is the most genuine way to break and trouble the soul. Beloved, lay yourself in the arms of Christ, on the bed of His love, and that is the way to break your flinty and stony heart. A child of God who knows his sins to be bathed in Christ's blood in a way of satisfaction cannot choose but to bathe his sins in the tears of contrition.

I now come to give you four consolatory rules. Is there comfort for a man who finds his heart hard, who seldom or never finds his soul disquieted under the sense of sin?

RULE 1. Be comforted if what you want in godly sorrow for sin you make up in holy care and watchfulness against sin. If a child of God does not have a weeping eye for sin, yet if he has a watchful heart against sin, that is pleasing to God. If tears are not in your eye for sin, yet if weapons of defense are in your hand to contest and conflict with corruptions, that is most pleasing to God. The captain of our salvation, Jesus Christ, would rather see a fighting weapon against sin than a weeping eye for sin. That is one comfort.

RULE 2. The want of trouble of soul for sin does not always arise from a stupefied conscience, but sometimes from an ignorant mind. If conscience had an eye to see sin, conscience would have a hand to smite for sin. Conscience therefore lacks a hand because man's judgment lacks an eye to discern what is evil.

RULE 3. Though a good man may not for some time be troubled for sin, yet at that time and in that case there is a great difference between him and a wicked man. He is not troubled, but he would be troubled. A wicked man is not disquieted, and he would never be disquieted; a godly man does not mourn, but he would mourn, and would love that minister who pierces his heart. A wicked man cannot endure him. There is a great difference between the one and the other. A good man dares not stifle the checks of conscience; a wicked man, when conscience begins to trouble him, does what he can to still the cries of conscience. When conscience arrests wicked men for debt, they run not unto God. They make conscience drunk with sensual pleasures and vain delights so that they may run away from conscience's arrest. Godly men dare not do this, but they cry to conscience, "Excuse me when I do well, and accuse me when I do ill." This is the behavior of a godly man.

4. Last, take this for comfort: though you do not have as much trouble for sin as you desire, yet you have as much as God accepts. It is a true rule in divinity that the desire for any grace is the grace itself; for to desire to believe is faith, and true desire to repent is repentance, and true desire to mourn for sin is mourning for sin. If you desire a troubled heart, that is a holy trouble.

It is a great mercy that Scripture accounts the desire of any grace as the grace itself. Worthy of your observation is Nehemiah 1:11: "O Lord, I beseech Thee, let now Thine ear be attentive to the prayer of Thy servant, and to the prayer of Thy servants, who desire to fear Thy name." Compare that passage with 5:15: "But the former governors that were before me were chargeable unto the people. But so did not I, because of the fear of the Lord." This notes that a desire to fear God is a fearing of God; a desire to repent is repenting; a desire to be troubled is a holy trouble, provided that it is solemn, sincere, and insatiable in seeking after any grace. Thus we read of Abraham. When God came to deal with

Abraham, what did God say to him? "Because thou hast done this deed, I will do so and so to you." But he had not actually done it. Divines gather that in God's account the desire and intention to do a good thing *is* the doing of it. Therefore, when Paul records Abraham's act, it is said that by faith he did it.

Beloved, it should be a great discomfort to ungodly men that the Scripture should say to us that a desire to do a sin is the sin. It is all one to God; therefore Christ tells you in Matthew 5:28, "He that looketh on a woman to lust after her hath committed adultery in his heart." The desire and the act are all one to God, though not to men. God looks on the lust of the eye to be the same as the uncleanness of the act. He who is angry with his brother, of him 1 John 3:15 says, "Whosoever hateth his brother is a murderer, and no murderer hath eternal life abiding in him." God looks on the desire to kill a man as if you had killed him.

Now, on the other hand, it should be a great comfort to godly men that the desire for grace is grace itself. I mention this to you who grieve because you cannot grieve, who do not mourn but would mourn. So much for the consolatory rules.

I shall only give you this use, and so shall finish this doctrine about the disquietings of the soul. And that is a use of caution to persuade you to take heed that you do not run into false mistakes touching disquiet of soul for sin. The devil may paint that which is not grace, and which is not true trouble of conscience and disquiet of mind for sin, as if it were. This is my caution to persuade you, that you may not be mistaken in this matter.

I shall give you cautions regarding several errors:

CAUTION 1. Take heed you do not mistake a natural melancholy for a godly sorrow and trouble of mind for sin. Many people whose tempers are sad, heavy, and dumpish apprehend melancholy to be a godly sorrow. There is a great difference between natural melancholy and spiritual trouble. First, natural melancholy has many apprehensions in the fancy, in the imagination; but spiritual trouble arises from the conscience upon the sense of God's wrath, the frowns of the Almighty, the greatness of sin, and the evil thereof.

Second, melancholy is cured by medicine. A physician is a proper help for a melancholy man, but all the medicine in the world cannot allay the disquiet of a godly man's soul.

Third, melancholy makes a man sad, but he cannot tell for what. But a man under spiritual trouble says, "This sin galls my conscience, and such a failing grieves my soul." This a melancholy man cannot do; he cannot identify a specific corruption that he is guilty of.

Fourth, melancholy is discerned by its natural complexion, a heavy eye or a grizzly look; but spiritual trouble on the conscience may be in the man who is of a merry, pleasant, amiable countenance. Therefore divines observe of David that the Scripture tells us he was a man of a ruddy complexion. The effect thereof is to be merry and pleasant; yet he grieved and roared under disquiet of soul for sin.

Again, melancholy impairs the health of the body, but sorrow for sin does not. A melancholy man cannot delight in God nor in duty, whereas a man under trouble of mind, though he is troubled for sin, can yet rejoice in God and delight in duty. Godly sorrow and spiritual joy are no way contradictory to each other, but rather subservient to each other.

CAUTION 2. Do not mistake that to be trouble of mind for sin which is only a trouble for some outward disaster in the world. When a man is troubled for the loss of a child or for the loss of an estate, many men deceive themselves and take that worldly sorrow to be spiritual trouble; if this were true, Ahithophel should be a troubled man for sin. He came home sad and hanged himself. Then Haman should have godly sorrow for he was troubled for crosses in the world. He came home sad and told all his friends what had befallen him. Beloved, you must not look upon worldly trouble to be spiritual trouble. Rather, when you find the heart overwhelmed with worldly trouble, oh, labor to direct it into spiritual trouble—to shed tears for sin as you shed tears for the loss of an estate! Why, turn that flood of tears to weep for sin, to turn the mill of godly sorrow, to grind your heart to powder in the sense of sin. It is a debasement to tears to be shed for every trifle. Beloved, to shed tears for worldly things is to be prodigal of your tears.

CAUTION 3. Do not conceive that to be trouble for sin that causes shame among men. Many reprobates are troubled for sin, but why? It is not because God receives dishonor by sin, but because they shall receive shame for their sin. This is not evangelical trouble.

Many men are like Judah, in Genesis 38:23: "And Judah said, 'Let her take it to her, lest we be ashamed; behold, I send this kid, and thou hast not found her.' " It is as if he had said, "If the woman should tell that I have committed adultery with her, I should be ashamed, so let her alone."

Thus men cry out that they would have conscience let them alone, and they would let sin alone lest they should be ashamed. If concealing a sin can conceal their shame, they care not. Why, heathens went beyond this! It is a saying of Seneca, "If I knew that all the men of the world were ignorant of what sin I had done, yet I would not sin because of the filthiness of sin." Tertullian had a notable passage, and it is to be wondered at that a heathen should go so far. He said that if we thought that all our sins could be concealed from all the world, yet we must do nothing covetously, nothing incontinently, nothing unjustly. We must do no evil though the world should never see us. Many men are more grieved for sin because it is a shame to them; this is not a gracious or evangelical trouble for sin.

CAUTION 4. Do not account that to be a right trouble for sin which is rather for the punishment of sin than for the evil nature of sin, or, which is more, because there is a hell *for* sin than that there is a hell *in* sin. Cain was more troubled for the punishment than for the sin. He cried out, "My punishment is more than I can bear." But Cain did not cry out, "My sin is greater that I have committed."

CAUTION 5. Do not account that to be a right disquiet and trouble of soul for sin which is only for great and gross acts of sin, without having any remorse for secret and lesser evils. Many men, if one stares them in the face, though all their other sins never trouble them, conclude that this is godly sorrow and evangelical remorse in them. Alas, beloved, Judas was troubled for one sin, but not for another sin. He was troubled for ill-gotten goods, but to be troubled for one sin and not for all sins is no gospel sorrow. He who is not troubled for every sin that he knows that he is guilty of is troubled for no sin.

Look upon wicked men, and you shall see them many times troubled for great evils, but never troubled for smaller evils. Those sins that disquiet a godly man's heart shall not seize a wink of sleep from the wicked man. He can go merrily and jocundly under the guilt of those sins which trouble the soul and break the peace of a godly, conscientious man all his days. Those sins that are ornaments to wicked men can be worn as a chain of gold about their necks. They wear and show their pride; they account sin to be their ornaments. But that which is one man's ornament is another man's torment. The wicked man's pride, lust, and oaths are his delight, but they are a torment to a godly man. Therefore do not account that disquiet of soul over great sins only to be a godly disquiet.

Again, do not account that to be an evangelical trouble for sin when it is not for original sin as well as actual sin. Mr. [Robert] Bolton tells you of a German in his time who was a great professor of religion, and he was once overtaken in drink. He says, "I went to this man to show him the evil of drunkenness, to let him see what a beast-like sin it was, what a swinish sin it was. I labored to show him what this was. I labored to make him see the evil of a drunken nature; and he would yield to me that drunkenness was a bad sin, but he would not admit to the wickedness of his nature." This man bewailed the act of drunkenness and fell to other sins; yet at last God troubled this man again and, being perplexed, he sent for the same man again and said, "Now I believe your words. I find an unclean heart, an adulterous heart, a drunken heart. I see it is now worse than a drunken act." And afterwards he never fell to those sins again.

Thus I have in seventeen sermons gone over the distresses the Psalmist here complains of: "Why art thou cast down, O my soul? and why art thou disquieted within me?"

A Treatise of Angels

"Are they not all ministering spirits, sent forth to minister for them who shall be heirs of salvation?"
Hebrews 1:14

A Treatise of Angels

The main scope of the apostle in this chapter is to show the excellent dignity of Jesus Christ surpassing the chiefest creatures, the angels, and that he proves by these six arguments:

1. He sets out the dignity of Jesus Christ above the angels in that He had a more excellent name than the angels had. And that is laid down in verse 4: "Being made so much better than the angels, as He hath by inheritance obtained a more excellent name than they." Jesus Christ had a better name than the angels. The angels are the servants of God, but Jesus Christ is called the Son of God.

2. Although the Scripture calls the angels the sons of God (Job 38:7: "When the morning stars sang together, and all the sons of God shouted for joy"), yet Jesus Christ is the Son of God in a more eminent manner than the angels are. Therefore you may read in verse 5: "To which of the angels said He at any time, 'Thou art My Son, this day I have begotten thee'?" And again, 'I will be to Him a father, and He shall be to Me a son'?" Although the angels are the sons of God, yet the Scripture does not say that they are the begotten sons of God, but about Jesus Christ it is said that He is the begotten Son of God. They are the sons of God by creation, but Jesus Christ is the eternal Son of God by eternal generation, and therefore is far above the angels.

3. Jesus Christ is higher than the angels because they are ordained by God the Father to worship Jesus

Christ the Son, and that you have expressed and laid down in verse 6: "And again, when He bringeth in the first-begotten into the world, He saith, 'And let all the angels of God worship Him.' " Jesus Christ's dignity and honor are far above the dignity of angels, because the angels themselves are commanded to fall down and worship, and yield obedience to Him.

4. Jesus Christ is far above the angels because the angels are made by Him, and they are but His ministering spirits; that is laid down in verse 7: "And of the angels He saith, 'Who maketh His angels spirits, and His ministers a flaming fire.' " Not only are angels made by Jesus Christ, but all things are made by Him that are made, both those which are in heaven and those on earth. He made His angels ministering spirits, and His ministers flames of fire, and therefore He must be above them.

5. It is said that Jesus Christ sat down at the right hand of the majesty on high, verse 13: "But to which of the angels said He at any time, 'Sit Thou at My right hand, till I make Thine enemies Thy footstool'?" The angels are not to sit at the right hand of God, but Christ has sat down on the right hand of God; they are to serve Jesus Christ, and that for the sake of the elect of God in the world.

6. This is how Jesus Christ is far above them in dignity and honor, for so says our text in verse 14: "Are they not all ministering spirits, sent forth to minister for them who shall be heirs of salvation?" And thus you see I have led you by the hand unto the words themselves.

"Are they not all ministering spirits?" This is not a doubtful interrogation, but a plain and strong affirmation that they are so. It is to be understood as if the words were spoken positively and affirmatively.

"All." There are no angels but those who are made ministering spirits to the elect, the people of God who shall be heirs of salvation. Indeed, the popish interpreters say that there are some angels of the higher orders who are like the cherubims; they serve God only, because they are of a higher nature. They cite Daniel 7:10: "A fiery stream issued and came forth before him; a thousand thousands ministered to him." But this is only a fancy. They serve God in serving us. Again you see that the Apostle tells you they are all ministering spirits without exception.

"Ministering spirits." The word here put for ministering signifies a public officer who puts himself out to the utmost, even with all his might, to do good in the place whereunto he belongs and whereunto he is cast. The same word you have in Romans 13:6: "For this cause pay you tribute; for they are God's ministers, attending continually upon this very thing." So these ministers make it their great work to do good to the people of God.

"Sent forth by God." The word is in the present tense in the Greek to show that it was not any transient act in God, but it was a continued act to all generations that they should be continually ministering spirits to the elect of God in the world.

"For those that shall be heirs of salvation." It is made their peculiar privilege to have angels to attend them. Those who are slaves and drudges to the devil shall not have good angels to attend them.

The papists say that wicked men have angels to attend them as well as the people of God. Daniel 10:20: "Knowest thou wherefore I am come unto thee? And now will I return to fight with the prince of Persia; and when I am gone forth, lo, the prince of Greece shall come in." In answer to this, consider that there is a question whether the angels there spoken of are the angels of God, or whether they were not to be understood as some great men who were sent by God to assist the Persian against the enemies of the people of God.

If it were an angel, yet this assistance was not for his own sake, but for the sake of the people of God. But I shall not trouble you with matters of controversy, but shall come more directly to the words themselves.

And in the text there are three parts, or three particulars, to be considered:

First, the nature of angels: they are spirits, not bodies, as Origen, Damascen, and others of the ancients thought.

Second, their office or work: they are ministering spirits; they are servants of Jesus Christ.

Third, the particular persons unto whom the angels do minister: not to all, but to those who are and shall be heirs of salvation.

These are the three particulars in the text. I intend not to trouble you with many metaphysical and philosophical notions concerning angels, such as their number, distinct orders, the apparition of angels, and whether they assume bodies. I shall only handle the doctrine of angels in that sense the apostle here points to.

DOCTRINE: The angels of heaven have a commission and charge from God to be useful and serviceable to the elect here upon the earth. "Are they not all ministering spirits sent out from God for them that are heirs of salvation?"

A Treatise of Angels

The doctrine is of great use and comfort to believers. Now in handling and prosecuting this doctrine, I shall do these three things:

First, I will show wherein the serviceableness of angels towards the elect consists.

Second, I will show why God gives His angels such a charge and commission to serve the elect, and to preserve them, seeing that God is able to preserve them Himself.

Third, I will show whether every elect person has one particular angel to attend him, or if they have more.

QUESTION 1. What benefit do the elect have by the service of angels?

I shall lay it down both negatively and positively.

Negatively. They are not our mediators; their work does not relate to any piece or part of mediatorship to God, to appear before God to plead there on our behalf, to present our prayers before God. That is Christ's office, not theirs. The papists suppose the angels to be mediators to God for us, and they ground this idea on Tobit 12:12: "Now therefore when thou didst pray, and Sara thy daughter-in-law, I did bring the remembrance of your prayers before the Holy One." But it is condemned by all interpreters that it should be the work of angels to carry our prayers for us. This is an old error, and there is another similar one, that they were sharers with God in the work of creation.

But so that none might be ensnared with this conceit, the apostle exhorts the Colossians against this in Colossians 2:18: "Let no man beguile you of your reward in a voluntary humility, and worshipping of angels, intruding into those things which he hath not seen, vainly puffed up by his fleshly mind." Here the apostle forewarns them that they should not be overtaken with the worshipping of angels and the mediation of angels. They are not ministering spirits in the sense of being our intercessors before God, for that is only the work of the angel of the covenant, the Lord Jesus Christ. It is His office alone to appear before God His Father for us on our behalf. It is He alone who appears before God for us, and by the sweet perfume of His incense He makes our persons and performances accepted before God. So no angel in heaven has any share in the mediation and intercession before the Father on behalf of the people of God.

Positively. The angels are ministering spirits to serve the people of God, the elect in the world. And to make this good, I shall commend to your consideration these particulars.

First, the angels are said to be servants to the people of God in this regard: they are a guard to preserve the elect of God here in the world from outward danger. Psalm 91:9–12: "Because thou hast made the Lord which is my refuge, even the Most High, thy habitation, there shall no evil befall thee, neither shall any plague come near thy dwelling. For He shall give His angels charge over thee to keep thee in all thy ways. They shall bear thee upon their hands, lest thou dash thy foot against a stone." These words are applied to Christ in the New Testament. In Matthew 4:6, when the devil came to tempt Christ to worship him, he quoted this passage: "For He hath given His angels charge over Thee; in their hands they shall bear Thee, lest at any time Thou dash Thy foot against a stone." Although this is applied to Jesus Christ, yet it is also to be applied to all believers in the Old Testament before Christ, as in the New Testament since Christ. Psalm 34:7: "The angel of the Lord encampeth round about them that fear Him, and delivereth them."

So likewise, in Genesis 32:1–2, you read that as Jacob went on his way the angels of the Lord met him. "And when Jacob saw them, he said, 'This is God's host.' " Here angels are called the Lord's host that guarded Jacob. So also you read that it was an angel that rescued Lot out of Sodom so that he was not buried with the wicked of that city, in Genesis 19:15.

Likewise, in Revelation it is said that John saw four angels in the four corners of the earth, and they were commanded not to hurt the earth until "we have sealed the servants of our God in their foreheads." It is in Revelation 7:1–3: "And after these things, I saw four angels standing on the four corners of the earth, holding the four winds of the earth, that the wind should not blow on the earth, nor on the sea, nor on any tree. And I saw another angel ascending from the east, having the seal of the living God; and he cried with a loud voice to the four angels to whom it was given to hurt the earth and the sea, saying, 'Hurt not the earth, neither the sea, nor the trees, till we have sealed the servants of our God in their foreheads.' " Here was a time of great persecution of the church and people of God on the earth, but persecution was not to come until the people of God were in a way of protection and safety. And after that, let it come and let them slay as soon as they would. This protection is given by the ministry of angels, whom God uses to preserve His people so that they are not hurt, to be a safeguard for them from outward dangers in this life.

Angels preserve us in all ages. Rogers said the angels are rockers of little children when in the cradle (Matthew 18:10). So in all places: at sea an angel comforted Paul (Acts 27:23–24); on land an angel guided Jacob in his journey to Mesopotamia (Genesis 28); in prison Peter had his fetters knocked off by an angel (Acts 12). As evil angels bring diseases, so good angels help to remove them.

Second, the serviceableness of angels consists in this: they avenge the injuries and wrongs that are done to the elect by their enemies. Hebrews 1:7: "Who maketh His angels spirits, and His ministers a flaming fire." The angels are called seraphim not only because they burn in love for God, but because they are ready to avenge the wrongs done to the elect and are ready to burn the enemies of the people of God. Therefore wicked men are exhorted to take heed how they wrong any of the people of God. Matthew 18:10: "Take heed that you despise not one of these little ones, for I say unto you that in heaven their angels do always behold the face of my Father which is in heaven."

Now how can that be a reason that they should not despise them, because angels behold the face of God? Because they behold the face of God, they are ready to avenge those who do them wrong; and they wait upon God to execute His wrath upon all those who do His people harm. In 2 Kings 19:35 you read that when Sennacherib came to destroy the people of God, an angel of God smote the Assyrians for it: "And it came to pass that night that an angel of the Lord went out and smote in the camp of the Assyrians an hundred fourscore and five thousand; and when they arose early in the morning, behold they were all dead corpses."

A Treatise of Angels

So likewise you read how Herod vexed the church of God in Acts 12:1–2: "Now about that time Herod stretched forth his hands to vex certain of the church, and he killed James the brother of John with the sword." And for this act of cruelty you find that it is said, in verse 23, that an angel of the Lord smote Herod: "And immediately an angel of the Lord smote him."

In Revelation 16, seven vials were to be poured out upon the earth, which work was done by the angels. For they are always ready to be the executioners of God's wrath for the people of God upon the enemies who do them wrong. And herein we have cause to bless God for the ministrations of angels, that angels should be so serviceable to the people of God who live on the earth, to be a guard to preserve them while they live in the world.

Third, the angels are serviceable to the people of God in that God has made them instruments to reveal a great part of God's will and mind to the church of God, which otherwise they would not have known. The law was ordained by angels in Galatians 3:19: "Wherefore then serveth the law? It was added because of transgressions, till the seed should come unto whom the promise was made, and it was ordained by angels in the hand of a mediator." So likewise in Acts 7:53: "Who have received the law by the disposition of angels, and have not kept it." Here you see that God used the ministry of angels at the giving of the law. So in Daniel 9:22 you read that the vision was made known to Daniel by an angel: "And he (the angel) informed me, and talked with me, and said, 'O Daniel, I am now come forth to give thee skill and understanding.'" As it was an angel that informed him of the vision, so it was an angel that told him of the death of Christ; and, had not an angel told him, he could not have known it in those days, which was so long before the coming of Jesus Christ in the flesh, but this was revealed to him by the ministration of angels.

The birth of Christ was made known by an angel (Luke 1:26, 2:10–11). The great doctrine of Jesus Christ's resurrection was revealed by angels in Matthew 28:5: "The angel said unto the women, 'Fear not, for I know that you seek Jesus which was crucified.' " We would not have known the manner of His coming in judgment if an angel had not told us in Acts 1:11: "This Jesus which is taken from you into heaven shall so come in like manner as you have seen Him go into heaven."

So by all this you may see how much we are beholden to the angels, and to bless God for them, in that He should by them make known so great a part of His will and mind to His people, which otherwise would not have been revealed to us.

Fourth, the angels have a great hand in bringing and settling faithful ministers to convert and edify the people of God. Acts 16:9–10: "And a vision did appear to Paul in the night; there stood a man of Macedonia, and prayed him, saying, 'Come over into Macedonia and help us.' And after he had seen the vision, immediately he endeavored to go into Macedonia, assuredly gathering that the Lord hath called us to preach the gospel to them." This man of Macedonia was an angel that appeared to Paul and bade him come over to Macedonia to preach the gospel. There was much work for him to do there, and by his going many were brought in unto the profession of the gospel; and this was a call from God by an angel.

Likewise you read that an angel directed Philip to preach the gospel in Acts 8:26: "And the angel of the Lord spake unto Philip, saying, 'Arise, and go toward the south unto the way that goeth down from Jerusalem unto Gaza, which is desert.' " And verse 35: "And Philip opened his mouth and preached unto him Jesus." Here an angel directed Philip to the eunuch to preach.

Likewise you read in Acts 10:3–6 of Cornelius, a devout man fearing God: "He saw in a vision, about the ninth hour of the day, an angel of God coming in to him, and saying unto him, 'Cornelius.' And when he had looked on him, he was afraid, and said, 'What is it, Lord?' And He said, 'Thy prayers and thine alms have come up as a memorial before God. And now send men to Joppa, and call for one Simon, whose surname is Peter; he lodgeth with one Simon a tanner, whose house is by the seaside, he shall tell thee what thou oughtest to do.' " Here you see that the angel did not preach to Cornelius, but directed him to call Peter to tell him what he must do. Cornelius was to go to Joppa to hear Peter preach to him, and Philip was to go to Gaza to preach to the eunuch, so that by this means they brought in souls to Jesus Christ. This Zanchius cites to prove that one special office of the angels is to preserve the ministers of the church and to guide them where their ministry shall do most good to souls.

Fifth, the angels rejoice at the conversion of an elect man in the world. The angels in heaven rejoice to see an elect man called home and brought in by conversion to Jesus Christ. This you have laid down in Luke 15:10: "Likewise, I say unto you, there is joy in the presence of the angels of God over one sinner that repenteth." Augustine said, "Your being good or doing good makes the angels rejoice and be glad, the devils sad; but when you do evil you please the devil and rob the angels of their comfort."

Sixth, the angels do unknown service in comforting and counseling the elect when they are in sorrows, troubles, and straits, God makes use of them in this way in Daniel 8:16: "Gabriel, make this man understand the vision." And in 9:22: "I am come to give thee wisdom and understanding." This you have laid down in Genesis 21:17. When Hagar was sad, it is said that an angel of the Lord came to comfort her: "And God heard the voice of the lad, and the angel of the Lord called to her, and said, 'What aileth thee, Hagar? Fear not, for God hath heard the voice of the lad where he is.' " In this sad distress she was in, the angel of God came to her and comforted her. So likewise you read in Luke 2:10 that when the shepherds were looking for Christ they were afraid when the glory of the Lord shone round about them: "And the angel of the Lord came unto them, and said, 'Fear not, for behold, I bring you tidings of great joy, which shall be to all people.' "

Likewise, in Matthew 28:5, when Mary went to the sepulcher of Christ, the angel appeared to her and said to the woman, "Fear not, for I know that ye seek Jesus which was crucified." And to comfort her heart under this fear he said in verse 6–7: "He is not here, but is risen, as He said. Come see the place where the Lord lay, and go quickly and tell His disciples that He is risen." All this is to show the great use and advantage that the people of God have by the ministration of angels, as in this case, to comfort them, and counsel them in any distress and danger.

Seventh, the ministrations of angels are used by God to keep the people of God from committing much sin against God, and herein they are of great use. Jude 9: "Yet Michael the archangel, when contending with the devil about the body of Moses, durst not bring against him a railing accusation, but said, 'The Lord rebuke thee.' " The angel would not tell where the body of Moses was, because the people would have been ready to make an idol of his body; and out of love for them he would not let the devil know where the body of Moses was, so that he might not show it to them lest the knowledge of it might have been an occasion of sinning against God.

Hagar fled from the face of her mistress in Genesis 16:6–9, but an angel of the Lord appeared to Hagar and bade her take heed of sinning: "And the angel of the Lord said unto her, 'Return to thy mistress, and submit thyself to her.' " If Hagar had continued in the way she was in, she might have committed much sin against God. So herein also appears the usefulness of angels in doing good to the people of God, in that they keep them from occasions of sinning against Him.

Eighth, the angels are present with us, beholding us in our church assemblies when we come to worship before God. When you are in the worship and service of God, the angels are with you, beholding you though you see them not. As the angels behold us in our sufferings (1 Corinthians 4:9), so they also behold our acts of worship. This is hinted at in 1 Corinthians 11:10: "For this cause ought the woman to have power on her head, because of the angels." Some refer these words to ministers, who are elsewhere called angels, but we may understand it of the angels themselves because they delight in the things of the gospel. Here the apostle speaks of women not coming into church without covering. Why? Because of the angels, not the ministers. It is meant of the angels of heaven, and therein the women are to take heed how they come into the church, because the angels are spectators and behold how you behave yourselves, they being fellow-worshippers of God with you in church assemblies. And this should make you take heed of your carriage; for although they do not know your hearts, yet they behold your carriage as you come into the presence of God. The angels behold your uncomely gestures, and they behold your wanton dresses; and therefore this should put an awe upon your spirits how you appear before God in public assemblies, so that you do not appear before God with your indecent dresses and naked breasts, like prostitutes, and naked arms, like inmates at an asylum—such fashions do not become those who worship God, especially seeing that angels behold us in our worshipping Him.

Ninth, the angels not only behold us in our church assemblies, but they are also instruments in the hand of God to provoke us to the worship of God. That is Zanchius's opinion on Revelation 22:9: "See thou do it not, for I am thy fellow-servant, and of thy brethren the prophets, and of them which keep the sayings of this book; worship God." John would have worshipped the angel and fallen down to him, but was told, no, worship God; and this interpretation is reasonable, for why may not good angels provoke men to worship God as well as evil angels stir up and provoke wicked men to sin

A Treatise of Angels

against God, and to make them grow weary of good duties? This may be done, and is no derogation from the Spirit working. He does it as the author, but they do it as instruments to provoke you to do the good that the Spirit of God is the author of.

Tenth, angels are instruments to wait upon you when you are dying, and not only so, but to carry the soul to eternal life after death (I put those two together). And this you have recorded in Luke 16:22: "And it came to pass that the beggar died, and was carried by the angels into Abraham's bosom." Here you see that Lazarus died, and the angels attended him and carried his soul into Abraham's bosom, into heaven. Oh, think then that when we are all to die God has made the angels ministering spirits to attend to you upon your sick beds, so that when you shall die they will take your souls and carry them into heaven.

Eleventh, the angels are serviceable to the elect in that they are sent out by Jesus Christ to gather together the bodies of the elect at the great day to be their guard, and to bring them before the Lord Jesus Christ so that they then and there may receive the sentence of absolution and be taken up to glory. This particular is clearly laid down in Matthew 24:31: "And He shall send His angels with a great sound of a trumpet, and they shall gather together His elect from the four winds, from one end of heaven unto the other." Mark 13:27: "And then shall He send His angels, and shall gather together His elect from the four winds, from the utmost parts of the earth to the utmost parts of heaven." Here you see clearly laid down the work of the angels for the elect in this particular. Also, they shall not only gather them from the utmost parts of the earth, but also they will carry you to heaven, even to the utmost parts of heaven.

I lay these things before you that you may see the great and high privilege that the elect are made partakers of by virtue of the interest they have in Jesus Christ. God ordains and gives a commission and charge to His angels to do all these eleven offices for you. That is what I have presented for your consideration.

OBJECTION. But there may arise an objection in some men's spirits: "It is true, we have read and heard that angels in times past have done such offices for men; but then they appeared to them in bodily shapes, as they did to Lot, David, and others. But do the angels do the same offices for the saints now as they did for the saints of old?"

ANSWER. There are two things to be considered in answering this objection.

1. The angels are no less present with us now than they were with the people of God of old, though they are less visible. The reason why the angels appeared visibly to the saints of old was that the people of God were but children, and they needed bodily appearances to make them believe, and to make them strong and strengthen them in the faith. But the presence of the angels is with us in these ages of the world as well as before, for they guard you in your house for your good and benefit if you are an elect man. Your house is full of angels though you cannot see them. You cannot lie down, nor rise up, nor do anything, but you have the angels to be your guard and protect you.

2. The Scripture does not say that the angels *were* ministering spirits, but that the angels *are* ministering spirits; not that they were so only in times past, but they

are so still; not that they are ministering spirits for the present, but that they shall be so even for them who shall be heirs of salvation. So for later ages the angels shall be ministering spirits as well as they have been in former times; and therefore the angels do not appear in human shapes now, yet they have their office and their administration in as full a measure now as they had in former ages when they were seen in visible shapes.

QUESTION 2. But why does the Lord use this ministration of angels in reference to His elect? Cannot the Lord preserve them Himself?

ANSWER. I answer that it is not a necessary good, but a voluntary one; not as if God stood in any need of angels, for God does not. He needs none of His angels. Without them He could accomplish His own glorious ends. But for God's good will and pleasure He will have them minister for the good of His elect people while they live in the world. And there are four glorious and gracious ends toward which God uses the ministration of angels in reference to His own people's good here in this world.

The first end is to manifest the reconciliation and agreement that is between the angels in heaven and the saints on earth. The fall of man made a distinction between angels and men. Man, being thus fallen and an enemy to God, was at enmity with and separated from angels. Jesus Christ, by His cross, reconciled both men and angels. Now God uses the ministration of angels to declare this, and to manifet the reconciliation that is between not only God and man, but angels and men. Colossians 1:20: "Having made peace through the blood of His cross, by Him to reconcile all things to Himself; by Him, I say, whether they be things in earth, or things in heaven."

The Scripture makes mention of two types of reconcilation. The first is the reconcilation of men with men, and so Jews and Gentiles were reconciled. Second, there was a reconciliation in heaven between the angels in heaven and men on earth by Jesus Christ, and so He reconciled both to God. This reconciliation being wrought and perfected between men and angels and man and man, God now uses angels to make it manifest. He makes use of the ministration of angels to declare to the world that there is an agreement and a reconciliation between the angels in heaven and the saints on earth.

The second end is to declare to the world His great love for His people and His good will towards them, that He should be so graciously pleased to give to His own people such noble attendants as angels are. If you serve God, angels shall serve you. This is to show the high, unspeakable love that God bears toward His own people, that those who are God's own attendants, waiting upon Him round about His glorious throne, should be ordained by God to attend those who shall be heirs of salvation.

The third end is the reparation of that ruin which befell some of the angels; for some of the angels fell and were cast out of heaven (the loss was great). Now the elect, all who are saved by Jesus Christ, supply the place of the fallen angels. Both saints and angels make up one body; both sing praises to God. And all the saints, when they go to heaven, are employed in the same work that the fallen angels once were in. Knowing that this was the reparation of the loss makes the angels so willing in their service to and preservation of the people of God while they live on earth.

The fourth end is that the Lord thinks it fit to use the ministration of angels for the good of His elect children. Wicked angels, the devils, attend the saints to do them hurt while they live in the world. Therefore God uses those angels for the preservation of His elect while they live in the world. For the wicked angels make it their work continually to tempt them, and, if it were possible, to damn them, and ruin their souls. Therefore God gives His angels charge to preserve them and keep the elect from the envy, rage, and malice of the devil who seeks to devour and destroy them.

And these are the four reasons why God thinks it fit to use the ministration of angels for the elect's sake.

QUESTION 3. But when the Scripture says that the angels are ministering spirits sent forth by God to minister to them who are heirs of salvation, does the Scripture intend that every elect man has his particular angel to attend upon him, or do they have more?

ANSWER. The Platonists hold that every man has his angel, which they call his genius, which still protected him, and did many other good offices. Some of the ancient fathers incline that way, and most of the schoolmen. Thomas Aquinas, Origen, Basil, and Theodoret were of this mind. Among the modern divines Zanchius seems to incline this way. The chief place he builds on is Acts 12:15: "Then they said, 'It is his angel.' " The story goes thus: When Peter was in prison, and the church made prayers for his liberty, in the meantime he came to the door, and a maid ran to them and told them that it was Peter. The text says in verse 15: "And they said unto her, 'Thou art mad,' but she constantly affirmed it that it was even so; then said they, 'It is his angel.' " So from this text they gather that every good man has his angel to attend him, to be his guard. Now to give you a true sense and exposition of this verse, I shall offer these particulars.

First, I shall give you this answer: the word there rendered "an angel" is as much as to say "his messenger." It is his messenger, for the word signifies a messenger as well as an angel. So you find in Luke 7:24: "When the messengers of John were departed." There is the same word; it signifies a messenger as well as an angel. When the Scripture says, "It is his angel," it is as much as if they had said, "It was some messenger sent from Peter from the prison."

This is the reason why Gualter judges these words to import the weakness of the disciples in following the superstition of the people of those times, and that they spoke according to the fancies of the heathen who held tutelar gods.

Diodati gives this interpretation. He says among the Jews were frequent apparitions of dead persons, who were thought to be the spirits of the persons whom they represented. So they followed the popular opinion and thought Peter's death was inevitable, seeing that his spirit began to appear.

Another gives this answer from the text, that it will not hold out to maintain this opinion upon these words, for it is said that "when they saw him, they were astonished." As they were confused in their conceptions, so they might be as confused in their expressions, and so they might not speak so properly when

A Treatise of Angels

they said, "It is his angel."

The reasons against this interpretation are these:

It seems to have its rise from a bad origin, to wit, from the delusions of the heathen who said that every man had his good and bad genius, or angel, to attend them—good angels to do them good and bad angels to do them hurt, good angels to reward them and bad angels to punish them.

As it has a bad rise, so it has bad effects and it produces bad effects.

First, it countenances the Cabalistic divinity of the doting Jews. They assigned angels to every planet—to the sun, Raphael; to the moon, Gabriel; to Mercury, Michael; and so forth—and also to the four parts of the world: to the east, Michael; to the west, Raphael; to the north, Gabriel; and to the south, Nariel.

It would seem to give way and footing to particular saints to be for particular places: St. James for Spain, St. Denis for France, St. Patrick for Ireland, St. George for England. And to hold this opinion about angels would be an inlet to that opinion.

More especially, maintaining that opinion would greatly eclipse and seem to diminish the privileges that God has given to all the elect, that all the angels are said to be ministering spirits to serve them. To single out one angel from all the rest of the angels in heaven to preserve and guard one particular person would derogate and diminish and lessen the saints' privileges.

It is said that the angels rejoice over one sinner who repents. Luke 15:10: "Likewise I say unto you, there is joy in the presence of the angels of heaven over one sinner that repenteth." So likewise in Luke 16:22: "And it came to pass that the beggar died, and was carried by the angels into Abraham's bosom." Now if there had been but one particular angel assigned to him, it would not have been rendered "angels," but "angel"; but it is said expressly that the angels carried his soul into Abraham's bosom.

Likewise, when Esau came with an army against Jacob, Jacob saw many angels and said that they were "the angels of God," the host of God. So it is in 2 Kings 6:17. When Elisha saw the multitude of the enemies who came against him, there were many angels that compassed him round about against them: "And Elisha prayed and said, 'Lord, I pray Thee, open his eyes that he may see.' And the Lord opened the eyes of the young man and he saw; and behold, the mountain was full of horses and chariots and fire round about Elisha." And these were the angels of God who were his guard to preserve him. One angel was sent to destroy Sennacherib's host, many angels to preserve one godly man.

The fourth reason why one angel is not the guard of one man alone is that wicked men have not only one wicked angel, but many wicked angels to attend them. And therefore, if wicked men have more than one wicked angel to accompany and attend them, then, similarly, good men must have more than one good angel to secure and guard them. For sometimes it is said that a wicked man has legions, that is, many to attend him, and many possessing one person, as in the case of Mary Magdalene. Then surely a good man has more angels than one to protect and save him from hurt; and if it is granted that particular angels have their commission to guard particular persons, then it will follow that there are some particular angels that are not employed for the good and benefit of the elect. For it must be supposed that there are more angels in heaven than there are men on earth, for if there are fewer angels than men, then every man cannot have his particular angel to protect him; and if there are more angels in heaven than there are men on earth, which certainly there are (as in Daniel 7:10: "A thousand thousands ministered unto him, and ten thousand times ten thousand stood before him"), then if only one angel should minister unto one man and no more, then all the rest of the angels that were more in number are of no use, and not at all employed for the good of the elect, the people of God. So consequently it overthrows this text, which affirms that they are all ministering spirits, sent forth to minister to those who shall be heirs of salvation.

And so much for this question. There is now only one particular more before I give you the use.

OBJECTION. "But," you may say, "you indeed speak much from the Scripture touching the service and benefit of angels to the elect servants of God; but it makes us question whether it is true or not, because we know not when or how they were created. For, indeed, Moses tells us of man's creation, but he never speaks of the creation of angels."

ANSWER. To answer this objection, I shall only lay down a word or two concerning the creation of angels. For though the Sadducees deny angels and spirits, yet there are such spiritual, incorporeal essences created by God for His glory and the good of the elect. Now as for the time when they were created, it was in one of the six days, and before man was made, else there would have been no devil to tempt man. Some place it on the second day, because the evil angels fell the day they were made. Therefore it is not said of that day, "God saw that what He had made was good." Others put it on the fourth day, because in Genesis 1:16 the heavens were then adorned and completed, but most probably it was on the third day when the heavens were made, just as man was made upon the sixth day when the earth was finished. Job 38:6–7: "When the foundations of the earth were laid, the morning stars sang together and all the sons of God shouted for joy." So Psalm 148:2–3. The psalmist invites the creatures to praise God, beginning with the angels: "Praise Him all ye His angels." But I only touch upon this.

Concerning the time of their creation, it matters not when they were created; there is no matter of scruple or great doubt arising from hence with regard to their ministration and office.

They are created for the good of the people of God. The text is clear that they are all ministering spirits sent forth for the good of those who shall be heirs of salvation. They were created for the glory of God and the good of His elect. So you see that the office of angels is to minister for the good of the elect in the world.

And thus I have covered the doctrinal part of the text, wherein I have shown you where the ministry of angels consists. I then gave you the reasons why God makes use of angels to minister to His people, and then I showed you that one elect man has not one particular angel to attend him, but more—all the angels are in commission to minister for the good of the elect.

I now come to give you the uses of this doctrine.

USE 1. If God has given a charge and commission to all the angels in heaven to minister to the elect of God for their good, oh, then, how should this allure you to labor to become heirs of salvation! Oh, why will you delight to continue to be objects of God's wrath, to be heirs of hell and damnation, and to be without this guard of the angels of heaven, who are ordained by God to minister unto such who shall be saved? Oh, why shall not this invite you, and so allure you to come in to have interest in Jesus Christ, that you thereby may come to lay claim to this ministration of angels, and to have this protection and guard from them? Why will you run into ways of sin and into paths of ungodliness and iniquity, and so shut yourself out from this guard of angels? "God hath given His angels charge to keep you in all your ways" (Psalm 91:11), if you will come in to Jesus Christ to embrace Him; if you will not go in this way, you may be sure you will never be under His angels' protection.

USE 2. This shows the dignity of the people of God, although they may be but poor and mean in this present world. What if you are a poor, despised person, a poor wretch in the eyes of the world, even the scorn of men in this world? Yet if you are an elect person, a man or woman in Jesus Christ, you are invested into high privileges; you are a person of high dignity and in high esteem, though not with the world, yet in the esteem and account of God and Jesus Christ. If you are in the condition of a poor servant in this world, yet you are an honorable person in the sight of God; and your honor is such that you have honorable attendants to protect and guard you. You have the angels of God to guard and keep you in all your ways. It is said that King Solomon had two hundred men with targets and three hundred men with shields of beaten gold every day to defend him. Yet you, O godly man and woman, have a greater guard than Solomon had. You, O man, have all the angels of God to be your guard and to be ministering spirits unto you to guard and guide you in all your ways.

USE 3. This teaches us to bless, praise, and admire God's goodness to us, that such excellent, glorious creatures as the angels of heaven serve us on earth.

And so, having spoken in general, I come to handle those particulars wherein God in a special manner uses the ministration of angels for the elect.

1. *The Lord has used the ministering of angels to preserve the elect from bodily sickness in the times of infection and common mortality.* I shall give you one text to prove this, Psalm 91:10–12: "There shall no evil befall thee, neither shall any plague come nigh thy dwelling. For He shall give His angels charge over thee, to keep thee in all thy ways. They shall bear thee up in their hands, lest thou dash thy foot against a stone." Although it is true that good men may die by sickness in a common calamity, yet, for all that, they are under such a protection that the rest of the world have not. For they are under the protection of the angels which God has promised, and He has given them a commission to protect them in all their ways.

Therefore it is very observable what the Scripture ascribes to the ministration of angels when there is a pestilence or some other great and sore disease among a people. The Scripture ascribes to wicked angels that

God suffers that they are able to bring and cause sickness among a people for the sins of the place wherein they live. This is expressed in Psalm 78:49–50: "He cast upon them the fierceness of His anger, wrath, and indignation, and trouble, by sending evil angels among them. He made a way for His anger; He spared not their souls from death, but gave them over unto the pestilence." Here you see that God suffers the evil angels to inflict diseases and slay the people by sickness. Now as God suffers the evil angels to do this, so He also has ordained the good angels to preserve His people in a special manner from these calamities.

The devil sometimes has permission from God to afflict the body, for he afflicted the body of Job with boils. In Luke 13:16 we read of a daughter of Abraham who was bound by Satan for eighteen years. And so God here suffered the evil angels to bring evils among His people. And as the Lord suffers and permits the evil angels to bring diseases and troubles upon His people, so God gives commission to the good angels to preserve them from sickness. The devil has power to stir up the blood, and to infect it by stirring up those evil humors that are in a man's body, and thereby to cause diseases in the body. And as the devils can do this by virtue of the permission that they have from God, so, on the contrary, God has given a commission unto good angels to preserve His people from those distempers and bodily diseases by being a safeguard to them in time of common infection.

2. The second particular office of angels for the good of God's elect is this: *they have a special influence in ordering and disposing of military affairs.* The angels not only stand as onlookers and spectators to behold af-

fairs, but they have a particular charge from God to preserve that side which stands most for His glory. And this you have laid down in 2 Kings 19:35. When the Assyrians came against Israel, it is said that the angel of the Lord smote them: "And it came to pass that night, that the angel of the Lord went out and smote in the camp of the Assyrians a hundred fourscore and five thousand, and when they arose early in the morning, behold, they were all dead corpses." Here you see how the angel of God preserved His people, and was an instrument of that great success they had against their enemies.

So also it was in Genesis 32:2. When Jacob was on his journey and in danger, the angels of God met him to comfort and preserve him, and he called them the host of God. Likewise in Psalm 68:17: "The chariots of God are twenty thousand, even thousands of angels." As the chariots in war were a defense to them, so the angels of God are called the chariots of God for the preservation of His people in their time of trouble. Therefore you read in 2 Kings 6:14–18 that the angels of God were a safeguard to His people in time of war. Elisha was in great straits, for the enemies had compassed him round about. "And he prayed to the Lord and said, 'Smite this people, I pray Thee, with blindness'; and the Lord smote them with blindness." That is, the angel of the Lord smote the enemies that His servants might be delivered.

There are many who hold that the angels had bodily shapes to decide the quarrel and controversy between the people of God and their enemies. So in Zechariah 1:8 you read that Zechariah saw in a vision a man standing among the myrtle trees: "I saw by night, and behold, a man riding upon a red horse; and he stood among the myrtle trees that were in the bottom, and behind him were red horses, speckled, and white." The scope of the prophet is to set out the low condition of the church by one standing in the bottom behind the myrtle trees. By the red, speckled, and white horses, are meant, said Junius, angels appointed for several works: the red horses for judgment, the white for mercy, the speckled horses set out those who were destined for mixed actions, at once to protect the godly and execute wrath upon the wicked.

3. *God uses the ministry of angels, in the disposing of the solemn state of marriage, for the comfort and good of His own people.* This you have laid down in Genesis 24:7: "The Lord God of heaven, which took me from my father's house, and from the land of my kindred, and which spake unto me, and that swore unto me, saying, 'Unto thy seed will I give this land,' He shall send His angel before thee, and thou shalt take a wife unto my son from thence." It is as if God would send His angels to get a wife for Isaac; the very angels so far honor this state that they think it not much to be employed in it.

4. *Their ministry is to suggest holy thoughts into the hearts of the people of God.* It is true that there is no express word for this, but there is reason for it; and divines give this reason to prove that the ministrations of angels tend to suggest holy thoughts into the hearts of the people of God. This is no derogation to the Spirit of God, because the Lord is the author of them; rather, the angels are the instruments in the Spirit's hand, because evil angels have permission by God to suggest evil thoughts into the hearts of men (Job 2:6; Acts 5:3), and therefore, on the contrary, good angels have commission from

God to suggest good thoughts into the hearts of the people of God. Or else it would follow that evil angels have more power to make you follow the ways of vanity, and run into sinful courses, than good angels have power to make you, by their good suggestions, walk in the ways of holiness, and thereby further your way in the course of salvation.

Certainly the nature of a good angel is as fit, and the power given to him is as great, to deal with our spirits as either the nature or power of an evil angel. A hint, if not a proof, of this the apostle gives in 2 Corinthians 11:14, where it says that the devil transforms himself into an angel of light; and this he does that he might tempt you to walk in a sinful course. He who is an angel of darkness transforms himself to be an angel of light that he might ensnare and draw you to miscarry, even by suggesting good things into your mind unseasonably, or for evil ends. And thus he cheats and deludes your soul, and causes you to sin in seeming to do good. For example, he is an angel of darkness when he tempts you to anything absolutely sinful, but he is a seeming angel of light by suggesting that you do that which is in itself good, but out of season. He tempts you to prayer when you are hearing a sermon, so as to draw off your affections from the Word preached by setting them on another duty. When you are praying he may tempt you to reading. And in this sense he may be called an angel of light; and by this reason they prove that as the evil angels tempt you to evil by suggesting evil thoughts into your heart, so good angels have a commission from God to suggest good thoughts into the hearts of God's people for their good.

5. *By angels the Lord by them spreads abroad and propagates*

the gospel of Jesus Christ, and in a special manner, to protect those ministers who preach the gospel more than any other men in the world.

The angels propagate the gospel. This you have laid down in Acts 16:9: "And a vision appeared to Paul by night; there stood a man of Macedonia, and prayed him, saying, 'Come over into Macedonia, and help us.' " This was an angel that called to Paul, and by that Paul gathered that he was called to preach the gospel to that people, and so accordingly he went. Likewise, in Acts 8:26, you read that an angel of the Lord spake to Philip to go and preach the gospel: "And an angel of the Lord spake unto Philip, saying, 'Arise and go toward the south, unto the way that goeth down from Jerusalem unto Gaza which is desert.' " Here Philip had a special call by an angel from heaven to preach and propagate the gospel. He did so, and by this means he propagated it in that place by converting a man who was a man in great power and authority, which would be a great means to countenance religion and godliness. "For he was a man of great authority under Candace, queen of the Ethiopians, who had charge of all her treasure" (verse 27). This great man Philip was called by an angel to convert to the faith of Christ.

So they likewise are to protect the ministers and preachers of the gospel from wrongs and troubles. Therefore Perkins had a good note on this. In Isaiah 6:7-8 we read that "one of the seraphim flew unto me, having a live coal in his hand which he had taken with the tongs from the altar; and he laid it upon my mouth, and said, lo, this hath touched thy lips, and thine iniquity is taken away, and thy sin is purged; and then I said, 'Lo, here I am, send me.' " Now [William] Perkins on this text speaks of the dignity of the ministry. When Isaiah had the touch by the angel, he was full of courage and assured of protection; he was forward in his work. Though angels are ministering spirits to protect the elect of God in the world, yet God gives them a special charge to protect ministers more than other men. For if God gives His angels charge to protect all who shall be saved, much more does God give His angels charge to protect not only those who shall be saved themselves, but those who are instrumental in saving others.

So likewise you read Paul's charge to Timothy, not to be careless and negligent in the discharge of his duty, but to be careful in his office in using discipline in the church. 1 Timothy 5:21: "I charge thee before God, and the Lord Jesus Christ, and the elect angels, that thou observe these things without preferring one before another, doing nothing by partiality." Here the apostle gives Timothy his charge before God, the Lord Jesus Christ, and all the elect angels. Why? What is the reason? Because the angels were to be his protection. Not only God and Jesus Christ, but the angels will be your protection if you go on faithfully to discharge your duty in preaching the gospel.

In 1 Corinthians 4:9, when Paul speaks of his suffering, and the suffering of the rest of the apostles, he said, "For I think that God hath set forth us the apostles last, as it were appointed to death. For we are made a spectacle (or, as it is in the Greek, "we are made a theater") unto the world, to angels, and to men." God beholds you, men behold you, and angels behold you in the course of your ministry. It is as if the apostle had said, "Although you think to do us wrong and lead us about with shame, yet God sees you; and angels see what wrong you do faithful ministers, and they will avenge our wrongs." Thus does God preserve those who teach the gospel.

Angels are called fellow servants in Revelation 22:9: "See thou do it not; I am thy fellow-servant." As angels are called ministers, so ministers are called angels.

6. *God uses the ministry of angels to preserve the elect in times of persecution from the rage and tyranny of cruel persecutors.* Compare Psalm 34:7 ("The angel of the Lord encampeth round about them that fear Him, and delivereth them") with the heading of that psalm. Now when was it that the angel of the Lord encamped about those who fear Him? If you look at the heading of that psalm you shall find that it was when David changed his behavior before Abimelech; he wrote this psalm when he made himself mad to save his life. You have the story in 1 Samuel 21:11–13: "And the servants of Achish said, 'Is not this David the king of the land? Did not they sing one to another of him in dances, saying, "Saul hath slain his thousand, and David his ten thousands?" ' And David laid up these words in his heart, and was sore afraid of Achish the king of Gath. And he changed his behavior before them, and feigned himself mad in their hands, and scribbled on the doors of the gate, and let his spittle fall down upon his beard." Here you see David's troubles, and yet it was notwithstanding that this was the time when he had a promise of the ministration of angels for his protection and preservation, even in this time of persecution.

Likewise Daniel was preserved by angels from the jaws of the lions in Daniel 6:22. When he was cast into the lion's den, he said, "My God has sent His angel to shut the lions mouths so that they have not hurt me." And Peter was delivered out of prison by an angel, from the rage, cruelty, and persecution of Herod in Acts 12:7–8. The three children were delivered out of the fiery furnace by an angel in Daniel 3:25. All of these examples clearly prove that God delivers His people from the rage of cruel men by the ministration of angels.

7. *The Lord uses the ministration of angels to preserve the elect in times of temptation from the temptations of the devil.* The devil tempts you and you see it not; and so good angels minister unto you and you see it not. When the devil tempts you by corrupt motions and corrupt thoughts to commit sin, then the good angels minister to keep these temptations from doing you harm. In Zechariah 3:1, you read that the devil stood at the right hand of his servant Joshua: "And he showed me Joshua the high priest standing before the angel of the Lord, and Satan standing at his right hand to resist him." Here the angel stood by Joshua to resist the devil who came to oppose and tempt him, to show that as the devil is very busy in following of the people of God with his temptations, so the Lord uses the ministration of angels to preserve them from these temptations.

8. *The Lord gives a charge to the angels in a more special manner to preserve the elect when they lie dying.* Then God uses the angels in a more peculiar manner to wait upon you at that time, and it is for this reason: because it is the last work that the angels can do for you in this world. You read in Luke 16:22 that Lazarus died and was carried by the angels into Abraham's bosom. If it is only a parable (which is disputable), it still is very applicable for our purpose, to show that the angels carry the souls of the elect to heaven when they come to die.

A Treatise of Angels

Now put all these particulars together, and then tell me what cause you have to admire and to adore that gracious God, that He should love you with such an endearing love through His Son as to ordain and give His angels a commission and charge to be your safeguard and preservation for you as long as you live in this world; and not only for you, but for all the elect who shall be heirs of salvation. And thus I have given you these eight particulars wherein God, in a special manner, preserves His elect children by the ministration of angels.

Now there are two more objections to be answered.

OBJECTION 1. I think I find this doctrine bubbling and boiling in many a man's spirit, and he may say, "If it is true that the Lord makes use of the ministration of angels in general and in particular, as you have delivered to us concerning the general and particular benefits that the elect have by them, then what is the reason why Moses, in describing the works of creation, does not make mentions of angels? He tells us of all the fowls of the air, of all the beasts of the field, the sun, moon, and stars, and all the creation, but there is not one word of angels. If they were as useful as you have delivered, why was no mention made of angels?"

ANSWER. The most skillful men have spent much time in untying this knot and determining this question. There are three great reasons why Moses did not speak of angels in one of the six days, when it is certain that they were created in one of these days.

First, Moses did not speak of the creation of angels because he wanted to take the Jews off from idolatry, not to worship angels. Had he told them of the excellence of the nature of angels, had he told them of their strength and power, their greatness and wisdom, and their glory and excellence, the Jews would have been so apt to fall into idolatry that they would have worshipped angels. For they worshipped great men who had great honor and power, and who were held in high esteem in the world. They worshipped them as gods. And that is the reason why God hid the body of Moses, and no man to this day can tell where it was laid. The devil and the angel contended about the body of Moses to this end: that the devil would fain have brought it to light, and the angel would not let him, because he knew that they would have worshipped his dead body.

Second, Moses concealed this doctrine of angels, of their creation, because in treating the creation he only treated things visible, things that may be seen with the eye and understood with the capacity of the people. The heavens you can see above you, and the earth you can see below you. You see the beasts of the field feed, you see the fowls of the air fly, and you see the fish of the sea swim. So the Apostle Paul tells you that God created things visible and invisible; and Moses did not speak of the creation of angels, but he left that to later ages.

Third, Moses did not make mention of the creation of angels lest, if he had spoken of their creation who are such excellent creatures and so far above men, the people would have been apt to think that the angels had borne a share and had a hand with God in making the world. Since the old philosophers held that angels were the movers of heaven, people might say that angels had a share with God in making heaven and earth. Notwithstanding the fact that their creation is concealed, this would not be any argument to lessen your belief of the truth that angels were created and made ministering spirits sent out by God to minister unto those who shall be heirs of salvation.

OBJECTION 2. "If God uses the ministration of angels to this end, then it must follow," say the papists, "that we are bound to worship them and to adore them." Bellarmine takes some pains to prove the worshipping of angels, and he brings in Genesis 48:16: "May the angel that redeemed me from all evil bless the lads, and let my name be named on them, and the name of my fathers Abraham and Isaac, and let them grow into a multitude in the midst of the earth." These are Jacob's words, from which Bellarmine would prove that he prayed to angels for a blessing, and, said he, his prayer is part of worship. Therefore worship belongs to angels as well as to God.

Now to answer this objection, I shall lay down three particulars.

First, by "angel" is not here meant, as Augustine said, the angel of the Lord, but *the* angel, the Lord. It is not to be understood of any created angel, but of the Creator of angels, Jesus Christ, who is in Scripture called "the angel of the covenant."

Second, this reason is given by Rivet: the article is emphatic, and because the word "bless" is in the singular number. It is not "an angel who redeemed me," but "the angel who redeemed me," which is meant of Jesus Christ. Besides, the text itself is clear that it means God and not an angel of God, in verse 15: "And he blessed Joseph, and said, 'God before whom my fathers Abraham and Isaac did walk, the God which fed me all my life long unto this day.' " This angel who redeemed me is He who is eternal. He is that God whom Jacob prayed to, who can keep us from all evil. It is the Lord of angels, not the angels of the Lord.

Third, it may as well be meant, and as truly said to be God, here as in other places of the Scripture. Therefore you read in Genesis 32:26 that Jacob strove and wrestled with an angel, and he said, "I will not let Thee go, except Thou bless me." By this angel is meant God, for we read in Hosea 12:4: "Yea, he had power over the angel and prevailed; he wept and made supplication unto him; he found him in Bethel, and there he spake with us." And this is spoken of Jacob's wrestling with God, who is called an angel. Therefore that expression in Genesis 48:16 must mean God likewise, for you see how one place of Scripture expounds another to be meant of the angels of God. Besides, Chaimer says that it was not a prayer but a desire. But Rivet rejects this.

We may pray to God for angels' protection, but not to angels for God's protection. And to prove this more plainly to you, I shall give you both scripture and reason.

1. We are not to worship angels because they are our fellow creatures. You read in Revelation 22:9 the angel's speech to John when John would have given worship to the angel. The angel said, "See thou do it not, for I am thy fellow-servant, and of thy brethren the prophets, and of them that keep the sayings of this book; worship God."

2. They themselves charge us to worship God and not them. Judges 13:15–16: "And Manoah said unto the angel, 'I pray thee, let us detain thee until we shall have made ready a kid for thee.' And the angel of the Lord said unto Manoah, 'Though thou detain me, I will not

eat of thy bread; and if thou wilt offer a burnt offering, thou must offer it unto the Lord.' " Here you see that an angel will not be worshipped by any, because we are to worship God alone.

3. The angels themselves are to worship Jesus Christ, and therefore we are not to worship them. Hebrews 1:6: "And again when He bringeth the first begotten into the world, He saith, and let all the angels of God worship Him."

4. The Scripture is expressly against it. You read in Deuteronomy 6 that "He is the Lord thy God, and Him only shalt thou serve." We are commanded not to do any homage and divine worship to anyone but God alone. So Colossians 2:18: "Let no man beguile you of your reward in a voluntary humility and worshipping of angels, intruding into those things which he hath not seen, vainly puffed up by his fleshly mind." The people were apt to worship them as gods, and this the Apostle exhorts the Colossians against so that they are not overtaken in this fault.

And thus I have done with these two objections. I now come to three uses to be made of this text:

USE 1. Of caution.
USE 2. Of instruction.
USE 3. Of reprehension.

USE 1. By way of caution take these three particulars into your consideration.

1. If it is so that God gives commission to His angels to serve those who are heirs of salvation, then take heed that you do not extend the ministry of angels beyond its due bounds. It is true that angels do good to the elect of God, yet do not extend their office beyond what God

would have us do. Take heed that you do not fall into the error of the church of Rome. For they say not only that the angels of God guard us here and carry our souls to heaven, but that we have one more benefit by them: the angels are intercessors to God for us, and we, for modesty's sake, must not go to God directly, but must go to the angels to pray that they would intercede to God for us.

This the book of Tobit shows, but that book is not canonical. There it is said that angels carry our prayers to God, and this shows that it is not canonical scripture, because it holds forth things that are contrary to Scripture. Some Protestants hold, as Willet affirms in his "Synopsis," that we may do it declaratively to manifest our sayings and doings, as one friend to another, but by no means as mediators. Therefore, let this caution remind you to take heed that you do not extend the office of angels beyond its due bounds. Though they are a guard to protect us from danger here in the world, yet they are not intercessors on our behalf to God.

Bellarmine takes great pains to prove the contrary, and brings in Revelation 8:3 to prove his opinion: "And another angel came and stood at the altar, having a golden censer, and there was given unto him much incense, that he should offer it with the prayers of the saints." So Bellarmine draws from hence that the angels offer our prayers to God.

Now by way of answer, though [Daniel] Brightman understands this verse as referring to Constantine, yet it is clear that the angel there spoken means Jesus Christ and not created angels, as Augustine interprets it. The Jesuit Blasius Viega says that the things here spoken apply to none but Christ, and that in these three regards:

First, because the Scripture tells us that none but Jesus Christ can do this office for us, to offer up our prayers to God and intercede for us; none but Christ can be our Mediator. "There is but one Mediator between God and man, the man Christ Jesus" (1 Timothy 2:5).

Second, it is above the ability of any creature to do this work for us, to take any prayers from the people of God to carry them to God, to make them accepted before Him, and to commend them to God for us.

Third, it appears to be Jesus Christ because the allusion of this text takes us clearly to Jesus Christ. It refers to Exodus 30:7–8. There you have the high priest burning incense upon the golden altar: "And Aaron shall burn thereon sweet incense every morning; when he dresseth the lamps he shall burn incense upon it. And when Aaron lighteth the lamps at evening he shall burn incense upon it, a perpetual incense before the Lord throughout the generations." The high priest was a type of Jesus Christ, the altar a type of His Godhead, the sacrifice a type of His manhood, and the incense a type of His intercession. Now the altar intends Christ, the sacrifice intends Christ, and the incense intends Christ; and therefore it must relate to Jesus Christ since He is the angel of the covenant, and He alone, by His death and passion, and by His righteousness, commends all our prayers to God His Father, that they may be accepted by Him in our behalf.

2. Take this caution: look not on the ministration of angels to be any derogation from the all-ordering providence of God for you. Though God can protect you

without angels, yet God thinks it fit to guard you by angels; and this magnifies God in His protection of His people, that He should have so much love and care towards His people as to give His angels a charge over you to protect you. This magnifies and brings glory to God, and that because all the good that good angels do us in this world, they do by God's commission.

They receive a commission from God to do good to His elect servants. Thus the angels of God were the attendants of Jesus Christ, for when Judas had betrayed Him into the hands of the scribes and Pharisees, Christ said in Matthew 26:53: "Thinkest thou that I cannot now pray unto My Father, and He shall give Me more than twelve legions of angels?" It is God who gives His angels charge over you to protect you, or else you would always be in danger of receiving hurt, and of being destroyed while you live in the world. Therefore God so protects you by angels, which is a great honor to God, and not any derogation from His providence.

3. Take heed of this: seeing that angels are ministering spirits to all who are the elect of God, do not once plead for any worshipping of them. Although the Scripture speaks much of the angels, concerning the excellence of their nature, the greatness of their power, and the excellence of their making, yet let no man beguile you about the ministration of angels, to plead for any adoration of them, for there is no warrant for any worshipping of them. And so much for the use of caution.

USE 2. This use is for instruction, and that in these eight particulars touching the commission that God gives to the angels to serve and to minister to the elect.

A Treatise of Angels

1. Are there good angels who have commission from God to do us good and minister to us? Then it will follow on the contrary that there are evil angels who labor to do harm to the bodies and souls of the people of God. The good angels' commission is to do good to and protect the bodies and souls of the godly; this strongly implies that there are evil angels that will do all the harm they can to God's people.

First, they will hurt the bodies of the elect. So they did, by the permission of God, hurt Job's body. They so sorely afflicted him that he lay on the dunghill scraping himself. So in Psalm 78:49–50: "He cast down upon them the fierceness of His anger, wrath, and indignation, and trouble, by sending evil angels among them. He spared not their souls from death, but gave their life over to the pestilence." So they are in our souls, to tempt us to sin, to disturb us in duty.

Diodati makes use of Genesis 15:11 to this purpose. When Abraham went to offer sacrifice to God, it is said that the birds came down and troubled him. Now, says Diodati, these birds were evil spirits that troubled Abraham in his service to God when he offered sacrifice. So the evil angels labor to interrupt, to hinder, and to disturb the people of God in their approaches towards Him in holy services.

Consider Job 1:6: "Upon a certain day the sons of God came before the Lord, and Satan came in the midst of them." Now some interpreters refer to these sons of God as the angels who came before God to see what God would have them to do for the elect in the world, and the devils came among them to see what permission they might have from God to afflict, trouble, disturb, molest, and hurt the people of God. The

Jews say it was the first day of every year when God called this general audit, wherein He convened His angels to give Him an account of what was done the year past. Mercer accounts that to be very gross and groundless. But, said Balducius, "sons of God" refers to the godly men in the world, that is, those godly men who lived in the days of Job. And he proves it by this: it is said that the sons of God saw that the daughters of men were fair and married them (Genesis 6:2). He thinks that it was on the Sabbath day. Now when the sons of God came before the Lord, the devil came with them to trouble them in the service and worship that they were to perform to God. And it was on a certain day, that is, on the Sabbath, even that Sabbath day when the people of God came to perform their solemn duties in their worship and service to God. Then the devil labored to disturb them in the discharge of their duties. He would have some men sleep during the hearing of a sermon, and some to do one thing and some another. He will take all occasions at all times to disturb you in your duties to God. So there are evil angels to disturb and hurt you, as well as good angels to save and protect you.

2. If the angels are ministering spirits to the elect, then the elect of God have no cause to fear the rage and malice of the devil and the evil angels. If the good angels minister unto you, then fear not the evil angels; for though the devils have permission by God sometimes to do some good men harm, yet good angels always have commission from God to do good men good. And God gives special charge to them to do good.

If God gave them commission to contend for the body of Moses, shall He not do so much more to contend about and for the souls of the elect? And therein the power of the good angels is greater than the power of the evil angels. Therefore, fear them not, because God has given charge to the good angels to be your guard and protector; for even the evil angels by their fall have lost much of their power, strength, and wisdom. But the good angels have lost nothing of their power, strength, and wisdom, but are confirmed, and shall put all forth, by virtue of their commission from God to save and guard the elect in the world.

3. If the angels are by God made ministering spirits to the elect, then good men have no cause to fear death, for that is the last part that the angels are to act for them: to take care for your soul, and to preserve it when you are dying. Luke 16:22: "It came to pass that the beggar died, and was carried by the angels into Abraham's bosom." If the angels have been faithful to you all your lifetime, do you think they will not be faithful to you at the hour of death? The devil shall never be able to take your soul away from you; therefore, O man, why do you fear dying?

You may say, "Though I have friends to weep with me, yet I am sure I have angels to safeguard me to heaven when I die." Oh, consider, have the angels a commission all your lifetime to save you and do you good, and will you think that they will fail at last to do the last and great work for you? Nay, Jesus Christ, the Angel of the covenant who has taken your nature upon Him, not only strengthens you against the curse of death, but against the fear of death (Hebrews 2:15). Therefore fear not to die.

4. As good men have no cause to fear death, so good men have no cause to fear danger in this life. A king in this world, when he has his guard about him, fears no

danger because he is preserved by them. Oh, how much more have you cause not to fear any danger! For you have not a guard of men to secure you, but a guard of angels to be your preservation. Solomon did not fear when he had three hundred sharpshooters to be his safeguard, but you have more than this for your preservation. You have more than three hundred men with targets, for you have all the angels of God in commission to secure and preserve you from danger in the world.

It is an observation of a modern divine that God's care for His church is greater than of old because the church is enlarged and the enemies enraged. Though the angels appeared in a more visible shape under the Old Testament than under the New, yet there is a fuller ministration in the New Testament than under the Old. And there are two Scriptures to prove this.

In Ezekiel 9:2 we read that at the gate of Jerusalem there were six angels who had charge of the city. In Revelation 21:12 we read that the city had twelve gates and twelve angels, and names written thereon which are the names of the twelve tribes of the children of Israel. From these two places divines gather that the Lord has more care of His people under the time of the gospel than He had under the law; and the angels of God fence and guard the people of God from fear and danger in the world.

5. This doctrine should leave an awe and dread, and give a check to wicked men, not to trouble, hurt, and disturb the people of God, and wrong them in the world. Why so? Because you wrong those who have the angels as their guard. It may be that you wrong a good man, and he may forgive you, but consider that his an-

gels will not forgive you. Matthew 18:10: "Take heed (said Christ) that you do not hurt one of these little ones." Why so? "Because their angels do behold My Father's face" to avenge them that do them wrong.

When Balaam was going to curse the people of God, it is said that an angel stopped him. Numbers 22:22: "And God's anger was kindled against him (that is, against Balaam) because he went, and the angel of the Lord stood in the way as an adversary against him. He was riding upon his ass and his two servants were with him." An angel smote the Sodomites with blindness when they compassed about Lot's house. Therefore, take heed that you do no wrong to the people of God; they may forgive you, but the angels of God will not forgive you, but will avenge their wrongs.

6. Be ashamed and afraid of any indecency in the public worship of God whenever you appear before Him. It is a great part of the angels' office to behold your carriage in church assemblies. 1 Corinthians 11:10: "For this cause ought the women to be covered, because of the angels." Because the angels see the carriage and behavior of the people of God in church assemblies, take heed of unseemly behavior in the public worship of God, either in your words, your attire, or your gestures when you appear before God, for the angels see it and know it.

In Proverbs 7:10 you read of the "attire of the harlot" (making the neck bare to the breast). That is the manner of harlots, said [Thomas] Cartwright, to have their necks open and bare, and their breasts naked. That was the fashion of harlots in those days, and it has become a fashion now in these days as it was of old. This is one cause of the judgments that are on the land.

Look into Isaiah 3, from verse 18 on. There you have a wardrobe of pride laid down by the prophet which caused judgments to come: "In that day I will take away the bravery of their tinkling ornaments about their feet, and their networks, and their round tires like the moon, the chains, and the bracelets, and the mufflers, the bonnets, and the ornaments of the legs, and the headbands, and the tablets, and the earrings, and the rings, and the nose jewels, the changeable suits of apparel, and the mantles, and the crisping pins, and the glasses, and the fine linen, and the hoods, and the veils."

Behold what abundance of fashions of pride were here used, but what followed? God brought judgments upon them for this. Verses 24–25: "And it shall come to pass that, instead of a sweet smell, there shall be a stink; and instead of a girdle, a rent; and instead of well-set hair, baldness; and instead of a stomacher, a girdle of sackcloth; and burning instead of beauty." See how this vanity and pride provoked God to bring judgments upon them. Thy men shall fall by the sword, and thy mighty men in the war." Psalm 138:1: "Before the gods I will sing praise unto Thee." The Septuagint translates it "before the angels," though others translate it "before the rulers and princes." Ecclesiastes 5:6: "Neither say thou before the angel that it was an error," an oversight or mistake; every indecent carriage, sleeping, smiling, slighting, and spurning the ordinances, the angels take notice of. And this I name to let you see that God takes special notice of your carriage; and the angels see your behavior in your approaches to God.

7. If it be so that angels are made ministering spirits to the elect, then this should teach the sons of men to

A Treatise of Angels

be humble before God. If the angels, who are creatures of such admirable dignity, serve us, the angels who are great in power and excellent in nature—if they serve us who are so exceedingly below them, should we disdain to serve one another? Oh, why should you look on your betters with envy and your inferiors with disdain?

You read in Romans 12:3: "For I say, through the grace given unto me, to every man among you not to think of himself more highly than he ought to think, but to think soberly, according as God hath dealt to every man the measure of faith." And verse 16: "Be of the same mind one towards another. Mind not high things, but condescend to men of low degree. Be not wise in your own conceits." Do not disdain to do good to poor men, though you are rich in the world.

There is greater difference between angels and the greatest men than there is between a prince on the throne and a beggar on the dunghill; yet the angels do not disdain to minister unto you. You read in John 13:14: "If I then, your Lord and your Master, do wash your feet, you ought also to wash one another's feet." Christ washed His disciples' feet as an example of humility to His people, that they may walk according to His example and do as He had done before. So I may say to you, if angels, who are so high and so excellent above men, do good to the people of God, and if they minister to them for their benefit, Oh, then, do not disdain your inferiors, and do not withhold yourselves from doing good to those when you have power to do it unto them.

Labor for humility. Some interpreters think that the sin of angels was pride, and therefore God, to prove the angels who remained to be free from pride, made use of them to serve the people of God who are below in the world, and who are so far below themselves.

8. If angels minister to the people of God, oh, be exhorted to be more and more forward in the service of God! Has God given all the creatures on the earth to serve you? Has God given you the sun in the heavens to give you light? Has God caused the earth to yield increase to give you food? Has God given the angels in heaven to minister to you for your good? Has God done all this for you? Oh, then, serve your God! O honor that God who has so honored you! And how should you live to the praise and service of that God who has made all His creatures for your service! You do not recompense and answer God's expectation if you do not serve that God who has done all this for you.

USE 3. The third use is for reprehension, and that to four sorts of men.

1. It reproves that error of the Sadducees who deny the resurrection, angels, and spirits. Acts 23:8: "For the Sadducees say that there is no resurrection, neither angel nor spirit." How could the scriptures say so much of angels if there were no angels?

2. It condemns those who, ever since they came into the world, never have thought that angels do good unto them, or how much they are beholden to God for this great mercy.

3. It reproves those who give and ascribe too much to angels—who, because angels minister to us by God's commission, yet for this adore and worship the angels. And this is to worship the servant and neglect to worship the Master, the great God of heaven and earth.

4. It reproves those who expect the ministration of

angels, and yet do not make it their care to walk in the imitation of angels. Though you say in the Lord's Prayer, "Thy will be done in earth as it is in heaven," yet you do not do God's will on earth as the angels do in heaven. Many men pray that God will protect them on earth by angels, but never labor to walk under this protection in the imitation of the angels. Oh, consider that the angels serve you who are far inferior to them. They are humble and willing to do you good in the world, but you, O man, live a proud life, and have a haughty carriage toward those who are in a lower degree than yourself, and carry an envious heart against those who are higher than yourself. Oh, herein you do not do God's will on earth. Though we cannot do the will of God as angels do it with regard to equality, yet we may do it as for quality; as the angels do God's will willingly, so must we. The angels do God's will speedily, and therefore strength is ascribed to angels, but we do not imitate them, for we are very sluggish in the service of God; we are slow and dull in the service of God.

You read in Psalm 103:20: "Bless the Lord, ye His angels which excel in strength, that do His commandments, hearkening to the voice of His words." Oh, here is the service and diligence of angels in doing the commandments of God speedily; but we are not speedy in the service of God or in doing His will. The angels of God are not content with what they have done for God, but are ready to do more for God. The angels of God hearken to His commands; they hearken to the voice of His words and are in readiness to do the will of God. But we are not as the angels in our duties to God; therefore we are blameworthy that we should look for protection from angels and yet never look to imitate the angels in our service to God, to make any conscience to perform duties to God, or to observe and do the commands of God.

And this shall serve for this text and time. "Are not they all ministering spirits, sent forth to minister unto them that shall be heirs of salvation?"